T0233334

Oracle SQL Revealed

Executing Business Logic in the Database Engine

Alex Reprintsev

Apress®

Oracle SQL Revealed

Alex Reprintsev
London, United Kingdom

ISBN-13 (pbk): 978-1-4842-3371-9   ISBN-13 (electronic): 978-1-4842-3372-6
https://doi.org/10.1007/978-1-4842-3372-6

Library of Congress Control Number: 2018937895

Copyright © 2018 by Alex Reprintsev

This work is subject to copyright. All rights are reserved by the Publisher, whether the whole or part of the material is concerned, specifically the rights of translation, reprinting, reuse of illustrations, recitation, broadcasting, reproduction on microfilms or in any other physical way, and transmission or information storage and retrieval, electronic adaptation, computer software, or by similar or dissimilar methodology now known or hereafter developed.

Trademarked names, logos, and images may appear in this book. Rather than use a trademark symbol with every occurrence of a trademarked name, logo, or image we use the names, logos, and images only in an editorial fashion and to the benefit of the trademark owner, with no intention of infringement of the trademark.

The use in this publication of trade names, trademarks, service marks, and similar terms, even if they are not identified as such, is not to be taken as an expression of opinion as to whether or not they are subject to proprietary rights.

While the advice and information in this book are believed to be true and accurate at the date of publication, neither the authors nor the editors nor the publisher can accept any legal responsibility for any errors or omissions that may be made. The publisher makes no warranty, express or implied, with respect to the material contained herein.

Managing Director, Apress Media LLC: Welmoed Spahr
Acquisitions Editor: Jonathan Gennick
Development Editor: Laura Berendson
Coordinating Editor: Jill Balzano

Cover designed by eStudioCalamar

Cover image designed by Freepik (www.freepik.com)

Distributed to the book trade worldwide by Springer Science+Business Media New York, 233 Spring Street, 6th Floor, New York, NY 10013. Phone 1-800-SPRINGER, fax (201) 348-4505, e-mail orders-ny@springer-sbm.com, or visit www.springeronline.com. Apress Media, LLC is a California LLC and the sole member (owner) is Springer Science + Business Media Finance Inc (SSBM Finance Inc). SSBM Finance Inc is a **Delaware** corporation.

For information on translations, please e-mail rights@apress.com, or visit http://www.apress.com/rights-permissions.

Apress titles may be purchased in bulk for academic, corporate, or promotional use. eBook versions and licenses are also available for most titles. For more information, reference our Print and eBook Bulk Sales web page at http://www.apress.com/bulk-sales.

Any source code or other supplementary material referenced by the author in this book is available to readers on GitHub via the book's product page, located at www.apress.com/9781484233719. For more detailed information, please visit http://www.apress.com/source-code.

Printed on acid-free paper

Table of Contents

About the Author

Alex Reprintsev has more than 10 years of experience in database development using various databases, including Oracle, Microsoft SQL Server, MySQL, DB2, and modern SQL engines for Big Data such as Hive and Impala. He has successfully delivered applications for various customers covering different workload types such as OLTP, OLAP, and mixed workloads. During his journey, Alex has faced a number of challenges related to implementing business logic and tuning SQL for performance. He believes that details really do matter, and that it is important to know and exploit the full feature set of whatever database engine you choose to build your business around.

Introduction

The main purpose of this book is to describe the capabilities of SQL for implementing complex logic and specific features of Oracle SQL dialect, in particular. SQL, and especially Oracle dialect, are extremely powerful languages that allow you to get the result in a highly scalable fashion with very little code.

The book is dedicated to readers who have working experience with any relational DBMS as well as basic SQL knowledge. In particular, it's good to understand that SQL is a declarative language so it describes what to get rather than how to get the result. Also it's highly desirable to know what a query plan is and how to read it.

The first part provides a thorough overview of SQL capabilities in Oracle for selecting data as well as some basic SQL concepts. Information regarding the Cost Based Optimizer intentionally was minimized so the reader is not getting bogged down in minutiae and can concentrate on features for implementing business logic and understanding mechanics of the SQL engine. However, it was impossible to skip some concepts so a separate chapter is dedicated to query transformations.

Oracle capabilities and features keep evolving from one version to another so sometimes different Oracle versions 10g (10.2.0.5), 11g (11.2.0.4), and 12c (12.1.0.2, 12.2.0.1) are referred to highlight these changes. While introducing new functionality Oracle also aims to fix existing bugs so I tried not to mention bugs that are already fixed and are not important for describing possibilities of SQL. It's very important to keep in mind that such Oracle evolution occurred because best practices, which were actual 5, 10, or 15 years ago, may be not the best approach at all on new versions.

The goal, on one hand, was to provide comprehensive analysis of the functionality but, on the other hand, to minimize the number of pages. So narration in almost every chapter quickly flows from basic concepts to complex details. Sometimes the reader may want to ask questions that will be answered later on in the text so just keep reading and hopefully you will find required clarifications or additional details.

The book's second part covers a number of real-life tasks that can be solved using Oracle SQL dialect. Sometimes PL/SQL solutions are also provided just to highlight current limitations of SQL or to demonstrate that PL/SQL may be a preferable solution from a performance point of view even if an SQL solution looks concise and easy. You can find a bunch of real cases when PL/SQL is better than Vanilla SQL in the first chapter of Part II.

I do not see a reason to collect algorithmic quizzes that require only PL/SQL programming because PL/SQL is yet another procedural language with some OOP extensions, so the reader can find various books dedicated to algorithms and programming and try to implement those programs in PL/SQL. To understand PL/SQL advantages to compare to an ordinary procedural language, please refer to note [8] in the Appendix. Also PL/SQL has a number of features to effectively interact with the SQL engine and note [9] in the Appendix may be a good source to begin with.

PART I

Features and Theory

Chapters 1-10 are organized to follow the list below of Oracle SQL features:

1. All joins can be implicitly specified in the query; however sometimes it makes sense to use subqueries, for example, for a more efficient way to implement an ANTI/EQUI join. Correlated scalar subqueries may be more efficient than outer joins because of scalar subquery caching.

2. Query transformations make it possible for two queries with quite different text to have the same plan and performance. On the other hand, query transformations are not a universal panacea and sometimes manual query refactoring is required to achieve the best performance.

3. Analytic functions are an invaluable feature that helps to implement tricky logic without joins. On the other hand, they almost always require a sort, which may be an issue on big data volumes.

4. Aggregate functions allow us to group data and calculate aggregate values as well as implement some complex flattening or pivoting logic.

5. Connect by is the best tool to traverse hierarchies or generate lists; however it should not be used to traverse graphs despite built-in capabilities to handle cycles if performance is critical.

6. Recursive subquery factoring extends capabilities of traversing hierarchies in a way that you can refer values calculated on a previous level. When recursive subquery factoring is used for iterative transformations of a dataset you should take into account that a new recordset is generated on each iteration, which leads to intensive memory consumption. A functional advantage in comparison to a model clause is that you can calculate multiple measures on each step. In case of a model clause, the first measure is evaluated for all specified rows, then the second one, one and so on.

7. Model is the most powerful SQL feature but it's shining in quite specific cases. Model may require intensive CPU and memory consumption and does not scale well enough for millions of rows; however performance can be dramatically improved in case of parallel execution of partitioned models.

8. Row pattern matching adds noticeable flexibility for analysis of recordsets. This feature is the only way to solve a wide range of tasks in pure SQL in a scalable and efficient manner, and in addition it demonstrates a bit better performance for those tasks that can also be solved using analytic functions.

9. One query block may contain various clauses including joins, aggregate and analytic, or even mixes of advanced features like model clause and pattern matching. It's important to understand how this will be executed from a logical point of view and what are the pros and cons of using inline views.

10. It was proven that SQL is Turing complete language and for academic purposes it was shown how to implement arbitrary algorithms using an iterative model. SQL is a declarative language though and was designed to manipulate data and not for iterative computations.

Tom Kyte wrote many times over the years, "You should do it in a single SQL statement if at all possible." I'd like to elaborate on this statement a little bit. Even if we remove from consideration advanced features like recursive subquery factoring, model clause, row pattern matching, and connect by, there are some tasks that can be solved more efficiently using PL/SQL. Various examples will be considered in Chapter 11 to provide more background.

CHAPTER 1

Joins

Most real-life queries combine data from multiple tables instead of querying a single table. Logic may be encapsulated in a view to hide complexity from the end user, but the database accesses multiple tables anyway to get the result set. It's not necessary that data from all tables in a query appear in the result; some tables may be used to filter out data from other tables, for example.

Data from two tables may be combined using join (a join keyword is not mandatory as it will be shown later), subquery (may be correlated or not), lateral view (starting with Oracle 12c), or set operators (union/union all/intersect/minus).

Any logic implemented using set operators or subqueries may be rewritten with joins, but this may not be always optimal from a performance point of view. Moreover, semantically equivalent queries may be rewritten into the same query after query transformations are applied (see details in Chapter 2, "Query Transformations") or may have the same execution plan even if they have not been rewritten into the same query. Lateral views can be imitated using a table operator on older versions.

Looking forward, let me mention that some queries that use only one table may be not very easy to understand and may contain quite complex logic, but that is a rare case (a lot of such queries you can find in Part II).

This chapter covers joins (both ANSI and traditional Oracle outer joins syntax) along with some details about subqueries, lateral views, and join methods.

© Alex Reprintsev 2018
A. Reprintsev, *Oracle SQL Revealed*, https://doi.org/10.1007/978-1-4842-3372-6_1

ANSI Joins

The following tables will be used for demonstration.

Listing 1-1. Tables for demonstration

```
create table t1(id, name) as
select 1, 'A' from dual union all select 0, 'X' from dual;

create table t2(id, name) as
select 2, 'B' from dual union all select 0, 'X' from dual;
```

- Cross join (also called Cartesian product). It returns all possible combinations of two table's rows.

Listing 1-2. Cross join

```
select *
  from t1
  cross join t2;

        ID N          ID N
---------- - ---------- -
         1 A           2 B
         1 A           0 X
         0 X           2 B
         0 X           0 X
```

- Inner join – join type that returns those and only those rows from both joined tables satisfying a join predicate (i.e., predicate evaluates into TRUE).

Listing 1-3. Inner join

```
select *
  from t1
  join t2
    on t1.id = t2.id;

       ID N          ID N
---------- - ---------- -
        0 X           0 X
```

The table before the join keyword is called a "left joined table," and the table after the join keyword is called a "right joined table." For an inner join it does not matter which table is left and which one is right, as the result will always be the same for the same tables and join predicate.

A predicate may not always be an equality condition; it can be any expression that evaluates into TRUE, FALSE, or UNKNOWN. UNKNOWN acts almost like FALSE; if a join predicate evaluates into UNKNOWN for given rows from two tables, then they will not be part of the result set. However, if atomic predicates are combined using AND, OR, NOT conditions, then the result may be different if the subexpression evaluates to UNKNOWN and not to FALSE. For example, NOT FALSE evaluates to TRUE, but NOT UNKNOWN evaluates to UNKNOWN.

Speaking about joins, the terms "condition," "predicate," and "criteria" are interchangeable.

It's not mandatory that columns from both tables should be used in the predicate. "t1.id > 0" is also a valid join condition. All rows from table t2 satisfy this condition and only one row from table t1 does.

Listing 1-4. Inner join with predicate containing only one table

```
select *
  from t1
  join t2
    on t1.id > 0;
```

```
        ID N          ID N
---------- - ---------- -
         1 A           2 B
         1 A           0 X
```

If a join condition evaluates into true for some row from one table and multiple rows from another one, then that row will be repeated in the result multiple times. For example, join condition «t1.id <= t2.id» in the below example evaluates to true for row with id = 0 from the left join table and two rows from the right joined table so row with id = 0 appears in the result twice. The same reasoning is valid for row with id = 2 from the second table.

Listing 1-5. Inner join with non-equality predicate

```
select *
  from t1
  join t2
    on t1.id <= t2.id;
```

```
ID N   ID N
---- - ---- -
   0 X    0 X
   0 X    2 B
   1 A    2 B
```

- Outer join – type of join that returns the same rows as inner join (i.e., rows from both tables that match join condition and) and rows from left joined table (for left join) or right joined table (for right join) or both tables (full join), which do not match the join condition along with NULL values in place of other table's columns.

Listing 1-6. Left outer join

```
select *
  from t1
  left join t2
  on t1.id = t2.id;

      ID N          ID N
---------- - ---------- -
       0 X           0 X
       1 A
```

Listing 1-7. Right outer join

```
select *
  from t1
  right join t2
  on t1.id = t2.id;

      ID N          ID N
---------- - ---------- -
       0 X           0 X
                     2 B
```

Listing 1-8. Full outer join

```
select *
  from t1
  full join t2
    on t1.id = t2.id;
```

```
        ID N          ID N
---------- - ---------- -
         0 X           0 X
                       2 B
         1 A
```

The unnecessary keyword "outer" was not used in Listings 1-6, 1-7, or 1-8 because keywords left/right/full indicate then that the join is outer. Similarly, if none of the keywords left/right/full are used in join, then it's inner, so it does not make sense to specify this explicitly using an "inner" keyword.

As a rule, developers do not use right join in real-life tasks because it's always possible to use left join instead, which makes the statement easier to understand and improves readability.

When multiple tables (data sets) are joined in a query, then Oracle joins the first two and after that joins the resulting data set with the third data set etc. In case of inner joins, there are no logical limitations on the order of joins and CBO (Cost Based Optimizer) can join tables in any order irrespective of how tables are listed in the query text. For ANSI outer joins, the order of joins in the query matters - see section "Clearness and Readability" for more details.

Other Types of Joins

- Equi joins. If all join conditions contain equality operators, then join is called equi join; otherwise join is called non-equi (Theta) join. Listing 1-3, Listing 1-6, Listing 1-7, and Listing 1-8 are examples for equi join. Listing 1-4 and Listing 1-5 are non-equi joins.

A special case of an equi join is a natural join. A Natural join uses an implicit join condition, which are equality predicates on common columns from both tables (i.e., columns with the same names). This introduces potential danger because if table structure changes, then the join condition may change as well.

Listing 1-9. Natural join

```
select * from t1 natural join t2;

        ID N
---------- -
         0 X
```

It's possible to specify whether a natural join is inner or outer.

Listing 1-10. Outer natural join

```
create table t(id, name, dummy) as select 1, 'A', 'dummy' from
dual;
select * from t1 natural left join t;

        ID N DUMMY
---------- - -----
         1 A dummy
         0 X
```

If there are no common columns in both tables, then natural join will be effectively cross join.

Another form of equi join on the same columns is named columns join. It allows us to list all columns for join conditions and preserve join conditions even if table structure changes.

Listing 1-11. Named columns join

```
select * from t1 join t2 using (id);

        ID N N
---------- - -
        0 X X
```

When using this syntax, a common column only from one table appears in the result. The same happens in case of a natural join in Listing 1-9 and Listing 1-10.

- Semi joins. This type of join happens in case of using conditions like "in (subquery)" or "exists (correlated subquery)". Result contains column only from one table and only one row is returned from that table even if multiple rows from the subquery satisfy the condition.

Listing 1-12. Semi join

```
create table t0(id, name) as
select 0, 'X' from dual union all select 0, 'X' from dual;

select t1.* from t1 where t1.id in (select id from t0);

        ID N
---------- -
        0 X

select t1.* from t1 where exists (select id from t0 where
t1.id = t0.id);

        ID N
---------- -
        0 X
```

```
select t1.* from t1 join t0 on t1.id = t0.id;

      ID N
---------- -
       0 X
       0 X
```

- Anti joins. Work similarly to semi joins but return rows
  with no matches from the second table. Anti join appears
  when using predicates "not in (subquery)" or "not exists
  (correlated subquery)." The result will have no rows when
  using "not in" and the subquery contains NULL values.
  If the condition evaluates to UNKWNOWN for some
  rows and the "not exists" condition, then those rows will
  not be part of results; but result is not necessarily empty
  if the table in the subquery has NULL values for joining
  columns. This logical difference can be seen in the query
  plan operation name – HASH JOIN ANTI **NA**.

Listing 1-13. Anti join

```
select t1.* from t1 where t1.id not in (select id from t0);
select * from table(dbms_xplan.display_cursor(format => 'basic'));
select t1.* from t1 where not exists (select id from t0 where
t1.id = t0.id);
select * from table(dbms_xplan.display_cursor(format => 'basic'));
```

```
------------------------------------
| Id | Operation          | Name |
------------------------------------
|  0 | SELECT STATEMENT   |      |
|  1 |  HASH JOIN ANTI NA |      |
|  2 |   TABLE ACCESS FULL| T1   |
|  3 |   TABLE ACCESS FULL| T0   |
------------------------------------
```

```
------------------------------------
| Id  | Operation           | Name |
------------------------------------
|   0 | SELECT STATEMENT    |      |
|   1 |  HASH JOIN ANTI     |      |
|   2 |   TABLE ACCESS FULL| T1    |
|   3 |   TABLE ACCESS FULL| T0    |
------------------------------------
```

Here and in many following examples, output from SQL*PLUS may be trimmed for readability and formatting purposes.

Some SQL engines allow us to explicitly specify SEMI/ANTI. For example, Cloudera Impala has keywords left/right semi join, left/right anti join.

Listing 1-14. Cloudera Impala ANTI join syntax

```
> select * from t1 left anti join t2 on t1.id = t2.id;
+----+
| id |
+----+
| 1  |
+----+
Fetched 1 row(s)
> select * from t1 right anti join t2 on t1.id = t2.id;
+----+
| id |
+----+
| 2  |
+----+
Fetched 1 row(s)
```

Oracle-Specific Syntax

The ANSI join syntax was introduced in Oracle 9i thus before that in order to join tables all of them should be specified in the from clause and join conditions in the where clause. Oracle-specific syntax (also called Oracle native syntax) for outer joins was available much earlier, including versions such as Oracle 5.

Listing 1-3 with inner join can be rewritten in the following way, as shown in Listing 1-15.

Listing 1-15. Another form of inner join

```
select * from t1, t2 where t1.id = t2.id;
```

Even though this statement does not have the keyword "join," it fully complies with the ANSI standard.

Before ANSI support, the only way to specify that join was left or right was to use Oracle-specific syntax. The construction (+) near column name indicates that join is outer. Left and right outer joins from Listing 1-6 and Listing 1-7 can be expressed in the following way, as shown in Listing 1-16.

Listing 1-16. Oracle native syntax for left and right outer join

```
select * from t1, t2 where t1.id = t2.id(+);
select * from t1, t2 where t1.id(+) = t2.id;
```

In the first case table t1 is an inner table and table t2 is a left outer table; in the second case table t1 is a right outer table and table t2 is an inner table.

A full outer join cannot be expressed using native syntax in a way so that each table is used only once. As a rule, developers imitated it using two queries combined using union all.

Listing 1-17. Imitation of full join using Oracle native syntax

```
select *
  from t1, t2
 where t1.id = t2.id(+)
union all
select *
  from t1, t2
 where t1.id(+) = t2.id
   and t1.id is null;
```

Speaking about outer joins, it's very important to understand concepts of "pre-join" and "post-join" predicates (Metalink Doc ID 14736.1). As it was mentioned earlier, in the ANSI outer join description, if there is no matching row in the outer table, then columns in the result set are populated with NULL values. The difference between pre-join and post-join predicates is that pre-join predicates are evaluated before NULL augmentation while post-join predicates are logically evaluated after it. In other words, pre-join can be considered as join predicates and post-join as filer predicates.

Listing 1-18. Pre-join and post-join predicates in Oracle native syntax

```
select *
  from t1, t2
 where t1.id = t2.id(+)
   and t2.id is null;

        ID N          ID N
---------- - ---------- -
         1 A
```

Expression "t1.id = t2.id(+)" in Listing 1-18 is a pre-join predicate and "t2.id is null" is a post-join predicate. Row with id = 1 from table t1 does not have a matching row from table t2 for the join condition "t1.id = t2.id(+)" so NULL values are populated for columns from t2 and after that filter by "t2.id is null" is applied.

It's important to mention that a filter predicate by an inner table may be (will be) applied before joining but this does not violate the definitions of pre-join and post-join predicates. This is part of optimization and you can find additional details at the end of Chapter 2, "Query Transformations" where the "selection" operation is mentioned.

Please analyze which predicates are pre-join and post-join in Listing 1-19 (answer will be given right after the code snippet).

Listing 1-19. Pre-join and post-join predicates

```
create table t3 as
select rownum - 1 id, mod(rownum, 2) sign from dual connect by
level <= 3;

1)

select *
  from t3
  left join t1
    on t1.id = t3.id
 order by t3.id;
```

ID	SIGN	ID	N
0	1	0	X
1	0	1	A
2	1		

2)

```
select *
  from t3
  left join t1
    on t1.id = t3.id
   and t1.id = 1
 order by t3.id;
```

```
        ID        SIGN          ID N
---------- ---------- ---------- -
         0         1
         1         0           1 A
         2         1
```

3)

```
select *
  from t3
  left join t1
    on t1.id = t3.id
 where t1.id = 1
 order by t3.id;
```

```
        ID        SIGN          ID N
---------- ---------- ---------- -
         1         0           1 A
```

4)

```
select *
  from t3, t1
 where t1.id(+) = t3.id
   and t1.id(+) = 1
 order by t3.id;
```

```
     ID          SIGN          ID N
---------- ---------- ---------- -

      0           1
      1           0            1 A
      2           1
```

5)

```
select *
  from t3, t1
 where t1.id(+) = t3.id
   and t1.id = 1
 order by t3.id;
```

```
     ID          SIGN          ID N
---------- ---------- ---------- -

      1           0            1 A
```

The first query simply demonstrates the left outer equi join. Predicate "t1.id = 1" in the third and fifth queries is post-join while a similar predicate in the second and fourth queries is pre-join. In the fourth query we use (+) to mark the predicate as pre-join while in the second case it's pre-join because it's part of the outer join clause.

The concept of pre/post predicates makes sense only in case of outer joins. The mandatory requirement for an outer join is to have a predicate that contains columns from both tables and (+) near one of those columns.

Let's consider the following two queries.

Listing 1-20. Outer joins and presence of (+)

```
select *
  from t3, t1
 where 0 = 0
   and t1.id(+) > 1
```

```
order by t3.id;
```

no rows selected

```
select *
  from t3, t1
 where nvl2(t3.id, 0, 0) = nvl2(t1.id(+), 0, 0)
   and t1.id(+) > 1
 order by t3.id;
```

ID	SIGN	ID	N
0	1		
1	0		
2	1		

The first query returned no rows because it was not specified that tables are an outer join. However, in the second query it's explicitly specified that t1 is the left outer table by using a predicate that always evaluates to TRUE.

If some columns from the table are marked with (+) while others are not, then Oracle may apply transformation "outer to inner join conversion" (more details about query transformations can be found in the next chapter).

Listing 1-21. Outer joins converted into inner ones

```
select * from t1 left join t2 on t1.id = t2.id where t1.name =
t2.name;
select * from t1, t2 where t1.id = t2.id(+) and t1.name =
t2.name;
```

Using the outer join syntax (whether it's ANSI or Oracle native) does not makes sense in such cases and it may be very misleading so it should always be avoided.

Sometimes it may be a bit challenging to specify that the predicate is pre-join using Oracle native syntax. If a pre-join predicate contains either both tables or the outer table, it's quite straightforward to specify it as was shown in Listing 1-19, the fourth case. However, if the pre-join predicate contains only an inner table then we need to use a column from the outer table as well to define pre-join nature of the predicate.

Listing 1-22. Pre-join predicates on inner table in ANSI syntax

```
select *
  from t3
  left join t1
    on t3.id = t1.id
  and t3.sign = 1
  order by 1;

        ID      SIGN            ID N
---------- ---------- ---------- -
         0         1          0 X
         1         0
         2         1
```

So to indicate that a predicate on an inner table is pre-join, we can use, for example, a trick with rowid of the outer table.

Listing 1-23. Pre-join predicate on inner table and trick with rowid

```
select *
  from t3, t1
 where t3.id = t1.id(+)
   and nvl2(t1.rowid(+), t3.sign, null) = 1
 order by 1;
```

```
     ID         SIGN           ID N
---------- ---------- ---------- -
        0          1          0 X
        1          0
        2          1
```

Another approach is to use a case expression (more details about this approach can be found in the next section – "Limitation of the Oracle Native Syntax"), which can be easily expressed with decode for equi conditions.

Listing 1-24. Pre-join predicate on inner table and approach with case (decode) expression

```
select *
  from t3, t1
 where case when t3.sign = 1 then t3.id end = t1.id(+)
 order by 1;
```

```
     ID         SIGN           ID N
---------- ---------- ---------- -
        0          1          0 X
        1          0
        2          1
```

```
select *
  from t3, t1
 where decode(t3.sign, 1, t3.id) = t1.id(+)
 order by 1;
```

```
     ID         SIGN           ID N
---------- ---------- ---------- -
        0          1          0 X
        1          0
        2          1
```

The left part of the case expression evaluates to t3.id only if the condition "t3.sign = 1" is met and right part of the expression indicates that tables are outer joined. Unlike trick with rowid, in this case both predicates from the original query are combined into a single predicate.

ANSI vs. Oracle Native Syntax

Both ANSI and native syntax have pros and cons. Some consider ANSI syntax as syntactic sugar, because it improves readability, but eventually queries are transformed into native syntax by an SQL engine. However, there are two exceptions: full join and outer join partition by. This means it's not possible to achieve the same execution plan by using Oracle native syntax. In all other cases, a query in ANSI syntax has a semantically equivalent form in native syntax with the same query plan; however, it was not always possible to use such an equivalent before Oracle 12c because some capabilities were not available for developers – in particular, lateral views. The current subsection is dedicated to a comprehensive comparison – ANSI vs Oracle native syntax – and if you are not interested in such details, then feel free to skip the comparison and proceed to the conclusion at the end of the chapter.

Limitation of the Oracle Native Syntax

1) IN, OR conditions are not allowed in pre-join predicates.

    The query from Listing 1-25 fails in Oracle 10g and works fine from Oracle 11g onward. A possible workaround may be using case-expression.

23

Listing 1-25. In-predicate in Oracle 10g

```
select *
  from t1, t2
 where t1.id = t2.id(+)
   and t2.id(+) in (1, 2, 3);
   and t2.id(+) in (1, 2, 3)
                 *
ERROR at line 4:
ORA-01719: outer join operator (+) not allowed in operand of OR
or IN

select *
  from t1, t2
 where t1.id = t2.id(+)
   and case when t2.id(+) in (1, 2, 3) then 1 end = 1;

        ID N           ID N
---------- - ---------- -
         1 A
         0 X
```

The query from Listing 1-26 works fine in Oracle 10g and it is equivalent to the original query if t2.id is an integer.

Listing 1-26. Between-predicate

```
select *
  from t1, t2
 where t1.id = t2.id(+)
   and t2.id(+) between 1 and 3
```

Some queries with in-predicates fail with ORA-01719 in all versions including Oracle 11gR2 and Oracle12cR2. Case-expression may be a workaround in such cases as well.

Listing 1-27. In-predicate in Oracle 11g, 12c

```
select * from t1 left join t2 on t2.id in (t1.id - 1, t1.id + 1);

        ID N          ID N
---------- - ---------- -
         0 X
         1 A         0 X
         1 A         2 B
select * from t1, t2 where t2.id(+) in (t1.id - 1, t1.id + 1);
select * from t1, t2 where t2.id(+) in (t1.id - 1, t1.id + 1)
                              *
ERROR at line 1:
ORA-01719: outer join operator (+) not allowed in operand of OR
or IN

select *
  from t1, t2
where case when t2.id(+) in (t1.id - 1, t1.id + 1) then 1
end = 1;
```

> An Oracle 12c query may be rewritten using a correlated inline view. The keyword "lateral" is used for this purpose.

Listing 1-28. Lateral view workaround for in-predicate

```
select *
  from t1,
       lateral (select *
                  from t2
                 where t2.id = t1.id - 1
                    or t2.id = t1.id + 1)(+) v;
```

The Oracle Optimizer team defines lateral view in the following way: A lateral view is an inline view that contains a correlation referring to other tables that precede it in the FROM clause.

The ANSI syntax for cross join (cross apply) and outer join (outer apply) with correlation support also has been added in Oracle 12c.

Listing 1-29. ANSI syntax for lateral views

```
select *
  from t1
 outer apply (select *
                from t2
               where t2.id = t1.id - 1
                  or t2.id = t1.id + 1) v
```

The following example also fails with ORA-01719 on all Oracle versions with ANSI support.

Listing 1-30. Another example of in-predicate in Oracle 11g, 12c

```
select *
  from t1
  left join t2
    on t1.id = t2.id
    or t1.id = 1;
```

```
        ID N          ID N
---------- - ---------- -
         0 X           0 X
         1 A           0 X
         1 A           2 B
```

```
select * from t1, t2 where t1.id = t2.id(+) or t1.id = 1;
select * from t1, t2 where t1.id = t2.id(+) or t1.id = 1
                              *
```

ERROR at line 1:
ORA-01719: outer join operator (+) not allowed in operand of OR
or IN

Workarounds are the same – case-expression or lateral/outer apply.

It's easier to explain the essence of the trick with case-expression if predicates are combined using the conjunction (AND) but not the disjunction (OR).

Listing 1-31. Conjunction predicates

```
select *
  from t1, t2
 where t1.id = t2.id(+) and t1.id = 1;

        ID N         ID N
---------- - ---------- -
         1 A
```

```
select *
  from t1, t2
 where t1.id = t2.id(+) and t1.id = nvl2(t2.id(+), 1, 1);

        ID N         ID N
---------- - ---------- -
         0 X
         1 A
```

```
select *
  from t1, t2
 where case when t1.id = t2.id(+) and t1.id = 1 then 1 end = 1;

        ID N         ID N
---------- - ---------- -
         0 X
         1 A
```

27

Predicate «t1.id = 1» was post-join in the first case, and in the second case the trick with nvl2 was used to specify that comparison with 1 is a pre-join predicate; and finally, case expression was used to specify inseparability of the predicates: one condition in a case cannot be pre-join while another one is post-join.

Let's proceed to disjunction predicates.

Listing 1-32. Disjunction predicates

```
select *
  from t1
  left join t2
    on t1.id = t2.id
    or t1.id = 1;

        ID N         ID N
---------- - ---------- -
         0 X          0 X
         1 A          0 X
         1 A          2 B
```

The join condition in this query means if t1.id = 1, then join this row with all the rows from t2; otherwise do an equi join.

The straightforward translation into native syntax may look as what is shown in Listing 1-33.

Listing 1-33. Disjunction predicates, native syntax

```
select *
  from t1, t2
 where t1.id = t2.id(+)
    or t1.id = 1;
 where t1.id = t2.id(+)
              *
```

```
ERROR at line 3:
ORA-01719: outer join operator (+) not allowed in operand of OR
or IN
```

Oracle does not allow you to execute this query; however we may notice that the query does not make sense if «t1.id = 1» is post-join, but the SQL engine is not supposed to take a logical meaning into an account.

So let's try to explicitly specify that both conditions are pre-join predicates but in this case query also fails with ORA-01719.

Listing 1-34. Disjunction, pre-join predicates, native syntax

```
select *
  from t1, t2
 where t1.id = t2.id(+)
    or t1.id = nvl2(t2.id(+), 1, 1);
```

Finally, if we use case-expression, it helps to specify the inseparability of the conditions and get the desired result.

Listing 1-35. Disjunction, case-expression workaround

```
select *
  from t1, t2
 where case when t1.id = 1 or t1.id = t2.id(+) then 1 end = 1;

        ID N         ID N
---------- - ---------- -
         0 X          0 X
         1 A          0 X
         1 A          2 B
```

2) Pre-join predicate cannot contain scalar subqueries (limitation removed in Oracle 12c).

Listing 1-36. Pre-join predicates containing scalar subqueries

```
select *
  from t3
  left join t1
    on t1.id = t3.id
   and t1.id = (select count(*) from dual)
 order by t3.id;

        ID          ID N
---------- ---------- -
         0
         1           1 A
         2
select *
  from t3, t1
 where t1.id(+) = t3.id
   and t1.id(+) = (select count(*) from dual)
 order by t3.id;
 order by t3.id
 *
ERROR at line 5:
ORA-01799: a column may not be outer-joined to a subquery
```

One of the following workarounds may be applied:

- Inline view with the filter by scalar subquery

- Inline view with scalar subquery in select list

- Outer join of the t1 to both t3 and scalar subquery (works from 12c onward; otherwise fails with ORA-01417)

Listing 1-37. Workarounds for outer join with predicate containing scalar subqery

```
select t3.id, v.id, v.name
  from t3,
       (select id, name from t1 where t1.id = (select count(*)
       from dual)) v
 where t3.id = v.id(+)
 order by t3.id;
select t3.id, t1.id, t1.name
  from (select t3.*, (select count(*) from dual) cnt from t3) t3, t1
 where t3.id = t1.id(+)
   and t3.cnt = t1.id(+)
 order by t3.id;
select t3.id, t1.id, t1.name
  from t3, t1, (select count(*) cnt from dual) v
 where t3.id = t1.id(+)
   and v.cnt = t1.id(+)
 order by t3.id;
```

3) Table may be outer joined to at most one other table (limitation removed in Oracle 12c).

Listing 1-38. Table outer joined with two tables. Native syntax

```
select *
  from t1, t2, t t3
 where t1.id = t2.id
   and t1.id = t3.id(+)
   and t2.name = t3.name(+);
   and t1.id = t3.id(+)
             *
ERROR at line 4:
ORA-01417: a table may be outer joined to at most one other table
```

Inline view can be used as a workaround (please see transformed query for Oracle 11g in Listing 1-40). The ANSI syntax may look as follows.

Listing 1-39. Table outer joined with two tables. ANSI syntax

```
select *
  from t1
  join t2
    on t1.id = t2.id
  left join t t3
    on t1.id = t3.id
   and t2.name = t3.name;

       ID N          ID N          ID N DUMMY
---------- - ---------- - ---------- - -----
        0 X           0 X
```

If we check the transformed query for ANSI syntax, then Oracle 11g will create an additional inline view (not lateral) with joined t1 and t2 while the query for Oracle 12c will be as the query above in native syntax. Transformed queries are shown below (details regarding how to see transformed queries will be provided in the next chapter – "Query Transformations").

Listing 1-40. Transformed queries for join with two tables

11g

```
select "from$_subquery$_003"."ID"    "ID",
       "from$_subquery$_003"."NAME" "NAME",
       "from$_subquery$_003"."ID"    "ID",
       "from$_subquery$_003"."NAME" "NAME",
       "T3"."ID"                     "ID",
       "T3"."NAME"                   "NAME",
       "T3"."DUMMY"                  "DUMMY"
```

```
   from (select "T1"."ID"    "ID",
                "T1"."NAME" "NAME",
                "T2"."ID"    "ID",
                "T2"."NAME" "NAME"
            from "T1" "T1", "T2" "T2"
           where "T1"."ID" = "T2"."ID") "from$_subquery$_003",
         "T" "T3"
   where "from$_subquery$_003"."NAME" = "T3"."NAME"(+)
     and "from$_subquery$_003"."ID" = "T3"."ID"(+)

12c
select "T1"."ID"    "ID",
       "T1"."NAME"  "NAME",
       "T2"."ID"    "ID",
       "T2"."NAME"  "NAME",
       "T3"."ID"    "ID",
       "T3"."NAME"  "NAME",
       "T3"."DUMMY" "DUMMY"
  from "T1" "T1", "T2" "T2", "T" "T3"
 where "T1"."ID" = "T3"."ID"(+)
   and "T2"."NAME" = "T3"."NAME"(+)
   and "T1"."ID" = "T2"."ID"
```

The last detailed example in this section is rather specific of native joins than limitation. If a table joined to one other table as inner and to another one as outer, then it may be not obvious how to specify the predicate that contains only a column from that table. So in the example below, table t2 joined with t1 as the outer table and with t3 as the inner table and the question is this: how to specify predicate "tt2.name is not null" in native syntax.

Listing 1-41. Inner/outer joined table

```
create table tt1 as select 'name' || rownum name from dual
connect by level <= 3;
create table tt2 as select 'x_name' || rownum name from dual
connect by level <= 2;
create table tt3 as select 'y_x_name' || rownum name from dual;
select tt1.name, tt2.name, tt3.name
  from tt1
  left join tt2
    on tt2.name like '%' || tt1.name || '%'
  left join tt3
    on tt3.name like '%' || tt2.name || '%'
  and tt2.name is not null;
```

```
NAME        NAME        NAME
----------  ----------  ----------
name1       x_name1     y_x_name1
name2       x_name2
name3
```

If we try to use native syntax, then we are getting wrong results regardless of whether we use (+) or not for "tt2.name is not null".

Listing 1-42. Inner/outer joined table and native syntax

```
select tt1.name, tt2.name, tt3.name
  from tt1, tt2, tt3
 where tt2.name(+) like '%' || tt1.name || '%'
   and tt3.name(+) like '%' || tt2.name || '%'
   and tt2.name is not null;
```

```
NAME        NAME        NAME
----------  ----------  ----------
name1       x_name1     y_x_name1
name2       x_name2
```

```
select tt1.name, tt2.name, tt3.name
  from tt1, tt2, tt3
 where tt2.name(+) like '%' || tt1.name || '%'
   and tt3.name(+) like '%' || tt2.name || '%'
   and tt2.name(+) is not null;
```

```
NAME        NAME        NAME
----------  ----------  ----------
name1       x_name1     y_x_name1
name2       x_name2
name3                   y_x_name1
```

To explicitly specify that that condition is a pre-join predicate for t2 and t3 we can use the approach described in the section "Oracle-Specific Syntax."

```
nvl2(tt2.name, 0, null) = nvl2(tt3.rowid(+), 0, 0)
```

So the predicate shows that t3 is outer joined to t2 and it evaluates to TRUE if "tt2.name" is not null.

Taking into account specifics of the query, we can combine the predicates below

```
   and tt3.name(+) like '%' || tt2.name || '%'
   and nvl2(tt2.name, 0, null) = nvl2(tt3.rowid(+), 0, 0)
```

into one

```
   and tt3.name(+) like nvl2(tt2.name, '%' || tt2.name || '%', null)
```

Another possible workaround for Oracle 12c is a lateral view; actually for this query Oracle creates a lateral view after transformation from ANSI syntax for all versions.

Unnesting Collections

Let's consider a table containing a nested table column.

Listing 1-43. Table with nested table column

```
create or replace type numbers as table of number
/
create table tc (id int, nums numbers) nested table nums store
as nums_t
/
insert into tc
select -1 id, numbers(null) nums from dual
union all select 0 id, numbers() nums from dual
union all select 1 id, numbers(1) nums from dual
union all select 2 id, numbers(1,2) nums from dual;
```

If we need to unnest a subtable if it's not empty, then it could be done using one of the approaches below.

Listing 1-44. Unnesting nested table

```
select tc.id, x.column_value
from tc, table(tc.nums) x -- 1
--from tc, lateral(select * from table(tc.nums)) x -- 2
--from tc cross apply (select * from table(tc.nums)) x -- 3
--from tc cross join table(tc.nums) x -- 4
;

        ID COLUMN_VALUE
---------- ------------
        -1
         1            1
         2            1
         2            2
```

The second and third approaches work starting with Oracle 12c.

Let's make the logic a bit more complicated: we need to unnest the table and return even those rows where a nested table is empty.

Listing 1-45. Unnesting nested table preserving rows where it's empty

```
select tc.id, x.column_value
from tc, table(tc.nums)(+) x -- 1
--from tc, lateral(select * from table(tc.nums))(+) x -- 2
--from tc cross apply (select * from table(tc.nums))(+) x -- 3
--from tc outer apply (select * from table(tc.nums)) x -- 4
--from tc, table(tc.nums) x where nvl2(x.column_value(+), 0, 0)
= nvl2(tc.id, 0, 0) -- 5
--from tc left join table(tc.nums) x on nvl2(x.column_value,
  0, 0) = nvl2(tc.id, 0, 0) -- 6
;

ID COLUMN_VALUE
---------- ------------
       -1
        0
        1            1
        2            1
        2            2
```

A couple of important notes about this approach:

- Mixed syntax of cross apply and (+) returns correct result but this is not documented and should be avoided.

- Always-true predicate containing two tables was used in options #5 and #6. Option #5 returned incorrect result because of bug on all versions up to Oracle 12cR1 (row with id = 0 is missing). On the Oracle 12cR2, all options return all rows from the original table along with unnested rows.

If the nested table is not stored, then option #6 returns an incorrect result on all versions including Oracle 12cR2.

Listing 1-46. Trying to unnest table using ANSI outer join

```
with tc as
(select -1 id, numbers(null) nums from dual
union all select 0 id, numbers() nums from dual
union all select 1 id, numbers(1) nums from dual
union all select 2 id, numbers(1,2) nums from dual)
select tc.id, x.column_value
from tc left join table(tc.nums) x on nvl2(x.column_value,
0, 0) = nvl2(tc.id, 0, 0);

        ID COLUMN_VALUE
---------- ------------
        -1
         1            1
         2            1
         2            2
```

One of the descriptions of this behavior is Bug 20363558 : WRONG RESULTS FOR ANSI JOIN ON NESTED TABLE.

A possible workaround for ANSI syntax for pre 12c versions is below:

Listing 1-47. Unnesting table using ANSI syntax on pre 12c versions

```
select tc.id, x.column_value
from tc cross join table(case when cardinality(tc.nums) = 0
then numbers(null) else tc.nums end) x
```

If we use a nested varray instead of a nested table table, for example:

Listing 1-48. Nested varray

```
create or replace type num_array as varray(32767) of number
/
create table tc (id int, nums num_array)
/
```

The result will be incorrect for option #6 irrespective whether varray is stored or constructed on the fly.

So the query returns a correct result if we use an outer correlated table operator – table(...)(+) or apply syntax for Oracle 12c. On the other hand, a query may return an incorrect result if we try to use outer join (both ANSI and native) and regardless of whether the nested table/varray is persisted or not.

Correlated Inline Views and Subqueries

It was already demonstrated several times how to implement correlated inline views by using keywords lateral/apply. Before 12c similar functionality could be achieved using a table operator and cast + multiset/collect (also undocumented option in Oracle 11g is event 22829). An obvious disadvantage of such approaches is necessity to create an SQL type for collection.

If we need to generate the number of rows equals to id for each row, then we can use the approaches below for Oracle 12c.

Listing 1-49. Correlated inline views, 12c

```
select t3.id, v.idx
  from t3,
       lateral (select rownum idx
                  from dual
                 where rownum <= t3.id
                 connect by rownum <= t3.id)(+) v;

select t3.id, v.idx
  from t3
```

```
outer apply (select rownum idx
                  from dual
                 where rownum <= t3.id
               connect by rownum <= t3.id) v;
```

Pre Oracle 12c it could be achieved as demonstrated in Listing 1-50.

Listing 1-50. Correlated inline views, 11g

```
select t3.id, v.column_value idx
  from t3,
       table(cast(multiset (select rownum
                    from dual
                   where rownum <= t3.id
                 connect by rownum <= t3.id) as sys.
                 odcinumberlist))(+) v;

select t3.id, v.column_value idx
  from t3,
       table (select cast(collect(rownum) as sys.
       odcinumberlist)
               from dual
              where rownum <= t3.id
            connect by rownum <= t3.id)(+) v;
```

Option with cast + multiset is more preferable for performance reasons.

In all cases, the result is the following:

```
       ID         IDX
---------- -----------
        0
        1           1
        2           1
        2           2
```

Strictly speaking, pre Oracle 12c we use an outer correlated table operator instead of an inline view.

Yet another limitation for correlated subqueries (table operator and cast + multiset/collect) for pre Oracle 12c versions was visibility of correlation names only for one level deep. In the example below, m2, m4, m5 can be calculated only in Oracle 12c (all expressions are logically equivalent).

Listing 1-51. Visibility of columns from main table in table expression

```
select id,
      greatest((select min(id) mid from t3 where t3.id >
      t.id), 1) m1,
      (select max(mid)
         from (select min(id) mid
                  from t3
                  where t3.id > t.id
               union
               select 1 from dual) z) m2,
      (select max(value(v))
         from table(cast(multiset (select min(id) mid
                              from t3
                              where t3.id > t.id
                           union
                           select 1 from dual) as sys.
                           odcinumberlist)) v) m3,
      (select max(value(v))
         from table (select cast(collect(mid) as sys.
         odcinumberlist) col
                        from (select min(id) mid
                                 from t3
```

```
                              where t3.id > t.id
                            union
                            select 1 from dual) z) v) m4,
        (select value(v)
            from table(cast(multiset (select max(mid)
                              from (select min(id) mid
                                  from t3
                                  where t3.id > t.id
                                union
                                select 1 from dual) z) as
                                sys.odcinumberlist)) v) m5
    from t3 t
  where t.id = 1;
```

ID	M1	M2	M3	M4	M5
1	2	2	2	2	2

It's not always possible to simplify a (scalar) subquery so that it contains only one level deep; a possible workaround in such cases for pre Oracle 12 was encapsulating logic in UDF and then specifying it in a select list or rewriting the query to use explicit joins instead of (scalar) subqueries. In Oracle 12c scalar subqueries also should be used after careful consideration because sometimes they may be incorrectly or inefficiently transformed by the SQL engine.

The last important point in this section - lateral/apply does not allow such a flexible correlation as collect/multiset. For example it's not possible to specify the column from the main table to start with. The last query from Listing 1-52 fails with "ORA-00904: "T1" . "ID": invalid identifier" if we uncomment "t1.id".

Listing 1-52. Visibility of columns from main table in table expression and lateral view

```
select t1.*,
       l.*
  from t1,
       table(cast(multiset (select id
                     from t3
                     start with t3.id = t1.id
                     connect by prior t3.id + 1 = t3.id) as
                     numbers)) l;

select t1.*, l.*
  from t1,
       table (select cast(collect(id) as numbers)
                from t3
                start with t3.id = t1.id
                connect by prior t3.id + 1 = t3.id) l;

select t1.*, l.*
  from t1,
       lateral (select id
                  from t3
                  start with t3.id = 0 -- t1.id
                  connect by prior t3.id + 1 = t3.id) l;
```

ANSI to Native Transformation

Let's use the following tables and query to demonstrate transformation.

Listing 1-53. Tables and query to demonstrate ANSI to native transformation

```
create table fact as (select 1 value, 1 dim_1_id, 1 dim_2_id,
'A' type from dual);
create table dim_1 as (select 1 id, 1 dim_n_id from dual);
create table dim_n as (select 1 id, 1 value from dual);
create table map as (select 1 value, 'DETAILED VALUE' category
from dual);

select fact.*, map.*
  from fact
  join dim_1
    on dim_1.id = fact.dim_1_id
  join dim_n
    on dim_1.dim_n_id = dim_n.id
  left join map
    on fact.type in ('A', 'B', 'C')
  and ((map.category = 'FACT VALUE' and map.value = fact.
      value) or
      (map.category = 'DETAILED VALUE' and map.value = dim_n.
      value));
```

Listing 1-54. Query after transformation into native syntax

```
select "FACT"."VALUE"              "VALUE",
       "FACT"."DIM_1_ID"           "DIM_1_ID",
       "FACT"."DIM_2_ID"           "DIM_2_ID",
       "FACT"."TYPE"               "TYPE",
       "VW_LAT_3C55142F"."ITEM_1_0" "VALUE",
       "VW_LAT_3C55142F"."ITEM_2_1" "CATEGORY"
  from "FACT" "FACT",
       "DIM_1" "DIM_1",
       "DIM_N" "DIM_N",
```

```
        lateral((select "MAP"."VALUE" "ITEM_1_0", "MAP"."CATEGORY"
        "ITEM_2_1"
                    from "MAP" "MAP"
                where ("FACT"."TYPE" = 'A' or "FACT"."TYPE" =
                'B' or
                        "FACT"."TYPE" = 'C')
                    and ("MAP"."CATEGORY" = 'FACT VALUE' and
                        "MAP"."VALUE" = "FACT"."VALUE" or
                        "MAP"."CATEGORY" = 'DETAILED VALUE' and
                        "MAP"."VALUE" = "DIM_N"."VALUE")))(+)
                        "VW_LAT_3C55142F"
    where "DIM_1"."DIM_N_ID" = "DIM_N"."ID"
     and "DIM_1"."ID" = "FACT"."DIM_1_ID"
```

The crucial point here is that Oracle creates a non-mergeable lateral view. A logically equivalent query in native syntax may be implemented as the following (it's not possible to implement a query without an additional inline view for pre Oracle 12c versions because map table cannot be outer joined to both fact and dim_n and query fails with "ORA-01417: a table may be outer joined to at most one other table").

Listing 1-55. Query manually rewritten into native syntax

```
select *
  from (select fact.*, dim_n.value as value_1
          from fact, dim_1, dim_n
        where dim_1.id = fact.dim_1_id
           and dim_1.dim_n_id = dim_n.id) sub,
      map
 where case when decode(map.rowid(+), map.rowid(+), sub.type)
in ('A', 'B', 'C') then 1 end = 1
   and decode(map.category(+), 'FACT VALUE', sub.value,
   'DETAILED VALUE', sub.value_1) = map.value(+);
```

The ANSI version has better readability, but in case of native syntax, Oracle does not create a non-mergeable correlated inline view so that it allows us to achieve better performance because the SQL engine can use HASH JOIN in such cases. This join method is not possible for lateral views.

A very important point is that if we use predicates for ANSI syntax in the same form as they were for native syntax, then a lateral view is not created.

Listing 1-56. ANSI syntax with predicates copied from native syntax

```
select fact.*, map.*
  from fact
  join dim_1
    on dim_1.id = fact.dim_1_id
  join dim_n
    on dim_1.dim_n_id = dim_n.id
  left join map
    on case when decode(map.rowid, map.rowid, fact.type) in
    ('A', 'B', 'C') then 1 end = 1
    and decode(map.category, 'FACT VALUE', fact.value, 'DETAILED
    VALUE', dim_n.value) = map.value
```

The query above transformed into the following and the VIEW operation is absent in the query plan, which means there are non-mergeable views in the query itself.

Listing 1-57. Transformed query for ANSI version with amended predicates

```
select "FACT"."VALUE"     "VALUE",
       "FACT"."DIM_1_ID" "DIM_1_ID",
       "FACT"."DIM_2_ID" "DIM_2_ID",
       "FACT"."TYPE"     "TYPE",
```

```
            "MAP"."VALUE"       "VALUE",
            "MAP"."CATEGORY"   "CATEGORY"
    from "FACT"   "FACT",
         "DIM_1" "DIM_1",
         "DIM_N" "DIM_N",
         "MAP"     "MAP"
  where case when decode("MAP".ROWID(+), "MAP".ROWID(+),
"FACT"."TYPE") in ('A', 'B', 'C') then 1 end = 1
    and "MAP"."VALUE"(+) = decode("MAP"."CATEGORY"(+),
         'FACT VALUE', "FACT"."VALUE", 'DETAILED VALUE',
         "DIM_N"."VALUE")
    and "DIM_1"."DIM_N_ID" = "DIM_N"."ID"
    and "DIM_1"."ID" = "FACT"."DIM_1_ID"
```

Transformation ANSI to native continuously evolves from one Oracle version to another, and some queries do not have lateral views after transformation even though they led to lateral view creation in older versions.

As it was mentioned earlier, full join and left/right join partition by are not transformed into native syntax.

To demonstrate the latter, let's consider the following requirement. For each presenter from the table "presentation" display all days of the week and number of presentations for each day.

Listing 1-58. Tables to demonstrate join partition by

```
create table week(id, day) as
select rownum,
       to_char(trunc(sysdate, 'd') + level - 1,
               'fmday',
               'NLS_DATE_LANGUAGE = English')
  from dual
connect by rownum <= 7;
```

```
create table presentation(name, day, time) as
select 'John', 'monday', '14' from dual
union all
select 'John', 'monday', '9' from dual
union all
select 'John', 'friday', '9' from dual
union all
select 'Rex', 'wednesday', '11' from dual
union all
select 'Rex', 'friday', '11' from dual;
```

The result can be achieved by using the query below.

Listing 1-59. Join partition by

```
select p.name, w.day, count(p.time) cnt
  from week w
  left join presentation p partition by (p.name)
    on w.day = p.day
 group by p.name, w.day, w.id
 order by p.name, w.id;
```

```
NAME DAY             CNT
---- --------- ----------
John monday            2
John tuesday           0
John wednesday         0
John thursday          0
John friday            1
John saturday          0
John sunday            0
Rex  monday            0
Rex  tuesday           0
Rex  wednesday         1
```

Rex	thursday	0
Rex	friday	1
Rex	saturday	0
Rex	sunday	0

14 rows selected.

Listing 1-60. Final query after transformations

```
select "from$_subquery$_003"."NAME_0" "NAME",
       "from$_subquery$_003"."QCSJ_C000000000300000_2" "DAY",
       count("from$_subquery$_003"."TIME_4") "CNT"
  from (select "P"."NAME" "NAME_0",
               "W"."ID"   "ID_1",
               "W"."DAY"  "QCSJ_C000000000300000_2",
               "P"."DAY"  "QCSJ_C000000000300001",
               "P"."TIME" "TIME_4"
          from "PRESENTATION" "P" partition by("P"."NAME")
          right outer join "WEEK" "W"
            on "W"."DAY" = "P"."DAY") "from$_subquery$_003"
 group by "from$_subquery$_003"."NAME_0",
          "from$_subquery$_003"."QCSJ_C000000000300000_2",
          "from$_subquery$_003"."ID_1"
 order by "from$_subquery$_003"."NAME_0", "from$_
subquery$_003"."ID_1"
```

"partition by (p.name)" means that all rows from the week table will be joined for each name from the presentation table. The same result can be achieved without this capability but it requires an additional join.

Listing 1-61. Workaround for join partition by

```
select w.name, w.day, count(p.time) cnt
  from (select p0.name, w0.*
          from (select distinct name from presentation) p0,
               week w0) w,
```

49

```
      presentation p
where w.day = p.day(+)
  and w.name = p.name(+)
group by w.name, w.day, w.id
order by w.name, w.id;
```

Let's consider final query after transformations for SEMI join "select t1.* from t1 where t1.id in (select id from t0)"

Listing 1-62. Transformed query for SEMI join

```
select "T1"."ID" "ID", "T1"."NAME" "NAME"
  from "M12"."T0" "T0", "M12"."T1" "T1"
 where "T1"."ID" = "T0"."ID"
```

There is no special notation for SEMI join predicates, thus a condition in a final query looks like a simple equality predicate; however the join method for the original query is HASH JOIN SEMI (similar reasoning applies to ANTI joins as well). If you try to build a plan for a transformed query, then the join method will be just HASH JOIN. So additional attention is required when working with final queries after transformation – they are just a representation of the transformed queries and may not be semantically equivalent in all cases to the original query. We can add distinct and t1.rowid to select a list to get what is required but performance is not the same as for SEMI join – joining and applying distinct on top of it is not the same as looking for one row satisfying a join condition for each row from t1.

It's possible to specify another join method (NESTED LOOPS SEMI in this case) for the query or to completely disable all transformations using optimizer hints.

```
select t1.* from t1 where t1.id in (select /*+ use_nl(t0) */ id
from t0);
select /*+ no_query_transformation */ t1.* from t1 where t1.id
in (select id from t0);
```

In the second case Oracle does a full scan of T0 for each row from T1 (it may be index access though if there is an index on T0(id)) to find the first match.

Listing 1-63. Query plan with disabled transformations

```
------------------------------------
| Id | Operation        | Name |
------------------------------------
|  0 | SELECT STATEMENT |      |
|  1 |  FILTER          |      |
|  2 |   TABLE ACCESS FULL| T1 |
|  3 |   TABLE ACCESS FULL| T0 |
------------------------------------

Predicate Information (identified by operation id):
----------------------------------------------------

   1 - filter( EXISTS (SELECT 0 FROM "T0" "T0" WHERE "ID"=:B1))
   3 - access("ID"=:B1)
```

In general case, plans for an original query and transformed query may be different and, as it was already mentioned, the final query after transformation is an SQL-like representation of what will be eventually executed.

In case of using a Cost Based Optimizer (CBO), original queries that look quite different may be transformed into the same final query and lead to the same execution plan because of query transformations.

On the other hand, the way a query is written has much considerable influence on the query plan while using Rule Based Optimizer (RBO) final query. In this case a query plan is built based on a predefined set of rules and a very limited number of transformations. Many of the join methods are not implemented for RBO; in particular, there is no SEMI JOIN.

Listing 1-64. Query plan when built by RBO

```
select /*+ rule */ t1.* from t1 where t1.id in (select id from t0);
```

```
-------------------------------------------
| Id | Operation            | Name      |
-------------------------------------------
|  0 | SELECT STATEMENT     |           |
|  1 |  MERGE JOIN          |           |
|  2 |   SORT JOIN          |           |
|  3 |    TABLE ACCESS FULL | T1        |
|* 4 |   SORT JOIN          |           |
|  5 |    VIEW              | VW_NSO_1  |
|  6 |     SORT UNIQUE      |           |
|  7 |      TABLE ACCESS FULL| T0       |
-------------------------------------------

Predicate Information (identified by operation id):
---------------------------------------------------

   4 - access("T1"."ID"="ID")
       filter("T1"."ID"="ID")
```

CBO was introduced in Oracle 7.3 and has been greatly improved since then; moreover RBO is deprecated since Oracle 10g and Oracle do not recommend using it in any cases. The above example was provided to demonstrate that some join methods were missing for RBO and also manual rewriting of the queries may not be that important as it was in the past.

Clearness and Readability

Let's use a simple model with a fact table containing two coordinates of a single dimension.

Listing 1-65. Trivial model for star schema

```
create table fact_ as (select 1 value, 1 dim_1_id, 2 dim_2_id
from dual);
create table dim_ as (select rownum id, 'name'||rownum name
from dual connect by rownum <= 2);
```

If we need to get dimensional attributes for both coordinates, it can be done using ANSI syntax as shown in Listing 1-66.

Listing 1-66. Using ANSI to join fact with dimensions

```
select *
from fact_ f
join dim_ d1 on f.dim_1_id = d1.id
join dim_ d2 on f.dim_2_id = d2.id
```

Clearness and readability highlights for ANSI:

1) Join conditions for each dimension are separated into a correspondent on clause. For inner joins and complex join conditions it may be not obvious where to specify predicates – in the where clause or in the on clause. In such cases the next rule may help: where clause should contain only filters by a fact table. For outer joins there is no need for such a rule.

2) There is no need to create additional inline/lateral views for outer joins. This feature also may be considered as a disadvantage because readability results in more problematic control on a query plan (see also the section "Controlling Execution Plan").

3) There is additional validation for join predicates. It's possible to use only those tables that listed before the current table. For example, the query below will fail with "ORA-00904: "D2". "ID": invalid identifier."

Listing 1-67. Validation for predicates for ANSI syntax

```
select *
from fact_ f
join dim_ d1 on f.dim_1_id = d2.id
join dim_ d2 on f.dim_2_id = d2.id
```

In case of native syntax, all predicates are listed in a where clause. Additional control may be achieved by using inline views.

Also we can introduce various standards for specifying predicates in a where clause but if a query contain joins of, let's say, 20 tables anyway, those predicates will look a bit messy. If we use ANSI for inner joins it's possible to cross join all the tables and then list all predicates in a where clause but no one follows this ridiculous approach because separating join conditions improves readability a lot.

4) ANSI syntax clearly defines for each predicate the specific join it belongs to. In case of native syntax it's not always easy to specify if a predicate contains only one table (that was shown in section "Limitation of the Oracle Native Syntax").

Flexibility of ANSI syntax allows us to write some cunning queries that are not that easy to understand. I would not recommend using these capabilities, but it's important to know they exist.

So, changing the order of tables in from and join clauses for ANSI syntax may impact the query result.

Results are different for the queries below because in in the first case, Oracle joins t1 with t2 and then the result set with t3, while in the second case it joins t2 with t3 and then the result set with t1.

Listing 1-68. Changing join order for ANSI syntax

```
select t1.*, t2.*, t3.*
  from t1
  full join t2
    on t1.id = t2.id
  join t3
    on t2.id = t3.id
  order by t1.id;

        ID N          ID N          ID
---------- - ---------- - ----------
       0 X          0 X           0
                    2 B           2

select t1.*, t2.*, t3.*
  from t2
  join t3
    on t2.id = t3.id
  full join t1
    on t1.id = t2.id
  order by t1.id;

        ID N          ID N          ID
---------- - ---------- - ----------
       0 X          0 X           0
       1 A
                    2 B           2
```

However, it's possible to change the order of joins without changing the order of tables in the query text.

Listing 1-69. Specifying join clause in place of table reference

```
select t1.*, t2.*, t3.*
  from t1
  full join (t2 join t3 on t2.id = t3.id) on t1.id = t2.id
 order by t1.id;
```

```
        ID N          ID N          ID
---------- - ---------- - ----------
         0 X           0 X           0
         1 A
                       2 B           2
```

This query may look even more ambiguous if we remove brackets. Nevertheless this functionality is documented and join_clause may be specified in place of the table reference. In a trivial case it looks like the following:

Listing 1-70. table_reference and join_clause

```
-- table_reference in ()
select * from (dual);
-- join_clause in ()
select * from (dual cross join dual);
```

Mixing Syntax

Some people prefer native syntax while others tend to use only ANSI syntax. In rare cases, it may be acceptable to use both ANSI and native in the same query but on different levels (or in different subqueries). This could happen, for example, if the development standard in the team is ANSI but it does not allow you to fix the plan because of inline views creation under the hood, or you faced some ANSI bug or limitation (see section "Limitations of ANSI").

It is more surprising that Oracle allows you to mix ANSI and native syntax even in single from clause. The following examples will demonstrate some bad practices. I do not think anyone should be using this but it's important to understand what is going on if you face such a query.

So, if you specify ANSI inner join and add operator (+) to a join condition, then, in fact, Oracle will execute it as an outer join.

Listing 1-71. Original and transformed queries for mixed syntax

```
select * from t1 join t2 on t1.id = t2.id(+)
select "T1"."ID"   "ID",
       "T1"."NAME" "NAME",
       "T2"."ID"   "ID",
       "T2"."NAME" "NAME"
  from "T1" "T1", "T2" "T2"
 where "T1"."ID" = "T2"."ID"(+)
```

Let's proceed to the following query in Listing 1-72.

Listing 1-72. Mixed syntax in from clause

```
select *
  from t1, t2
  left join t3
    on t3.id = t2.id + 1;
```

ID N	ID N	ID
0 X	0 X	1
1 A	0 X	1
0 X	2 B	
1 A	2 B	

Please note that tables t1 and t2 are listed using a comma while t3 was added using an ANSI join. The transformed query looks as shown in Listing 1-73.

Listing 1-73. Transformed query for mixed syntax in from clause

```
select "T1"."ID"    "ID",
       "T1"."NAME" "NAME",
       "T2"."ID"    "ID",
       "T2"."NAME" "NAME",
       "T3"."ID"    "ID"
  from "T1" "T1", "T2" "T2", "T3" "T3"
 where "T3"."ID"(+) = "T2"."ID" + 1
```

Let's specify all joins in ANSI style and add one more condition.

Listing 1-74. Mixed query rewritten into ANSI along with additional predicate

```
select *
  from t1
 cross join t2
  left join t3
    on t3.id = t2.id + 1
   and t3.id = t1.id;
```

ID	N	ID	N	ID
1	A	0	X	1
0	X	0	X	
1	A	2	B	
0	X	2	B	

If we try to use mixed syntax for the above query, it will fail, which means that only t2 is visible in an on clause for join with t3.

Listing 1-75. Mixed syntax and complex predicate

```
select *
  from t1, t2
  left join t3
    on t3.id = t2.id + 1
    and t3.id = t1.id;
    and t3.id = t1.id
            *
ERROR at line 5:
ORA-00904: "T1"."ID": invalid identifier
```

If we try to specify a predicate for joining t1 and t3 using (+) in a where clause, then the query fails with ORA-25156.

Listing 1-76. Mixed syntax and predicates in where and on clauses

```
select *
  from t1, t2
  left join t3
    on t3.id = t2.id + 1
 where t3.id(+) = t1.id;
 where t3.id(+) = t1.id
         *
ERROR at line 5:
ORA-25156: old style outer join (+) cannot be used with ANSI
joins
```

It would be reasonable to raise «ORA-25156» always when a from clause contains ANSI syntax and (+) operator or raise another exception, then different join styles are used in a from clause but demonstrated examples with mixed syntax work successfully on Oracle 10g, 11g, and 12c.

Controlling Execution Plan

As already mentioned, some hints may become invalid while using ANSI syntax because of lateral/inline views creation under the hood. Moreover, some hints cannot be used with ANSI, particularly, qb_name. This hint may be very useful when someone tries to specify tables from an inline view in the main query hint.

Let's check aliases for the queries below using "select * from table(dbms_xplan.display_cursor(format => 'BASIC ALIAS'));".

Listing 1-77. Specifying qb_name hint

```
select --+ qb_name(q)
  *
  from t1
  join t2
    on t1.id = t2.id;

select --+ qb_name(q)
  *
  from t1, t2
 where t1.id = t2.id;
```

The result is shown below (hint became invalid for ANSI syntax) in Listing 1-78.

Listing 1-78. Aliases after using qb_name

```
Query Block Name / Object Alias (identified by operation id):
-------------------------------------------------------------

  1 - SEL$695B99D2
  2 - SEL$695B99D2 / T1@SEL$1
  3 - SEL$695B99D2 / T2@SEL$1
```

```
Query Block Name / Object Alias (identified by operation id):
-----------------------------------------------------------------

   1 - Q
   2 - Q / T1@Q
   3 - Q / T2@Q
```

Limitations of ANSI

Before Oracle 12c there was a limitation in using ANSI syntax in subqueries. However I'd say that it was a bug rather than a limitation.

If we use a column from the main query in a join condition, then it fails with ORA-00904.

Listing 1-79. Using column from main query in ANSI join predicate

```
select t3.id,
       (select count(t2.rowid) + count(t1.rowid)
          from t2
          join t1
            on t2.id = t1.id
          and t2.id = t3.id) x
  from t3
 order by t3.id;
          and t2.id = t3.id) x
                    *
ERROR at line 6:
ORA-00904: "T3"."ID": invalid identifier
```

We can get rid of the correlated scalar subquery and use explicit joins instead to avoid error (t3.rowid is added to group by because there is no guarantee that t3.id is unique).

Listing 1-80. Using explicit joins instead of correlated scalar subquery

```
select t3.id, count(t2.rowid) + count(t1.rowid) x
  from t3
  left join(t2 join t1 on t2.id = t1.id) on t3.id = t2.id
 group by t3.rowid, t3.id
 order by t3.id;
```

```
        ID             X
---------- ----------
         0             2
         1             0
         2             0
```

Scalar subqueries may be preferable for performance reasons because of scalar subquery caching if t3.id has low cardinality.

If we move predicate "t2.id = t3.id" into the where clause, then the query works fine.

Listing 1-81. Moving predicate with column from main query into where clause

```
select t3.id,
       (select count(t2.rowid) + count(t1.rowid)
          from t2
          join t1
            on t2.id = t1.id
         where t2.id = t3.id) x
  from t3
 order by t3.id;
```

This workaround is not always possible though, because the join may be outer and with a condition containing column from the main query. Query from Listing 1-82 was executed on Oracle 12c (it fails on older versions).

Listing 1-82. ANSI outer join in scalar subquery

```
select t3.id,
       (select count(t2.rowid) + count(t1.rowid)
          from t2
          left join t1
            on t2.id = t1.id
           and t3.id > 0
         where t2.id = t3.id) x
  from t3
 order by t3.id;

        ID          X
---------- ----------
         0          1
         1          0
         2          1
```

We can avoid an error in 11g if we move the logic into a select list expression, but this approach cannot be considered a proper workaround. See Listing 1-83.

Listing 1-83. Avoiding error for ANSI outer join in scalar subquery

```
select t3.id,
       (select count(t2.rowid) + decode(sign(t3.id), 1,
       count(t1.rowid), 0)
          from t2
          left join t1
```

```
            on t2.id = t1.id
         where t2.id = t3.id) x
  from t3
 order by t3.id;
```

```
       ID              X
---------- ----------
        0              1
        1              0
        2              1
```

A better approach would be to use an outer correlated table operator (type numbers was defined in section "Unnesting Collections") as shown in Listing 1-84.

Listing 1-84. Using table operator with ANSI join in scalar subquery

```
select t3.id,
       (select count(t2.rowid) + count(tt.column_value)
          from t2
          left join table(cast(multiset (select nvl2(t2.rowid,
          1, null)
                                            from t1
                                           where t2.id = t1.id
                                             and t3.id > 0) as
                                            numbers)) tt
           on 1 = 1
          where t2.id = t3.id) x
  from t3
 order by t3.id;
```

And finally a query may be rewritten to use native joins, as shown in Listing 1-85.

Listing 1-85. Using native join instead of ANSI in scalar subquery

```
select t3.id,
       (select count(t2.rowid) + count(t1.rowid)
          from t2, t1
         where t2.id = t3.id
           and t2.id = t1.id(+)
           and decode(sign(t3.id), 1, 0) = nvl2(t1.id(+), 0, 0)) x
  from t3
 order by t3.id;
```

The same issues occur while using ANSI and correlated subqueries in a where clause, so this is not specific for scalar subqueries in a select list.

Summary

As a rule, a query returns data from many tables (or one table occurs multiple times) and data sets from different tables must be joined into a single result set (except in cases when they are combined using set operators - union/union all/intersect/minus). Joins may be explicitly specified using a join keyword or implicitly using an Oracle native syntax or subqueries. (ANTI) SEMI joins may be specified by using conditions (not) in/exists.

The same logic may be implemented in a very different fashion, but it's not always possible to get the same plan for different but semantically equivalent queries. During execution of a query, it's getting converted into native syntax and various transformations are applied – additional details will be explained in the next chapter.

Speaking about ANSI vs. native syntax, it's worth to mention that ANSI provides better readability and clearness; however, native syntax allows better control over an execution plan. Two types of ANSI joins – full and outer partition by – cannot be expressed in native syntax, so that they have the same execution plan as an ANSI equivalent.

ANSI syntax was introduced much later than the native one and initially had a huge number of bugs. However, as it was shown in the section "Unnesting Collections," some bugs still exist even in Oracle 12c and may appear for both ANSI and native syntaxes.

CHAPTER 2

Query Transformations

The same logic can be implemented using various but semantically equivalent queries that look quite different but have the same plans and performance. This is achieved as a result of query transformations – original queries transform into the same final query.

For instance, the queries from Listing 2-1 have the same performance and plans. The last one has minor difference though – the join method is HASH JOIN ANTI NA while for all other queries it is HASH JOIN ANTI, so the result set for the last query will be empty if t2.id has null values.

Listing 2-1. Different ways to implement ANTI join

```
select t1.* from t1 left join t2 on t1.id = t2.id where t2.id
is null;

select t1.* from t1 where not exists (select t2.id from t2
where t1.id = t2.id);

select t1.* from t1, t2 where t1.id = t2.id(+) and t2.id is
null;

select t1.* from t1 where t1.id not in (select t2.id from t2);
```

© Alex Reprintsev 2018
A. Reprintsev, *Oracle SQL Revealed*, https://doi.org/10.1007/978-1-4842-3372-6_2

To check applied transformations and final queries, one needs to set an event 10053 or enable SQL Optimizer tracing before executing the statement (detailed descriptions of these commands is out of the scope of this book, additional information can be found in [1]).

Listing 2-2. Enabling tracing for transformations

```
alter session set events 'trace[rdbms.SQL_Optimizer.*]';
alter session set events '10053 trace name context forever,
level 1';
```

Final query text will be in a tracing file in the section «Final query after transformations:******* UNPARSED QUERY IS *******». For all above queries it will be exactly the same (schema name was manually removed from the statement) as shown in Listing 2-3:

Listing 2-3. Transformed query for ANTI join

```
SELECT "T1"."ID" "ID","T1"."NAME" "NAME" FROM "T2", "T1" WHERE
"T1"."ID"="T2"."ID"
```

If you execute this query it will not return the expected result. That is because there is no special notation for an ANTI join in a tracing file - even though it exists in relational algebra. ANTI (or SEMI) joins are not the only case when a query plan for a final query does not match the query plan for the original query. There are many other examples and one of them will be shown in Chapter 5, "Hierarchical queries: connect by" while explaining how connect by + join + where works.

To check the final query after transformations, you can also use stored procedure dbms_utility.expand_sql_text added in Oracle 12c (starting with Oracle 11.2.0.3 there was undocumented dbms_sql2.expand_sql_text for the same purpose); however, its output may differ from what we see in trace file so I would recommend using trace files as a more reliable source.

The transformation engine is part of the query optimizer and the general schema of the optimizer is shown in Figure 2-1. It consists of three main components: the transformer, estimator, and plan generator.

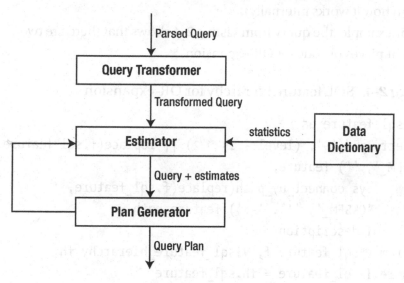

Figure 2-1. *Query optimizer components*

Transformations are also known as logical optimization while the plan generator (searches through different access paths, join methods, and join orders) is responsible for physical optimization. Please see further details in [2], [3].

Transformations are divided into two main categories (additional information can be found in documentation and [4]):

- Cost-based transformations – applied based on cost, for example, or-expansion;

- Heuristic-based transformations – applied based on heuristics, for instance, simple/complex view merging.

So cost-based transformations are applied only if the cost of the transformed query is lower than the cost of the original query while heuristic-based transformations are applied always when some conditions are met (conditions differ from one transformation to another).

Most of the transformations come into play only when CBO is enabled; however, some of them may be applied even if RBO is used (let me remind you that RBO is deprecated and this information is provided to shed some light on how it works internally).

For example, the query from Listing 2-4 shows that there are two different pieces of code for OR-expansion.

Listing 2-4. SQL feature hierarchy for OR-expansion

```
with sql_feature as
 (select lpad(' ', (level - 1) * 2) || replace(f.sql_feature,
 'QKSFM_', '') feature,
         sys_connect_by_path(replace(f.sql_feature,
         'QKSFM_', ''), '->') feature_path,
         f.description
    from v$sql_feature f, v$sql_feature_hierarchy fh
   where f.sql_feature = fh.sql_feature
  connect by fh.parent_id = prior f.sql_feature
   start with fh.sql_feature = 'QKSFM_ALL')
select *
  from sql_feature
 where lower(replace(description, '-', ' ')) like 'or %';

FEATURE       FEATURE_PATH                            DESCRIPTION
----------    ----------------------------------      -----------
OR_EXPAND     ->ALL->COMPILATION->CBO->OR_EXPAND      OR expansion
USE_CONCAT    ->ALL->COMPILATION->TRANSFORMATION
              ->HEURISTIC->USE_CONCAT                 Or-optimization
```

Let's move on to a specific example of or-expansion.

Listing 2-5. OR-expansion

```
create table tr(id primary key, name) as
select rownum, lpad('#',rownum,'#') from dual connect by level
<= 1e5;
```

Table created.

```
explain plan for select * from tr where id = nvl(:p, id);
```

Explained.

```
select * from table(dbms_xplan.display(format => 'basic
predicate'));
```

PLAN_TABLE_OUTPUT

Plan hash value: 2631158932

```
--------------------------------------------------------------
| Id  | Operation                    | Name         |
--------------------------------------------------------------
|   0 | SELECT STATEMENT             |              |
|   1 |  CONCATENATION               |              |
|*  2 |   FILTER                     |              |
|*  3 |    TABLE ACCESS FULL         | TR           |
|*  4 |   FILTER                     |              |
|   5 |    TABLE ACCESS BY INDEX ROWID| TR          |
|*  6 |     INDEX UNIQUE SCAN        | SYS_C0011913 |
--------------------------------------------------------------
```

Predicate Information (identified by operation id):

```
   2 - filter(:P IS NULL)
   3 - filter("ID" IS NOT NULL)
```

```
4 - filter(:P IS NOT NULL)
6 - access("ID"=:P)
```

If the value of the bind variable is null, then Oracle will do a full scan of TR; otherwise it will do an index unique scan. Semantically, this query is equivalent to the next one:

Listing 2-6. Manual OR-expansion

```
select *
  from tr
 where id is not null
   and :p is null
union all
select *
  from tr
 where id = :p
   and :p is not null
```

Listing 2-7 shows the final query after transformations:

Listing 2-7. Final query after OR-expansion

```
SELECT "TR"."ID" "ID","TR"."NAME" "NAME" FROM "TR" WHERE
"TR"."ID"=NVL(:B1,"TR"."ID")
```

As you see it's impossible to figure out whether transformation was applied or not based on the query text. This transformation could not have been applied in other circumstances – for example, if there is no index on ID or if it is not selective. If you want to force the optimizer to do (or not to do) OR-expansion, you can use hints use_concat/no_expand.

Let's now turn on RBO and consider an example that is a bit simpler.

Listing 2-8. RBO and OR-expansion

```
explain plan for
select /*+ rule */ * from tr where id = any (:bind1, :bind2);
```

Explained.

```
select * from table(dbms_xplan.display(format => 'basic
predicate'));
```

PLAN_TABLE_OUTPUT
```
--------------------------------------------------------------
```

Plan hash value: 2176406400

```
--------------------------------------------------------------

| Id  | Operation                    | Name         |
--------------------------------------------------------------

|   0 | SELECT STATEMENT             |              |
|   1 |  CONCATENATION               |              |
|   2 |   TABLE ACCESS BY INDEX ROWID| TR           |
|*  3 |    INDEX UNIQUE SCAN         | SYS_C0011913 |
|   4 |   TABLE ACCESS BY INDEX ROWID| TR           |
|*  5 |    INDEX UNIQUE SCAN         | SYS_C0011913 |
```

PLAN_TABLE_OUTPUT
```
--------------------------------------------------------------

----------------------------------------------------------
```

Predicate Information (identified by operation id):
```
----------------------------------------------------------
```

```
   3 - access("ID"=TO_NUMBER(:BIND2))
   5 - access("ID"=TO_NUMBER(:BIND1))
       filter(LNNVL("ID"=TO_NUMBER(:BIND2)))
```

19 rows selected.

So in this case OR-expansion also has been triggered but this transformation is not part of CBO, and it is implemented in a different way. This transformation cannot be cost-based because cost is not considered when RBO is turned on.

Let's proceed to heuristic transformations and consider view merging. To reproduce it in Oracle 12c, it may be necessary to disable adaptive plans using the statement "alter session set optimizer_adaptive_ reporting_only = true;".

Listing 2-9. View merging

```
explain plan for
select name, cnt
  from t3
  join (select id, max(name) name, count(*) cnt from tr group
  by id) sub
    on sub.id = t3.id;

Explained.

select * from table(dbms_xplan.display(format => 'basic
predicate'));

PLAN_TABLE_OUTPUT
-----------------------------------------------------------------
Plan hash value: 1900897066

---------------------------------------------------------
| Id  | Operation            | Name           |
---------------------------------------------------------
|   0 | SELECT STATEMENT     |                |          |
|   1 |  HASH GROUP BY       |                |          |
|   2 |   NESTED LOOPS       |                |          |
```

```
|   3 |     NESTED LOOPS              |               |
|   4 |      TABLE ACCESS FULL        | T3            |
|*  5 |      INDEX UNIQUE SCAN        | SYS_C0011582  |
|   6 |   TABLE ACCESS BY INDEX ROWID| TR            |
-------------------------------------------------------
```

Predicate Information (identified by operation id):
----

    5 - access("ID"="T3"."ID")

18 rows selected.

So what happens here? Oracle scans table T3 and then uses the index access to get correspondent rows from TR, and as a last step it applies group by. The final query looks like the following shown in Listing 2-10:

Listing 2-10. Final query after view merging

```
SELECT MAX("TR"."NAME") "NAME",COUNT(*) "CNT" FROM "T3", "TR"
WHERE "TR"."ID"="T3"."ID" GROUP BY "TR"."ID","T3".ROWID
```

View merging transformation may be affected using hints merge/ no_merge; however if we turn off this transformation for the above query, then another one will be applied – filter push down. To completely disable all the transformations we can use a no_query_transformation hint. The original and final query after transformations in this case is below in Listing 2-11.

Listing 2-11. Original and final query with disabled transformations

```
select --+ no_query_transformation
 name, cnt
  from t3
  join (select id, max(name) name, count(*) cnt from tr group
  by id) sub
```

```
    on sub.id = t3.id;

select "from$_subquery$_004"."NAME_0" "NAME",
       "from$_subquery$_004"."CNT_1"  "CNT"
  from (select "SUB"."NAME" "NAME_0", "SUB"."CNT" "CNT_1"
          from "T3",
               (select "TR"."ID" "ID",
                       max("TR"."NAME") "NAME",
                       count(*) "CNT"
                  from "TR"
                 group by "TR"."ID") "SUB"
         where "SUB"."ID" = "T3"."ID") "from$_subquery$_004"
```

As you see, ANSI syntax was converted into Oracle native syntax even though all the transformations are disabled. This will be more than 100 times slower than the original one with enabled transformations.

In some rare cases both cost-based and heuristic transformations may lead to degraded performance; however it's better to narrow down the root case and disable specific transformations rather than all of them.

Let's assume we have tables fact_ and dim_ without referential integrity constraints and our goal is to check whether all the IDs from the fact table exist in the dimension table.

Listing 2-12. fact_ and dim_ tables

```
create table fact_ as
select rownum value, rownum - 1 dim_1_id, rownum dim_2_id from
dual connect by rownum <= 1e6;
create table dim_ as
select rownum id, 'name'||rownum name from dual connect by
rownum <= 1e6;
```

If we check separately for each column in the fact table, then the query is getting transformed to HASH JOIN ANTI NA and runs very fast.

Listing 2-13. Checking existence for dimension IDs separately

```
select * from fact_ f where dim_1_id not in (select id from dim_);
select * from fact_ f where dim_2_id not in (select id from dim_);
```

However, if we try to check that using query from Listing 2-14, it will be extremely slow. This query cannot be transformed to use HASH JOIN ANTI twice - because of current implementation limitations.

Listing 2-14. Checking existence for dimension IDs. Slow version

```
explain plan for
select *
  from fact_ f
 where dim_1_id not in (select id from dim_)
    or dim_2_id not in (select id from dim_);

Explained.

select * from table(dbms_xplan.display(format => 'basic
predicate'));


PLAN_TABLE_OUTPUT
-------------------------------------------------------------------
Plan hash value: 481481104


------------------------------------
| Id | Operation           | Name  |
------------------------------------
|  0 | SELECT STATEMENT    |       |
|* 1 |  FILTER             |       |
|  2 |   TABLE ACCESS FULL| FACT_ |
|* 3 |   TABLE ACCESS FULL| DIM_  |
|* 4 |   TABLE ACCESS FULL| DIM_  |
------------------------------------
```

```
Predicate Information (identified by operation id):
----------------------------------------------------

  1 - filter( NOT EXISTS (SELECT 0 FROM "DIM_" "DIM_" WHERE
              LNNVL("ID"<>:B1)) OR  NOT EXISTS (SELECT 0 FROM
              "DIM_" "DIM_" WHERE
              LNNVL("ID"<>:B2)))
  3 - filter(LNNVL("ID"<>:B1))
  4 - filter(LNNVL("ID"<>:B1))
```

```
20 rows selected.
```

If we rewrite the query manually and create an inline view, then it will be fast again, as shown in Listing 2-15.

Listing 2-15. Checking existence for dimension IDs. Fast version

```
explain plan for
select *
  from (select * from fact_ f where dim_1_id not in (select id
  from dim_))
 where dim_2_id not in (select id from dim_);
```

```
Explained.
```

```
select * from table(dbms_xplan.display(format => 'basic
predicate'));
```

```
PLAN_TABLE_OUTPUT
--------------------------------------------------------------
Plan hash value: 1918822958

-----------------------------------------------
| Id  | Operation                 | Name  |
-----------------------------------------------
|   0 | SELECT STATEMENT          |       |
|*  1 |  HASH JOIN ANTI NA        |       |
|*  2 |   HASH JOIN RIGHT ANTI NA|        |
|   3 |    TABLE ACCESS FULL      | DIM_  |
|   4 |    TABLE ACCESS FULL      | FACT_ |
|   5 |    TABLE ACCESS FULL      | DIM_  |
-----------------------------------------------

Predicate Information (identified by operation id):
---------------------------------------------------

   1 - access("F"."DIM_2_ID"="ID")
   2 - access("DIM_1_ID"="ID")

18 rows selected.
```

You may have noticed an interesting detail about the filter operation – it has three child operations. In our case, one operation is for the fact table and two operations are for the dimension table to check both IDs. The first child operation for the filter is row-source, which is filtered and others are row-sources to check filter conditions. Once first match is found for the current row then Oracle proceeds to the next one from the main row-source.

Speaking about joins, there are only three join methods in Oracle - MERGE JOIN, HASH JOIN, NESTED LOOPS – and all of them can operate with only two row-sources unlike filter operation.

The number of query transformations keeps increasing from one release to another, and their capabilities evolve more and more as well; for example, scalar subquery unnesting transformation that can dramatically improve the performance of some queries was added in Oracle 11gR2. On the other hand, it will unlikely be possible to make the transformation engine so intelligent that we can completely avoid manual query rewriting.

Besides query transformation, there are a lot of other conversions applied to query during the optimization phase starting from ANSI to native translation to column projection. Important details to note:

- Transformation may impact the query plan and query performance, but it's not always possible to figure out whether transformation was applied or not based on final query text. For detailed analysis, you can start with the "Query Transformations (QT)" section of the optimizer trace.

- It's important to distinguish query optimizer transformation and other transformations like ANSI to native syntax translation. The latter one applies for all queries regardless of whether query optimizer transformations are enabled or not.

- ANSI syntax may appear in the final query if original query has:

  - full join;

  - left/right join partition by.

- Another very important CBO feature is automatic generation of additional predicates, also referred as transitive closure (Metalink Doc ID 68979.1). Simply speaking, if we remove the second or third predicate from a condition like "where t1.id = t2.id and t1.id = 1 and t2.id = 1" then it will be generated automatically.

- The next transformation to mention is column projection. Projection is one out of five relation algebra operations: selection, projection, union, difference, join. Great introductional articles about relational algebra written by Iggy Fernandez: SQL Sucks [5], Explaining the EXPLAIN PLAN [6].

To demonstrate column projection let's execute the query below:

```
with t_ as (select id, id, name from t)
select name from t_;
```

It returned a result without any errors because, in fact, it's translated to the query below (only name column remains after projection is applied):

```
SELECT "T"."NAME" "NAME" FROM "T" "T"
```

On the other hand, Oracle does not allow us to create a view using the factored query above because of obvious reasons.

Like many other popular RDBMS, Oracle applies heuristics like the following:

- do a projection "elimination of unnecessary columns from row-source" as early as possible;

- do a selection "filtering out unnecessary rows" as early as possible. In fact this means that the post-join predicate on the inner table will be applied before join.

In context of CBO this means "as early as possible if it leads to the plan with lower cost."

- The final query in the optimizer trace is only an SQL-like
  representation of what will be eventually executed
  and may not be semantically equivalent to the original
  query in all cases. In some cases, plans for the original
  and final query may differ. Also, the final query may
  not return the same result as the original query, for
  example, because there is no special notation for ANTI/
  SEMI joins and predicates for them are displayed
  simply like equality predicates.

- As you see on Figure 2-1, transformations happen
  before plan generation and query hints may become
  unusable after transformations. For example, if inline
  view has been eliminated after view merging and you
  used its alias in the hint, then the hint is no longer valid.

Summary

Query transformations allow to provide significant flexibility for developers
in writing queries, and they make it possible for queries with considerably
different query texts to have eventually the same query plan and, possibly,
the same final query text. Thanks to query transformations, it's not
necessary to care about the order of query operations. For example, if you
join two tables and calculate some aggregates, Oracle will decide what to
do first – group by or join if that is possible. Also transformations allow us
to avoid code duplication – for instance, or-expansion may expand one
query into several branches with union all, and transitive closure helps to
avoid "unnecessary" predicates.

However, the transformation engine is not a "silver bullet" and developers should follow best practices when writing queries to help optimizer make the right decisions and build optimal plans. The transformation engine will unlikely ever be so intelligent that manual query rewriting can be completely avoided.

In additional to query transformations, the SQL engine applies a lot of other conversions, for example, translation ANSI to native and heuristics like column projection or column selection.

CHAPTER 3

Analytic Functions

Basic SQL provides row-level visibility, and aggregate functions allow us to analyze data in groups so that each row corresponds to one specific group according to group by expressions (more details about aggregate functions provided in the next chapter, "Aggregate Functions").

Analytic functions introduce window-level visibility. Window defines the subset of rows used to apply a function for each input row, and its definition is the same for all rows and is specified in the analytic clause of the function. Analytic functions are evaluated after all operations like joins, where, group by, having but before order by so they can appear only in select list or in order by clause but not in where clause, for example. The number of rows in a recordset remains the same after the analytic function is applied, unlike the number of rows after aggregate function is applied where each group is represented by one row in a result set.

It's easier to explain how it works based on an example, as shown in Listing 3-1.

Listing 3-1. Analytic functions

```
with t as
 (select rownum id, trunc(rownum / 4) part from dual connect by
 rownum <= 6)
select t.*,
       sum(id) over(partition by part order by id) sum1,
       sum(id) over(partition by part) sum2
```

© Alex Reprintsev 2018
A. Reprintsev, *Oracle SQL Revealed*, https://doi.org/10.1007/978-1-4842-3372-6_3

```
from t
order by id;
```

ID	PART	SUM1	SUM2
1	0	1	6
2	0	3	6
3	0	6	6
4	1	4	15
5	1	9	15
6	1	15	15

```
6 rows selected.
```

"partition by part" means that we apply an analytic function for each part independently. If it's omitted, then the whole recordset is treated as one partition. Without an "order by" clause, window for each row covers all the rows for the current partition so the result is the same for all rows. With an "order by" clause, window for each row covers all rows from the beginning of the partition to the current row. This can be adjusted by specifying a windowing clause after "order by" while the default behavior is "range between unbounded preceding and current row" (or simply "range unbounded preceding") when "order by" is specified; otherwise it's "range between unbounded preceding and unbounded following."

Partition by clause is not mandatory as well as a windowing clause may not be specified after an order by; however, for some functions "order by" must be always provided – for example, in case of row_number or rank.

The logic that can be implemented using analytic functions and single table access would otherwise require additional joins or subqueries. Listing 3-2 shows how logic from Listing 3-1 can be implemented without analytic functions.

Listing 3-2. Rewriting query without analytic functions

```
with t as
 (select rownum id, trunc(rownum / 4) part from dual connect by
 rownum <= 6)
select t.*,
       (select sum(id) from t t0 where t0.part = t.part and
       t0.id <= t.id) sum1,
       (select sum(id) from t t0 where t0.part = t.part) sum2
  from t
 order by id;

    ID        PART       SUM1        SUM2
---------- ---------- ---------- ----------
     1         0          1          6
     2         0          3          6
     3         0          6          6
     4         1          4          15
     5         1          9          15
     6         1          15         15

6 rows selected.
```

Back to query transformations, Oracle cannot rewrite this query to use analytic functions and avoid unnecessary joins and table scans. Such an intelligence unlikely will be added in the near future.

Analytic functions can help to avoid joins even if different columns are used in a join condition. In Listing 3-3, the same value is calculated using a correlated scalar subquery and analytic functions.

Listing 3-3. Avoiding joins by using analytic functions

```
exec dbms_random.seed(99);

create table ta as
select rownum id,
       trunc(dbms_random.value(1, 5 + 1)) x1,
       trunc(dbms_random.value(1, 5 + 1)) x2,
       trunc(dbms_random.value(1, 5 + 1)) x3
  from dual
connect by level <= 10;
select (select sum(x3) from ta t0 where t0.x2 = ta.x1) s,
       case
         when x1 > x2 then
           sum(x3) over(order by x2 range between greatest
           (x1 - x2, 0)
                       following and greatest(x1 - x2, 0) following)
         else
           sum(x3) over(order by x2 range between greatest
           (x2 - x1, 0)
                       preceding and greatest(x2 - x1, 0) preceding)
       end sa,
       ta.*
  from ta
 order by id;
```

S	SA	ID	X1	X2	X3
4	4	1	3	1	2
10	10	2	1	5	4
1	1	3	2	5	1
9	9	4	5	3	4

4	4	5	3	1	1
		6	4	5	1
		7	4	5	3
4	4	8	3	1	5
9	9	9	5	2	1
9	9	10	5	1	2

```
10 rows selected.
```

In order to calculate a sum of x3 for rows where x2 equals to x1, we use a window with a range shift that equals the difference between x1 and x2. Depending on whether x1 is greater or less than x2, we consider the following or preceding rows. For each row we are interested only in one sum, but Oracle needs to calculate both for all rows, so to avoid an exception when x1-x2 or x2-x1 is negative we apply the greatest function.

In addition to a logical offset by range, a window may be specified with a physical offset by rows. To highlight the difference let's consider the following task. There is a table containing information about cash withdrawals from an ATM and we need to calculate for each withdrawal the following:

- For how many transactions the amount was not less than 50 considering the current transaction and the 5 preceding transactions – 6 withdrawals in total (cnt1);

- For how many transactions the amount was not less than 50 considering the range between the current transaction and 5 preceding minutes (cnt2).

Listing 3-4. Implementing logic using windowing clause

```
exec dbms_random.seed(11);

create table atm as
select trunc(sysdate) + (2 * rownum - 1) / (24 * 60) ts,
       trunc(dbms_random.value(1, 20 + 1)) * 5 amount
```

```
   from dual
connect by level <= 15;
select to_char(ts, 'mi') minute,
       amount,
       count(nullif(sign(amount - 50), -1))
        over(order by ts rows 5 preceding) cnt1,
       count(nullif(sign(amount - 50), -1))
        over(order by ts range interval '5' minute preceding) cnt2
  from atm;
```

MI	AMOUNT	CNT1	CNT2
01	85	1	1
03	15	1	1
05	100	2	2
07	40	2	1
09	30	2	1
11	50	3	1
13	85	3	2
15	60	4	3
17	5	3	2
19	100	4	2
21	25	4	1
23	30	3	1
25	80	3	1
27	5	2	1
29	35	2	1

15 rows selected.

A bit simpler example to highlight the difference between offset by range and by rows is in Listing 3-5.

Listing 3-5. Difference between a logical offset and a physical offset

```
with t as
(select rownum id, column_value value from table(numbers
(1,2,3,4.5,4.6,7,10)))
select t.*,
       last_value(value)
       over (order by value range between unbounded preceding
       and 1 preceding) l1,
       last_value(value)
       over (order by value rows between unbounded preceding
       and 1 preceding) l2
  from t;

       ID       VALUE          L1         L2
---------- ----------- ---------- ----------
        1           1
        2           2           1          1
        3           3           2          2
        4         4.5           3          3
        5         4.6           3        4.5
        6           7         4.6        4.6
        7          10           7          7

7 rows selected.
```

L1 and L2 differ for id = 5 because the upper bound for the last_value in the first case is 3.6 (4.6 – 1) while in the second case it's simply the value from the previous row - 4.5.

A windowing clause doesn't make sense for some analytic functions so it cannot be specified for lag/lead, for example.

Despite all the flexibility, analytic functions have some limitations:

1) Only the unbounded preceding, current row, unbounded following boundaries are allowed when sorting by multiple columns. For example, if we have a table containing information about points (coordinates x and y), then it's not possible to calculate for each row how many points exist within a given shift by x and y from the current point.

2) Attributes from the current row cannot be referred to in a function. For example, if we want to sum the distances from the current point to all other points, then it's not doable using analytic functions. However, if the goal is to sum the distances to some specific point, then it can be easily done for different ranges of rows.

The specifics with brief comments inline are below.

Listing 3-6. Limitations of analytic functions

```
with points as
 (select rownum id, rownum * rownum x, mod(rownum, 3) y
    from dual
  connect by rownum <= 6)
, t as
(select p.*,
       -- the number of points within the distance of 5 by x
          coordinate
       -- cannot be solved with analytic functions for more
          than one coordinate
       count(*) over(order by x range between 5 preceding and 5
       following) cnt,
```

```
       -- sum of the distances to the point (3, 3) for all rows
       -- between unbounded preceding and current row ordered by id
       -- cannot be solved using analytic functions if required
          to calculate
       -- distance between other rows and current row rather
          than a constant point
       round(sum(sqrt((x - 3) * (x - 3) + (y - 3) * (y - 3)))
             over(order by id),
             2) dist
   from points p)
select t.*,
(select count(*)
   from t t0 where t0.x between t.x-5 and t.x + 5) cnt1,
(select count(*)
   from t t0 where t0.x between t.x-5 and t.x + 5 and t0.y
   between t.y-1 and t.y + 1) cnt2,
(select round(sum(sqrt((x - 3) * (x - 3) + (y - 3) * (y - 3))), 2)
   from t t0 where t0.id <= t.id) dist1,
(select round(sum(sqrt((x - t.x) * (x - t.x) + (y - t.y) *
(y - t.y))), 2)
   from t t0 where t0.id <= t.id) dist2
from t
 order by id;
```

ID	X	Y	CNT	DIST	CNT1	CNT2	DIST1	DIST2
1	1	1	2	2.83	2	2	2.83	0
2	4	2	3	4.24	3	2	4.24	3.16
3	9	0	2	10.95	2	1	10.95	13.45
4	16	1	1	24.1	1	1	24.1	34.11
5	25	2	1	46.13	1	1	46.13	70.2
6	36	0	1	79.26	1	1	79.26	125.28

6 rows selected.

93

So values cnt2 and dist2 cannot be calculated using analytic functions.

Also it's worth mentioning that if a type of the sort key does not support arithmetic operations then the logical offset (range) cannot be used. Obviously, there is no such limitation for physical offset (rows).

Most analytic functions can also act as aggregate functions (if "over" is not specified); however some of them are purely analytic, for example, row_number or rank. As was mentioned previously, "order by" is mandatory for such functions.

A special case of an analytic function is listagg. First, it's not commutative, which means that concatenation of the first and second values is not the same as concatenation of the second and first, unlike sum or average, for example. Second, "order by" cannot be specified in analytic clause. Third, it's not possible to use distinct keyword in a function. Some differences between listagg and UDF stragg (source code available on AskTom) are shown in Listing 3-7.

Listing 3-7. Differences between listagg and stragg

```
with t as
 (select rownum id, column_value value
    from table(sys.odcinumberlist(2, 1, 1, 3, 1))),
t0 as
 (select t.*, row_number() over(partition by value order by id)
 rn from t)
select t1.*,
       (select listagg(value, ',') within group(order by value)
          from t t_in
          where t_in.id <= t1.id) cumul_ord
  from (select t0.*,
               listagg(value, ',') within group(order by value)
               over() list_ord,
```

```
        listagg(decode(rn, 1, value), ',') within
        group(order by value) over() dist_ord,
        stragg(value) over(order by id) cumul,
        stragg(distinct value) over() dist,
        stragg(decode(rn, 1, value)) over(order by id)
        cumul_dist
    from t0) t1
order by id;
```

ID	VALUE	RN	LIST_ORD	DIST_ORD	CUMUL	DIST	CUMUL_DIST	CUMUL_ORD
1	2	1	1,1,1,2,3	1,2,3	2	1,2,3	2	2
2	1	1	1,1,1,2,3	1,2,3	2,1	1,2,3	2,1	1,2
3	1	2	1,1,1,2,3	1,2,3	2,1,1	1,2,3	2,1	1,1,2
4	3	1	1,1,1,2,3	1,2,3	2,1,1,3	1,2,3	2,1,3	1,1,2,3
5	1	3	1,1,1,2,3	1,2,3	2,1,1,3,1	1,2,3	2,1,3	1,1,1,2,3

In short, it's not possible to get cumulative concatenation with window ordering for listagg. On the other hand, window ordering can be specified for stragg, but in this case it's not possible to specify a concatenation order for result.

So if the goal is to concatenate values with window ordering and specify the order of the result itself, then it cannot be achieved using analytic functions and a single table scan. In the above example it was calculated using scalar subquery.

The important point is that analytic functions is not a panacea. Sometimes it may be more efficient to use joins instead. Let's consider the following case. Data batches identified by batch_id are written into a stream table with an index on batch_id. Our goal is to calculate the sum(value) for the last batch_id. See Listing 3-8.

Listing 3-8. Different approaches: analytic functions vs joins

```
create table stream as
select batch_id, value
  from (select rownum value from dual connect by rownum <=
  10000) x1,
       (select rownum batch_id from dual connect by level <= 1000)
 order by 1, 2;

create index stream_batch_id_idx on stream(batch_id);

exec dbms_stats.gather_table_stats(user, 'stream');
alter session set statistics_level = all;

select sum(s.value)
  from stream s
 where batch_id = (select max(s0.batch_id) from stream s0);
select * from table(dbms_xplan.display_cursor(null,null,
'IOSTATS LAST'));

select sum(value)
  from (select s.*, dense_rank() over(order by batch_id) drnk
  from stream s)
 where drnk = 1;
select * from table(dbms_xplan.display_cursor(null,null,
'IOSTATS LAST'));
```

Execution plans are shown in Listing 3-9 (columns Name and Starts have been cut out for formatting purposes). So the version with a scalar subquery a in where clause (which requires additional join) is 35 times faster than a version with analytic functions – 0.09 vs 3.48 seconds. Most of the time for the analytic query was spent on the ordering – 3.47 – 1.40 = 2.07 seconds not to mention that number of logical reads increased by more than 400 times.

Listing 3-9. Analytic functions vs joins: executions plans

Id	Operation	E-Rows	A-Rows	A-Time	Buffers	Reads
0	SELECT STATEMENT		1	00:00:00.09	43	40
1	SORT AGGREGATE	1	1	00:00:00.09	43	40
2	TABLE ACCESS BY INDEX ROWID	10000	10000	00:00:00.09	43	40
* 3	INDEX RANGE SCAN	10000	10000	00:00:00.06	25	22
4	SORT AGGREGATE	1	1	00:00:00.05	3	3
5	INDEX FULL SCAN (MIN/MAX)	1	1	00:00:00.05	3	3

Id	Operation	E-Rows	A-Rows	A-Time	Buffers	Reads
0	SELECT STATEMENT		1	00:00:03.48	17823	17820
1	SORT AGGREGATE	1	1	00:00:03.48	17823	17820
* 2	VIEW	10M	10000	00:00:03.47	17823	17820
* 3	WINDOW SORT PUSHED RANK	10M	10001	00:00:03.47	17823	17820
4	TABLE ACCESS FULL	10M	10M	00:00:01.40	17823	17820

In some cases, a sort operation caused by analytic queries may be so inefficient that approaches with additional joins would have better performance even without any indexes. Even though such cases are quite rare, it always makes sense to consider different ways to get the desired result set.

Differences and Interchangeability of Functions

This section is not dedicated to describing differences between row_ number and rank or, let's say, between rank and dense_rank. Instead of that, we will consider how different functions can be used to implement the same logic, taking into account specifics of the functions and windowing clause.

Sometimes you may come across code demonstrated in Listing 3-10.

Listing 3-10. Order by with unbounded range

```
max(version) over (partition by dt order by version
rows between unbounded preceding and unbounded following)
latest_version
```

In this case it does not make any sense to specify the order because the window for each row is the whole partition so Listing 3-11 shows logically identical expression.

Listing 3-11. Max value by partition

```
max(version) over (partition by dt) latest_version
```

However, sometimes it makes sense to specify order even if the window is the whole partition.

Let's consider the following task: for each row we need to derive a max value corresponding to a max date. This is implemented in expressions for m2 and m3 below.

Listing 3-12. Max value for max date

```
with t(id, value, dt, part) as
(
select 1, 10, date '2015-07-01', 1 from dual
union all select 2, 3, date '2015-08-01', 1 from dual
union all select 3, 2, date '2015-09-01', 1 from dual
union all select 4, 0, date '2016-11-01', 1 from dual
union all select 5, 5, date '2016-11-01', 1 from dual
union all select 6, 9, date '2017-01-01', 1 from dual
union all select 7, 4, date '2017-01-01', 1 from dual
)
select
 t.*,
 max(value) over (partition by part) m1,
 max(value) keep (dense_rank last order by dt) over (partition
 by part) m2,
 last_value(value)
 over (partition by part order by dt, value
     rows between unbounded preceding and unbounded following) m3,
 max(value)
 over (partition by part order by dt, value
     rows between unbounded preceding and unbounded following) m4
 from t
order by id;
```

ID	VALUE DT	PART	M1	M2	M3	M4
1	10 01.07.15	1	10	9	9	10
2	3 01.08.15	1	10	9	9	10
3	2 01.09.15	1	10	9	9	10
4	0 01.11.16	1	10	9	9	10
5	5 01.11.16	1	10	9	9	10
6	9 01.01.17	1	10	9	9	10
7	4 01.01.17	1	10	9	9	10

7 rows selected.

So the max date is 01.01.2017 and it has two corresponding values - 4 and 9. The result can be calculated as "max(value)" with "last" function specified after the keyword keep and ordering by dt or by using the "last_value" function and ordering by dt and value.

If we need to get the min value then we can use min function instead of max or simply specify descending order for the value in last_value function.

Listing 3-13. Min value for max date

```
min(value) keep (dense_rank last order by dt) over (partition
by part) m2,
last_value(value)
over (partition by part order by dt, value desc
    rows between unbounded preceding and unbounded following) m3
from t
```

So in the first case we used another function while in the second one only the ordering direction by value has changed.

The last example highlights specifics of the "last_value" function and construction "ignore nulls." It was impossible to specify "ignore nulls" before 10g but the workaround is quite straightforward.

Listing 3-14. Last_value + ignore nulls and workaround for old versions

```
with t(id, value, part) as
(
select 1, null, 1 from dual
union all select 2, 'one', 1 from dual
union all select 3, null, 1 from dual
union all select 1, 'two', 2 from dual
union all select 2, null, 2 from dual
union all select 3, null, 2 from dual
union all select 4, 'three', 2 from dual
)
select t.*, max(value) over(partition by part, cnt) lv0
  from (select t.*,
              last_value(value ignore nulls) over(partition by
              part order by id) lv,
            count(value) over(partition by part order by id) cnt
        from t
        order by part, id) t;

    ID VALUE      PART LV          CNT LV0
---------- ----- ----------- ----- ----------- ---
     1            1                 0
     2 one        1 one             1 one
     3            1 one             1 one
     1 two        2 two             1 two
     2            2 two             1 two
     3            2 two             1 two
     4 three      2 three           2 three

7 rows selected.
```

We used count in the inline view to build partitions containing the current value and all subsequent rows with blank values and max function on top of that to mimic behavior of the last_value + ignore nulls. So apparently functions with completely different purposes can be used to implement the same logic.

Summary

Analytic functions are very powerful tool that can be used to get the result that otherwise would require self joins or subqueries. They have been introduced in Oracle 8i and has significantly evolved since then; however, their capabilities continue developing in many versions including Oracle 12c. Oracle provides a flexible definition of the windowing clause to adjust the default definition of the analytic window, and such a feature has its own limitations but for most of the practical tasks, built-in flexibility is more than enough.

CHAPTER 4

Aggregate Functions

Aggregate functions return one row for each group defined in a group by clause. Both column names and expressions can be used to define groups, and one group is a set of rows with the same values for all expressions specified in "group by." Each row belongs to one and only one group. If "group by" is not specified, then the entire recordset is a single group, and in this case query always returns one row even if the recordset to be grouped is empty.

Listing 4-1 shows how to calculate the total amount of presentations and count of working days for all authors based on tables introduced in Listing 1-58 in Chapter 1.

Listing 4-1. Aggregate functions. Simple example

```
select p.name,
       count(*) cnt_all,
       count(distinct p.day) cnt_day,
       listagg(p.day || ' ' || p.time || ':00', '; ') within
       group(order by w.id) details
  from presentation p, week w
 where p.day = w.day
 group by p.name;

NAME    CNT_ALL    CNT_DAY DETAILS
----    ----------    ---------- ------------------------------------
John        3          2 monday 14:00; monday 9:00; friday 9:00
Rex         2          2 wednesday 11:00; friday 11:00
```

© Alex Reprintsev 2018
A. Reprintsev, *Oracle SQL Revealed*, https://doi.org/10.1007/978-1-4842-3372-6_4

Only distinct values are passed to an aggregate function when a distinct keyword is specified. Listagg function was used to display details for all presentations, as this was pointed out in the previous chapter – listagg is not commutative and order must be specified after "within group" keywords. There are some other aggregate functions whose result depends on the order within a group, for instance - percentile_cont (see quiz "Percentile with Shift" in Part II for a more complicated example).

Most of the aggregate functions return a result of the atomic type, which is the same as a type of argument – for example, number, date, varchar2, etc. However, some functions just combine values together instead of calculating a result value based on input – for example, collect and xmlagg.

UDFs can be applied on top of the collect function to process elements for each group. The collagg function below may be used to concatenate collection elements.

Listing 4-2. Concatenating collection elements

```
create or replace function collagg(p in strings) return varchar is
  result varchar2(4000);
begin
  for i in 1 .. p.count loop
    result := result || ', ' || p(i);
  end loop;
  return(substr(result, 3));
end collagg;
/
```

Where strings is a collection defined as

```
create or replace type strings as table of varchar2(4000)
/
```

Listing 4-3 shows how to get a list of all days with presentations per presenter as well as a list of distinct days.

Listing 4-3. Using collect function

```
select name,
       collagg(cast(collect(p.day order by w.id desc) as
       strings)) days,
       collagg(set(cast(collect(p.day order by w.id desc) as
       strings))) days_unique
  from presentation p, week w
 where p.day = w.day
 group by p.name;
```

```
NAME DAYS                                 DAYS_UNIQUE
---- ------------------------------- ----------------------------
John friday, monday, monday              friday, monday
Rex  friday, wednesday                   friday, wednesday
```

Unlike listagg, order by is specified in the function itself, and distinct keyword is not allowed in collect but the set function can be used to eliminate duplicates. Even though set function seems to preserve the order of elements – there is no guarantee that it's true in all cases.

Similar logic including ordering can be implemented using xmlagg as shown in the expression below, but elimination of duplicates is not possible in this case without an additional inline view.

```
substr(xmlagg(xmlelement("x", ', ' || p.day) order by w.id
desc)
    .extract('//x/text()')
    .getstringval(), 3) x
```

In addition to built-in aggregate functions, Oracle (since version 9i Release 1) provides an interface for user-defined aggregates (UDAG) that can be leveraged to implement any complex logic for grouping. For example, there is a single-row function bitand which does not have an aggregate analog. If necessary this logic can be implemented using UDF + collect or UDAG.

In a previous chapter it was shown how analytic functions may help to avoid joins, and aggregate functions can also be used for this purpose.

For example, a requirements table contains information about positions and corresponding skills. The goal is to get positions that require Oracle knowledge without Linux.

```
create table requirements(position, skill) as
(
select 'Data Scientist', 'R' from dual
union all select 'Data Scientist', 'Python' from dual
union all select 'Data Scientist', 'Spark' from dual
union all select 'DB Developer', 'Oracle' from dual
union all select 'DB Developer', 'Linux' from dual
union all select 'BI Developer', 'Oracle' from dual
union all select 'BI Developer', 'MSSQL' from dual
union all select 'BI Developer', 'Analysis Services' from dual
union all select 'System Administrator', 'Linux' from dual
union all select 'System Administrator', 'Network Protocols'
                                         from dual
union all select 'System Administrator', 'Python' from dual
union all select 'System Administrator', 'Perl' from dual
);
```

A straightforward solution is shown below.

```
select position
  from requirements r
 where skill = 'Oracle'
   and not exists (select null
           from requirements r0
          where r0.position = r.position
            and r0.skill = 'Linux');
```

```
POSITION
--------------------
BI Developer
```

The main disadvantage of this solution is a correlated subquery in a where clause that causes an additional scan of the requirements table.

An alternative approach would be to calculate counts for Oracle and Linux skills and filter out those that do not satisfy.

```
select position
  from requirements
 group by position
having count(decode(skill, 'Oracle', 1)) = 1
   and count(decode(skill, 'Linux', 1)) = 0;
```

```
POSITION
--------------------
BI Developer
```

This solution is more preferable from a performance point of view, and you may notice that aggregate functions are used only for filtering purposes and not in a select list.

Let's consider a more generic example. A tables entity and property are used to implement an entity–attribute–value (EAV) model – this approach is used in database design to store entities with variable number of attributes in a single table.

Listing 4-4. EAV model

```
with entity(id, name) as
(select 1, 'E1' from dual
union all select 2, 'E2' from dual
union all select 3, 'E3' from dual),
property(id, entity_id, name, value) as
(select 1, 1, 'P1', 1 from dual
union all select 2, 1, 'P2', 10 from dual
union all select 3, 1, 'P3', 20 from dual
union all select 4, 1, 'P4', 50 from dual
union all select 5, 2, 'P1', 1 from dual
union all select 6, 2, 'P3', 100 from dual
union all select 7, 2, 'P4', 50 from dual
union all select 8, 3, 'P1', 1 from dual
union all select 19, 3, 'P2', 10 from dual
union all select 10, 3, 'P3', 100 from dual)
```

Our goal is to select entities with values for attributes P1, P2, P3 equal to 1, 10, 100 correspondingly, and properties are supposed to be unique for each entity. Sometimes developers use multiple joins to achieve this, which is very inefficient – in fact, the number of joins equals to the number of attributes we are interested in.

```
select e.name
  from entity e
  join property p1 on p1.entity_id = e.id and p1.name = 'P1'
  join property p2 on p2.entity_id = e.id and p2.name = 'P2'
  join property p3 on p3.entity_id = e.id and p3.name = 'P3'
 where p1.value = 1 and p2.value = 10 and p3.value = 100;

NAME
-----
E3
```

If we required getting values for 20 attributes, this would cause 20 joins, which is not a viable solution at all.

Taking into account that for each property there may be either one value or no values at all, we can flatten properties for each entity in one row and apply a filter on top of that.

Listing 4-5. Flattening EAV model using group by

```
select name
  from (select e.name,
               max(decode(p.name, 'P1', value)) p1_value,
               max(decode(p.name, 'P2', value)) p2_value,
               max(decode(p.name, 'P3', value)) p3_value
          from entity e
          join property p
            on p.entity_id = e.id
         group by e.name)
 where (p1_value, p2_value, p3_value) in ((1, 10, 100));
```

Finally, flattening is not really necessary so we can simply calculate the number of properties with specified values.

```
select e.name
  from property p
  join entity e on p.entity_id = e.id
 where (p.name, p.value) in (('P1', 1), ('P2', 10), ('P3', 100))
 group by e.name
having count(*) = 3;
```

Pivot and Unpivot Operators

Listing 4-5 demonstrates flattening logic implemented using group by; however starting with Oracle 11g, the same can be achieved using a pivot operator.

Listing 4-6. Flattening EAV model using pivot operator

```
create table entity_flattened as
select *
  from (select e.name name, p.name p_name, value
          from entity e
          join property p
            on p.entity_id = e.id)
pivot(max(value) for p_name in('P1' p1_value, 'P2' p2_value,
'P3' p3_value));
```

Table entity_flattened contains a recordset identical to the one in the inline view with group by. One of the most important points regarding the pivot operator is that all columns must be listed in a query because Oracle defines all the columns of a result set during the parsing phase. Saying that, it's not possible to dynamically create columns in a recordset based on data in a table or other conditions, so if you have such a requirement, then you can use ODCItable interface (or polymorphic table functions starting with Oracle 18c). Pivot XML allows you to generate XMLs for a dynamic number of columns, but if you want to get a result in a relational form you need to list all of them for XML parsing. This technique is demonstrated in Listing 4-7.

Listing 4-7. Parsing pivot XML

```
select name, x.*
  from (select *
          from (select e.name name, p.name p_name, value
                  from entity e
```

```
                join property p
                  on p.entity_id = e.id)
        pivot xml(max(value) value for p_name in(any))),
        xmltable('/PivotSet' passing p_name_xml
                columns
                name1 varchar2(30)
                path '/PivotSet/item[1]/column[@name="P_NAME"]/
                text()',
                value1 varchar2(30)
                path '/PivotSet/item[1]/column[@name="VALUE"]/
                text()',
                name2 varchar2(30)
                path '/PivotSet/item[2]/column[@name="P_NAME"]/
                text()',
                value2 varchar2(30)
                path '/PivotSet/item[2]/column[@name="VALUE"]/
                text()',
                name3 varchar2(30)
                path '/PivotSet/item[3]/column[@name="P_NAME"]/
                text()',
                value3 varchar2(30)
                path '/PivotSet/item[3]/column[@name="VALUE"]/
                text()') x;
```

NAME	NAME1	VALUE1	NAME2	VALUE2	NAME3	VALUE3
E1	P1	1	P2	10	P3	20
E2	P1	1	P3	100	P4	50
E3	P1	1	P2	10	P3	100

Given that this logic relates to presenting a result, sometimes it makes sense to implement it on the client side.

The reverse operation can be done using the unpivot operator as shown in Listing 4-8.

Listing 4-8. Unpivot operator

```
select *
from entity_flattened
unpivot (value for p_name in
        (p1_value as 'P1', p2_value as 'P2', p3_value as 'P3'));
```

```
NAME  P_NAME      VALUE
----- ------ -----------
E1    P1             1
E1    P2            10
E1    P3            20
E3    P1             1
E3    P2            10
E3    P3           100
E2    P1             1
E2    P3           100

8 rows selected.
```

It creates new rows for each column listed in unpivot clause and replicates values for all remaining columns. In the example above it's "p1_value, p2_value, p3_value" and name correspondingly. There is no need for "any" keyword for unpivot because the recordset to be unpivoted always contains fixed and predefined number of columns. Oracle could have introduced syntactic sugar like "unpivot (value for p_name in (any except name))" but there is no strong necessity for this.

Unpivot can be implemented using Cartesian jon.

```
select name,
       p_name,
       decode(p_name, 'P1', p1_value, 'P2', p2_value, 'P3',
       p3_value) value
  from entity_flattened,
       (select 'P1' p_name from dual
         union all select 'P2' from dual
         union all select 'P3' from dual)
 where decode(p_name, 'P1', p1_value, 'P2', p2_value, 'P3',
 p3_value) is not null
 order by 1, 2;
```

Cube, Rollup, Grouping Sets

Oracle provides additional capabilities for calculating totals and subtotals. Let's consider a table with information about orders.

```
create table orders(order_id, client_id, product_id, quantity) as
(
select 1, 1, 1, 1 from dual
union all select 1, 1, 2, 2 from dual
union all select 1, 1, 3, 1 from dual
union all select 2, 2, 1, 1 from dual
union all select 2, 2, 5, 1 from dual
union all select 3, 1, 1, 1 from dual
union all select 3, 1, 4, 1 from dual
union all select 3, 1, 4, 1 from dual
union all select 4, 2, 4, 1 from dual
union all select 4, 2, 5, 1 from dual
);
```

"Rollup" allows us to calculate subtotals from right to left and "cube" allows us to calculate all possible subtotals for listed columns.

```
select client_id, product_id, sum(quantity) cnt
  from orders
 group by rollup(client_id, product_id)
 order by client_id, product_id;
```

CLIENT_ID	PRODUCT_ID	CNT
1	1	2
1	2	2
1	3	1
1	4	2
1		7
2	1	1
2	4	1
2	5	2
2		4
		11

```
10 rows selected.
```

```
select client_id, product_id, sum(quantity) cnt
  from orders
 group by cube(client_id, product_id)
 order by client_id, product_id;
```

CLIENT_ID	PRODUCT_ID	CNT
1	1	2
1	2	2
1	3	1
1	4	2

1		7
2	1	1
2	4	1
2	5	2
2		4
	1	3
	2	2
	3	1
	4	3
	5	2
		11

15 rows selected.

The same can be done using respectively.

```
grouping sets ((), (client_id), (client_id, product_id))
```

and

```
grouping sets ((), (client_id), (product_id), (client_id, product_id))
```

Functions grouping and grouping_id can be used to identify subtotals. Grouping accepts only a single expression as a parameter while grouping_id can accept multiple expressions.

```
select decode(grouping(client_id), 1, 'all clients', client_id)
as client_id,
     decode(grouping(product_id), 1, 'all products', product_id)
     as product_id,
     sum(quantity) cnt,
     decode(grouping_id(client_id, product_id),
           bitand(grouping_id(client_id, product_id), bin_
           to_num(0, 0)),
           'client, product',
```

```
                bitand(grouping_id(client_id, product_id),
                bin_to_num(0, 1)),
                'client',
                bitand(grouping_id(client_id, product_id),
                bin_to_num(1, 1)),
                'grand total') slice
   from orders
 group by rollup(client_id, product_id)
 order by client_id, product_id;
```

CLIENT_ID	PRODUCT_ID	CNT	SLICE
1	1	2	client, product
1	2	2	client, product
1	3	1	client, product
1	4	2	client, product
1	all products	7	client
2	1	1	client, product
2	4	1	client, product
2	5	2	client, product
2	all products	4	client
all clients	all products	11	grand total

10 rows selected.

There is also a function group_id that can be used to distinguish the same slices.

```
select decode(grouping(client_id), 1, 'all clients', client_id)
as client_id,
        decode(grouping(product_id), 1, 'all products', product_id)
        as product_id,
        sum(quantity) cnt,
        group_id() group_id
```

```
 from orders
group by grouping sets(client_id, product_id,(),())
order by client_id, product_id;
```

CLIENT_ID	PRODUCT_ID	CNT	GROUP_ID
1	all products	7	0
2	all products	4	0
all clients	1	3	0
all clients	2	2	0
all clients	3	1	0
all clients	4	3	0
all clients	5	2	0
all clients	all products	11	0
all clients	all products	11	1

9 rows selected.

Without these capabilities, the same result can be achieved using multiple table scans and groupings for each grouping set. On the other hand, it's doable using a single table scan and Cartesian join with slices, but performance of built-in functionality will be better because it's optimized to calculate aggregates by different attributes for the same recordset.

```
select client_id, product_id, sum(quantity) cnt, slice
  from (select decode(instr(slice, 'client'), 0,
                      'all clients', client_id) as client_id,
               decode(instr(slice, 'product'), 0,
                      'all products', product_id) as product_id,
               quantity,
               slice
          from orders,
               (select 'client, product' slice from dual
                union all select 'client' from dual
```

```
                union all select 'grand total' from dual))
group by client_id, product_id, slice
order by client_id, product_id;
```

So pivot can be rewritten with group by, unpivot can be imitated with a Cartesian product, and group by cube/rollup/grouping sets can be replaced with a Cartesian product and simple group by. However, built-in capabilities not only make queries more concise and easier to understand but have noticeably better performance.

The last thing to mention in this chapter is that aggregate functions can be nested or mixed up with analytic functions, which is explained in more detail in Chapter 9, "Logical Execution Order of Query Clauses."

Summary

Aggregate functions allow us to calculate a single result row for each group. In addition to various built-in aggregates, developers can implement their own UDAG (which also can be used as analytic functions with "over" clause) or use the collect function to aggregate rows into collection and apply any logic on top of it using UDF. Most of the built-in aggregates are commutative so order of rows within a group does not matter; however, some of them, like listagg or percentile_cont, require order that is specified after "within group" keywords. Order also matters for collect or xmlagg functions and may be specified in a function itself.

In a similar manner as it was shown for analytic functions, Oracle allows us to access first (or last) values from the group according to a specified order using the keyword keep and functions first/last. This is very helpful when it's required to find a min or max value from the group and corresponding attributes.

Sometimes grouping may help to avoid additional joins; however, such cases are quite rare. Also grouping can be used instead of pivot to "flatten" data, but using built-in capabilities are more preferable.

CHAPTER 5

Hierarchical Queries: Connect by

The connect by clause is used to query hierarchies if they are stored as parent-child relationships, also known as an adjacency lists model. Simply speaking, this model means that a parent – child pair is stored for each child. In general adjacency lists can represent directed graphs, not only hierarchical trees; in this case the list describes the set of neighbors of a vertex in the graph. So an adjacency list model is much wider and a parent-child model is one of its implementations.

Listing 5-1 shows the query for building hierarchy based on a parent-child relationship and using Oracle hierarchical query pseudocolumns.

Listing 5-1. Querying parent-child relationship

```
create table tree as
select 2 id, 1 id_parent from dual
union all select 3 id, 1 id_parent from dual
union all select 4 id, 3 id_parent from dual
union all select 5 id, 4 id_parent from dual
union all select 11 id, 10 id_parent from dual
union all select 12 id, 11 id_parent from dual
union all select 13 id, 11 id_parent from dual;
```

© Alex Reprintsev 2018
A. Reprintsev, *Oracle SQL Revealed*, https://doi.org/10.1007/978-1-4842-3372-6_5

```
select connect_by_root id_parent root,
       level lvl,
       rpad(' ', (level - 1) * 3, ' ') || t.id as id,
       prior id_parent grand_parent,
       sys_connect_by_path(id, '->') path,
       connect_by_isleaf is_leaf
  from tree t
 start with t.id_parent in (1, 10)
connect by prior t.id = t.id_parent;
```

ROOT	LVL	ID	GRAND_PARENT PATH	IS_LEAF
1	1	2	->2	1
1	1	3	->3	0
1	2	4	1 ->3->4	0
1	3	5	3 ->3->4->5	1
10	1	11	->11	0
10	2	12	10 ->11->12	1
10	2	13	10 ->11->13	1

The following must be specified for building a hierarchy:

- Root – in the example we build two trees with root parent IDs equal 1 and 10;

- Relationship between parents and children. «prior» is a unary operator that returns a value of a given expression (which is column as a rule) for an immediate parent for the current row.

Other hierarchical queries features demonstrated in Listing 5-1:

- connect_by_root – unary operator that returns an expression value for the root row.

- level and connect_by_isleaf – pseudocolumns, which return level (hierarchical depth) and flag whether a node is leaf or not for each row.

- sys_connect_by_path – function that returns path from root to node with given separator.

prior operator can be used not just in "connect by" clause but in a select list as well, but it can be applied to a given expression only once. For example, if the goal is to select a parent id two levels up, then the prior can be applied to the id_parent column - see expression for grand_parent in Listing 5-1.

Connect by traverses a hierarchy using a depth-first search approach, so all descendants for the current node are processed before the next node on the same level. "Order siblings by" can be used to specify the order within the same level. In this case, Oracle also will use a depth-first search but the order of the children for the parent may change. Listing 5-2 shows the result after specifying «order siblings by t.id desc» in the previous query. There is no guarantee that first level nodes will be ordered as specified in "order siblings by" because we cannot say they have a common parent.

Listing 5-2. Ordering siblings

ROOT	LVL ID	----GRAND_PARENT PATH	IS_LEAF
10	1 11	->11	0
10	2 13	10 ->11->13	1
10	2 12	10 ->11->12	1
1	1 3	->3	0
1	2 4	1 ->3->4	0
1	3 5	3 ->3->4->5	1
1	1 2	->2	1

If connect by is specified in the same query block as joins, then Oracle processes hierarchical queries as follows: joins (including those specified in where clause), connect by, all remaining where clause predicates.

Let's create the following tables for a demonstration:

```
drop table tree;
drop table nodes;
create table tree(id, id_parent) as
select rownum, rownum - 1 from dual connect by level <= 4;
create table nodes(id, name, sign) as
select rownum, 'name' || rownum, decode(rownum, 3, 0, 1)
  from dual connect by rownum <= 4;
```

In the second and third queries from Listing 5-3, the filter by sign was applied before building the hierarchy while in the first query it was applied after the hierarchy was built.

Listing 5-3. Connect by and joins

```
select t.*, n.name
  from tree t, nodes n
 where t.id = n.id
   and n.sign = 1
 start with t.id_parent = 0
connect by prior t.id = t.id_parent;

        ID   ID_PARENT NAME
---------- ---------- ------------------------------------------
         1          0 name1
         2          1 name2
         4          3 name4

select *
  from (select t.*, n.name
          from tree t, nodes n
         where t.id = n.id
           and n.sign = 1) t
```

```
start with t.id_parent = 0
connect by prior t.id = t.id_parent;

        ID  ID_PARENT NAME
---------- ---------- ----------------------------------------

         1          0 name1
         2          1 name2

select t.*, n.name
  from tree t
  join nodes n
    on t.id = n.id
   and n.sign = 1
 start with t.id_parent = 0
connect by prior t.id = t.id_parent;

        ID  ID_PARENT NAME
---------- ---------- ----------------------------------------

         1          0 name1
         2          1 name2
```

The final query after transformations for the original query with an ANSI join contains a Cartesian join while join predicate moved to the "start with" and "connect by" clauses. However, more logically it would be to expect an inline view and connect by on to top it in the transformed query. So if you build a plan for a transformed query, it will differ from the original plan for an original query and the join type will be "MERGE JOIN CARTESIAN."

```
select "T"."ID" "ID", "T"."ID_PARENT" "ID_PARENT", "N"."NAME"
"NAME"
  from "TREE" "T", "NODES" "N"
 start with "T"."ID_PARENT" = 0
        and "T"."ID" = "N"."ID"
```

```
        and "N"."SIGN" = 1
connect by "T"."ID_PARENT" = prior "T"."ID"
        and "T"."ID" = "N"."ID"
        and "N"."SIGN" = 1
```

The transformed query for the first query from Listing 5-3 also looks a bit unexpected – as you see the join condition moved from the where clause to "start with" and "connect by."

```
select "T"."ID" "ID", "T"."ID_PARENT" "ID_PARENT", "N"."NAME"
"NAME"
  from "TREE" "T", "NODES" "N"
 where "N"."SIGN" = 1
 start with "T"."ID_PARENT" = 0
        and "T"."ID" = "N"."ID"
connect by "T"."ID_PARENT" = prior "T"."ID"
        and "T"."ID" = "N"."ID"
```

Let me emphasize again that plans for these transformed and original queries are different; and even though they are semantically equivalent, performance for queries with transformed text will be much worse because the hierarchy will be built on top of Cartesian joins.

Speaking about outer joins, there is no difference whether they specified in "join" or "where" clause because the predicate containing (+) will be evaluated before building the hierarchy.

Also it's worth mentioning that if the goal is to get all the descendants up to a specific level, then it makes sense to specify a filter by "level <= n" in "connect by" condition instead of a where clause because in this case, building a hierarchy will stop at a specific level. Otherwise the hierarchy will be built for all levels and the where filter will be applied after that.

Another important point is that the connect by condition evaluates only for nodes with a level greater than 1. A first level node must be filtered using a "start with" clause. For example, all first level nodes will be returned regardless of whether you specify "level <= 1" or "level <= 0" in the connect by condition.

Connect by allows you to traverse directed graphs even if they contain cycles. See Figure 5-1.

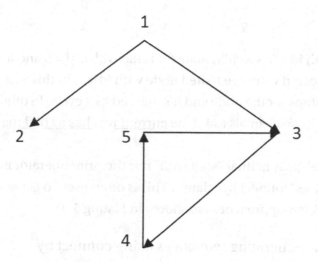

Figure 5-1. *Directed graph*

```
with graph (id, id_parent) as
(select 2, 1 from dual
union all select 3, 1 from dual
union all select 4, 3 from dual
union all select 5, 4 from dual
union all select 3, 5 from dual)
select level lvl, graph.*, connect_by_iscycle cycle
   from graph
 start with id_parent = 1
connect by nocycle prior id = id_parent;
```

LVL	ID	ID_PARENT	CYCLE
1	2	1	0
1	3	1	0
2	4	3	0
3	5	4	1

Node with id = 3 is a child node for node with c id = 5 and it was already processed when we visited node with id = 5. In this case, building a hierarchy stops for the node and it's marked as a cycle. In other words, connect_by_iscycle equals to 1 if the <u>current row has a child that is also its ancestor.</u>

In general case, neither "start with" nor the prior operator is mandatory when using the "connect by" clause. This is often used to generate sequences. A few approaches are shown in Listing 5-4.

Listing 5-4. Generating sequences using connect by

```
select level id from dual connect by level <= 10;
select rownum id from dual connect by rownum <= 10;
select rownum id from (select * from dual connect by 1 = 1)
 where rownum <= 10;
```

No cycles are identified for these queries because the parent record is not referred to in the connect by condition using the prior operator. So the cycle cannot exist when there is no parent-child relationship. Try to execute any of the queries from Listing 5-4 after adding the predicate «prior 1 = 1» to "connect by" condition.

Documentation says that "in a hierarchical query, one expression in [connect by] condition must be qualified with the PRIOR operator to refer to the parent row." So if you want to refer to the parent row then you must use the prior operator but you are not forced to refer to it – that is, connect by can be used not only to traverse hierarchies.

The key point for the prior operator is that the value referenced in it must exist before building the hierarchy. Also when you use a prior operator you cannot refer columns calculated in a hierarchical query. This is saying that it's not possible to calculate values for child nodes cumulatively. However, there is no such limitation for Recursive subquery factoring as will be shown in the next chapter.

To demonstrate this limitation let's consider a task when the goal is to generate the same sequence as function f returns (type numbers was defined in the section "Unnesting Collections").

```
create or replace function f(n in number) return numbers as
  result numbers := numbers();
begin
  result.extend(n + 1);
  result(1) := 1;
  for i in 2 .. n + 1 loop
    result(i) := round(100 * sin(result(i - 1) + i - 2));
  end loop;
  return result;
end f;
/
```

So the function returns a recursive sequence such as current value equals to sine of the sum of previous value and its index multiplied by 100 and rounded to integer. i-2 is used in the code because the elements indexed starting with zero.

To highlight the recursive nature of the sequence, it also can be defined using the recursive function.

```
create or replace function f(n in number) return numbers as
  result numbers;
begin
  if n = 0 then return numbers(1);
  else
    result := f(n - 1);
    result.extend;
    result(n + 1) := round(100 * sin(result(n) + n - 1));
    return result;
  end if;
end f;
/
```

Given that sine values fall in a range [-1; 1] and function values are multiplied by 100 and rounded to integers, it's possible to generate all possible values for the sequence – range [-100; 100]. With this assumption the sequence can be generated using "connect by."

The query in Listing 5-5 generates only the first 14 values instead of 21 because the 14th row is identified as a cycle.

Listing 5-5. Generating values of the recursive sequence using connect by

```
with t as
 (select -100 + level - 1 result from dual connect by level <= 201)
select level - 1 as id, result, connect_by_iscycle cycle
  from t
 start with result = 1
connect by nocycle round(100 * sin(prior result + level - 2)) =
result
        and level <= 21;
```

ID	RESULT	CYCLE
0	1	0
1	84	0
2	-18	0
3	29	0
4	55	0
5	64	0
6	-11	0
7	96	0
8	62	0
9	77	0
10	-92	0
11	-31	0
12	-91	0
13	44	1

The trick with adding "prior sys_guid() is not null" to "connect by" clause helps if we want to avoid cycles and generate all the elements. sys_guid() returns unique values so none of the rows generated so far are considered the same as a child row for the current row; thus no cycles are identified. Please refer to Listing 5-6 to see this approach in action.

Listing 5-6. Handling elements with the same values while generating the recursive sequence

```
with t as
 (select -100 + level - 1 result from dual connect by level <= 201)
select level - 1 as id, result, connect_by_iscycle cycle
  from t
 start with result = 1
```

```
connect by nocycle round(100 * sin(prior result + level - 2)) =
result
        and prior sys_guid() is not null
        and level <= 21;
```

ID	RESULT	CYCLE
0	1	0
1	84	0
2	-18	0
3	29	0
4	55	0
5	64	0
6	-11	0
7	96	0
8	62	0
9	77	0
10	-92	0
11	-31	0
12	-91	0
13	44	0
14	44	0
15	99	0
16	78	0
17	-25	0
18	-99	0
19	63	0
20	31	0

Now we see that no cycles were identified and so we can remove the nocycle keyword.

Summarizing the details of cycle identification:

- Cycle can be identified only if the "connect by" condition contains a "prior" operator.

- If we apply a "prior" operator to any function retuning unique values, then the cycle will not be identified because in this case rows with the same values are not considered as the same nodes of the hierarchy.

The demonstrated approach for running over pre-generated values can be used even if the recursive formula refers values on two previous iterations, but in this case it's necessary to generate all the possible pairs of previous element and the one before it. Listing 5-7 shows how to generate Fibonacci numbers using this approach.

Listing 5-7. Generating Fibonacci numbers using connect by

```
with t as
 (select rownum id from dual connect by rownum <= power(2, 15)
/ 15),
pairs as
 (select t1.id id1, t2.id id2
    from t t1, t t2
   where t2.id between (1 / 2) * t1.id and (2 / 3) * t1.id
  union all
  select 1, 0 from dual
  union all
  select 1, 1 from dual)
select rownum lvl, id2 fib
  from pairs
 start with (id1, id2) in ((1, 0))
connect by prior id1 = id2
       and prior (id1 + id2) = id1
       and level <= 15;
```

```
        LVL          FIB
---------- ----------
          1          0
          2          1
          3          1
          4          2
          5          3
          6          5
          7          8
          8         13
          9         21
         10         34
         11         55
         12         89
         13        144
         14        233
         15        377
```

15 rows selected.

We may notice that $F_i < 2^i/i$ and F_{i-1} between $\frac{1}{2} * F_i$ and $\frac{3}{4} *F_i$ for all elements greater than 1 and these conditions were used to reduce the number of pre-generated pairs. Unlike the previous example, there is no need to use a trick with prior sys_guid because the sequence is monotonically increasing for all elements greater than 1 so it's not possible to face a cycle.

Elapsed time grows exponentially depending on the level and such an approach cannot be used in real-life tasks; the main intention was to demonstrate specifics of the "connect by" clause.

The trick with sys_guid can also be used to generate the number of copies for each row.

```
with t as
  (select 'A' value, 2 cnt from dual
   union all
   select 'B' value, 3 cnt from dual)
select *
  from t
connect by level <= cnt
        and prior value = value
        and prior sys_guid() is not null;

V          CNT
-  ----------
A            2
A            2
B            3
B            3
B            3
```

As you can see, there is no "start with" condition in a query so the first level contains all the rows and connection is performed in the scope of each value until the cnt rows are generated. The trick with sys_guid was used to avoid cycles, given that all the rows for each root have the same values. There are many other ways to generate a specified number of copies for each row and connect by is not the best way to do that.

We can also use this trick while traversing directed graphs. It prevents Oracle from identifying cycles so the same cycle may be traversed multiple times. The cycle column equals to zero for all rows as expected.

```
select level lvl, graph.*, connect_by_iscycle cycle
  from graph
 start with id_parent = 1
```

```
connect by nocycle prior id = id_parent
        and prior sys_guid() is not null
        and level <= 10;
```

LVL	ID	ID_PARENT	CYCLE
1	2	1	0
1	3	1	0
2	4	3	0
3	5	4	0
4	3	5	0
5	4	3	0
6	5	4	0
7	3	5	0
8	4	3	0
9	5	4	0
10	3	5	0

If the goal is to select all the edges including the one closing the cycle, then we can add the condition "prior id_parent is not null" as shown in Listing 5-8. In this case the cycle will be identified if we visited the same node twice. Additional details can be found in the section "Once Again About Cycles" in the next chapter.

Listing 5-8. Affecting cycle detection by adding "prior id_parent is not null"

```
select level lvl, graph.*, connect_by_iscycle cycle
  from graph
 start with id_parent = 1
connect by nocycle prior id = id_parent
        and prior id_parent is not null;
```

LVL	ID	ID_PARENT	CYCLE
1	2	1	0
1	3	1	0
2	4	3	0
3	5	4	0
4	3	5	1

Pseudocolumn Generation in Detail

We already considered how join, connect by, and where clauses work in hierarchical queries. When a query contains pseudocolumns it's not possible to say that their values are generated before or after a specific query clause, but we can state the following rules:

- level is incremented when a row for a new level is generated

- rownum is incremented when a new row is added to a result set

Listing 5-9 demonstrates the above statements, based on an example

Listing 5-9. Specific of level and rownum pseudocolumns generation

```
create table t_two_branches(id, id_parent) as
(select rownum, rownum - 1 from dual connect by level <= 10
union all
select 100 + rownum, 100 + rownum - 1 from dual connect by
level <= 10
union all
select 0, null from dual
```

```
union all
select 100, null from dual);
select rownum rn,
       level lvl,
       replace(sys_connect_by_path(rownum, '~'), '~') as path_rn,
       replace(sys_connect_by_path(level, '~'), '~') as path_lvl,
       sys_connect_by_path(id, '~') path_id
  from t_two_branches
 where mod(level, 3) = 0
start with id_parent is null
connect by prior id = id_parent;
```

RN	LVL	PATH_RN	PATH_LVL	PATH_ID
1	3	111	123	~0~1~2
2	6	111222	123456	~0~1~2~3~4~5
3	9	111222333	123456789	~0~1~2~3~4~5~6~7~8
4	3	444	123	~100~101~102
5	6	444555	123456	~100~101~102~103~104~105
6	9	444555666	123456789	~100~101~102~103~104~105 ~106~107~108

6 rows selected.

For each of the two branches Oracle generated 9 levels and 3 rows: rows 1-3 for the first branch and rows 4-6 for the second branch. Columns path_rn and path_lvl help us to understand how values for pseudocolumns were generated. Technically, the "where" clause evaluates when a hierarchy is being built, not afterward.

Also it's interesting to point out the difference when a rownum/level is used in a "connect by."

Listing 5-10. Difference between using level and rownum in "connect by" condition

```
select rownum rn,
       level lvl,
       replace(sys_connect_by_path(rownum, '~'), '~') as path_rn,
       replace(sys_connect_by_path(level, '~'), '~') as path_lvl,
       sys_connect_by_path(id, '~') path_id
  from t_two_branches
start with id_parent is null
connect by prior id = id_parent
and rownum <= 2;
```

RN	LVL	PATH_RN	PATH_LVL	PATH_ID
1	1	1	1	~0
2	2	12	12	~0~1
3	1	3	1	~100

```
select rownum rn,
       level lvl,
       replace(sys_connect_by_path(rownum, '~'), '~') as path_rn,
       replace(sys_connect_by_path(level, '~'), '~') as path_lvl,
       sys_connect_by_path(id, '~') path_id
  from t_two_branches
start with id_parent is null
connect by prior id = id_parent
and level <= 2;
```

RN	LVL	PATH_RN	PATH_LVL	PATH_ID
1	1	1	1	~0
2	2	12	12	~0~1
3	1	3	1	~100
4	2	34	12	~100~101

In the first case Oracle returns two rows for the first branch and a root row for the second branch. Although the "connect by" condition is false for it, "start with" is true; thus all the roots are present in the result. In the second case Oracle simply traverses all the branches up to a specified level, and obviously the rownum monotonically increases.

Summary

The "connect by" clause is one of Oracle's specific features and can be used for traversing parent-child hierarchies or generating sequences without parent-child dependencies. In general, this feature allows traversing any directed graphs and a nocycle keyword can be used to handle cycles.

CHAPTER 6

Recursive Subquery Factoring

A subquery factoring clause (sometimes also referred to as a "with clause" or CTE – common table expression) was introduced in Oracle 9.2. At that time it did not allow us to define recursive subqueries and was mainly used to decompose the logic into named queries – factor out subqueries and reference them by names in the main query. CBO can decide whether to materialize results of factored out subqueries or plug them in as inline views. In the former case it can improve performance if the named query is referenced multiple times in the main query, while in the latter case it may have a negative impact on the performance because the transformation engine doesn't treat named queries in the same way as inline views. For example, on older versions Oracle could have merged an inline view but not the named query with exactly the same text.

Starting with Oracle 11.2, the subquery factoring clause allows us to execute a query recursively if a subquery references its own name, which is presented schematically in Listing 6-1.

Listing 6-1. Recursive subquery factoring

```
with rec as
(
anchor_query_text - anchor member
union all
```

© Alex Reprintsev 2018
A. Reprintsev, *Oracle SQL Revealed*, https://doi.org/10.1007/978-1-4842-3372-6_6

```
recursive_query_text - recursive member referencing rec
)
select *
from rec
```

The following algorithm is used for execution:

1. Run anchor member to get base result set Set_0.

2. Execute recursive member with result set Set_{i-1} from previous iteration.

3. Repeat step 2 until empty result set is returned.

4. Return final result set, which is the union all of Set_0 ... Set_n.

The query in Listing 6-2 traverses the trees from the tree table introduced in the previous chapter (Listing 5-1). You may notice that the order of the result differs from the "connect by" approach.

Listing 6-2. Building hierarchies using recursive subquery factoring

```
with rec(lvl, id, path) as
(
select 1 lvl, id, cast('->' || id as varchar2(4000))
  from tree where id_parent in (1, 10)
union all
select r.lvl + 1, t.id, r.path || '->' || t.id
  from tree t
  join rec r on t.id_parent = r.id
)
select lvl,
       rpad(' ', (lvl - 1) * 3, ' ') || id as id,
       path
  from rec;
```

```
 LVL  ID          PATH
----------- ----------- -----------
    1 2           ->2
    1 3           ->3
    1 11          ->11
    2    4        ->3->4
    2    12       ->11->12
    2    13       ->11->13
    3       5     ->3->4->5
```

To return the result in the same order as "connect by" does, you must specify "search depth first" – in this case all the descendants for the node will be returned before the other nodes on its level – see Listing 6-3. Default ordering is "search breadth first" so all nodes from previous levels are returned before nodes on the current level. As it will be shown in section "Traversing Hierarchies," order impacts only how results are returned, not the way of traversing a hierarchy.

Listing 6-3. Getting the same result as connect by

```
with rec(root, lvl, id, id_parent, grand_parent) as
(
select id_parent, 1 lvl, id, id_parent, cast(null as number)
  from tree where id_parent in (1, 10)
union all
select r.root, r.lvl + 1, t.id, t.id_parent, r.id_parent
  from tree t
  join rec r on t.id_parent = r.id
)
search depth first by id set ord
select root,
       lvl,
       rpad(' ', (lvl - 1) * 3, ' ') || id as id,
```

```
        id_parent,
        grand_parent,
        ord,
        decode(lvl + 1, lead(lvl) over(partition by root order
        by ord), 0, 1) is_leaf
    from rec;
```

ROOT	LVL	ID	ID_PARENT	GRAND_PARENT	ORD	IS_LEAF
1	1	2	1		1	1
1	1	3	1		2	0
1	2	4	3	1	3	0
1	3	5	4	3	4	1
10	1	11	10		5	0
10	2	12	11	10	6	1
10	2	13	11	10	7	1

7 rows selected.

There are no predefined pseudocolumns for recursive subquery factoring so the calculation logic should be implemented manually. For example, a node is not a leaf node if it's followed by node on the next level when search depth first is specified – this logic was used to calculate is_leaf column.

Mechanics of calculating a path from the previous example is a bit more interesting. An expression for a path references a path from a previous iteration. This is one of the most important differences from "connect by," which allows referencing only existing columns (not calculated ones). So if the goal is to calculate a path not from the root to the current node but in the opposite direction – from current node to root, then it can be done by replacing "r.path || '->' || t.id" with "'->' || t.id || r.path". On the other hand, it's not possible with connect by and built-in capabilities.

Listing 6-4 shows how recursive sequences from the previous chapter can be generated using recursive subquery factoring. In the first case the current value depends only on the previous value while in the second case it depends on the previous value and the one before it. Recursive subquery factoring allows referring only values from previous iteration so in order to be able to use values from an i-2 iteration, we introduced an auxiliary column.

Listing 6-4. Generating of recursive sequences

```
with t(id, result) as
(
select 0 id, 1 result from dual
union all
select t.id + 1, round(100 * sin(t.result + t.id))
  from t
 where t.id < 20
)
select * from t;

with t (lvl, result, tmp) as
(
select 1, 0, 1 from dual
union all
select lvl + 1, tmp, tmp + result
  from t
 where lvl < 15)
select lvl, result from t;
```

If we need to use values from several previous iterations, we can either add multiple auxiliary columns or use a collection column.

Anyway, such approaches are much more efficient than "connect by" because there is no need for running over pre-generated values to generate each new row.

As it was already mentioned, recursive subquery factoring allows referring values calculated on a previous iteration. This technique can be used for root-finding using the bisection method. This method is demonstrated purely to highlight capabilities of the SQL language, and there is no practical need to use SQL for this task.

Let's consider function y, which has different signs in points 1 and 2.

```
create or replace function y(x in number) return number as
begin return x*x - 2; end;
```

Listing 6-5 shows how to find the root in the range [1; 2] with precision 0.01.

Listing 6-5. Finding the root using bisection method and recursive subquery factoring clause

```
with t(id, x, x0, x1) as
(
  select 0, 0, 1, 2
    from dual
  union all
  select t.id + 1,
         (t.x0 + t.x1) / 2,
         case
           when sign(y(x0)) = sign(y((t.x0 + t.x1) / 2))
           then (t.x0 + t.x1) / 2
           else x0
         end,
         case
           when sign(y(x1)) = sign(y((t.x0 + t.x1) / 2))
           then (t.x0 + t.x1) / 2
           else x1
         end
```

```
  from t
  where abs((t.x0 + t.x1) / 2 - t.x) > 1e-2
)
select t.*, (x0+x1)/2 result from t;
```

ID	X	X0	X1	RESULT
0	0	1	2	1.5
1	1.5	1	1.5	1.25
2	1.25	1.25	1.5	1.375
3	1.375	1.375	1.5	1.4375
4	1.4375	1.375	1.4375	1.40625
5	1.40625	1.40625	1.4375	1.421875
6	1.421875	1.40625	1.421875	1.4140625

The algorithm divides the range on each step according to following rule: if sign of the function in the midpoint is the same as at the right border, then move the right border to the midpoint or else move the left border to the midpoint. Repeat iterations unless the difference between the midpoint on the current step and the midpoint on the previous step is less than 0.01.

Required precision was satisfied on the 6th iteration and the found root is a midpoint on the next iteration, which is **1.4140625**.

Range borders on each iteration were calculated using values from a previous iteration. It would not be possible to use "connect by" to implement this approach. The term "iteration" instead of level was used to highlight the iterative nature of the algorithm.

Traversing Hierarchies

Documentation says that the «subquery_factoring_clause supports recursive subquery factoring (recursive WITH) and lets you query hierarchical data. **This feature is more powerful than CONNECT BY in that it provides depth-first search and breadth-first search**, and supports multiple recursive branches». It sounds like "connect by" always does depth-first search while a traversing algorithm for recursive subquery factoring can be affected by specifying depth-first or breadth-first in search_clause. Let's check whether this is the correct impression or not.

Function stop_at sets a flag if a specific node was visited and returns a not null value if the flag is set.

```
create or replace function stop_at(p_id in number, p_stop in
number)
  return number is
begin
  if p_id = p_stop then
    dbms_application_info.set_client_info('1');
    return 1;
  end if;
  for i in (select client_info from v$session where sid =
userenv('sid')) loop
    return i.client_info;
  end loop;
end;
```

Listing 6-6. Specifying breadth-first and depth-first search

```
exec dbms_application_info.set_client_info('');

PL/SQL procedure successfully completed.

with rec(lvl, id) as
(
select 1, id
  from t_two_branches where id_parent is null
union all
select r.lvl + 1, t.id
  from t_two_branches t
  join rec r on t.id_parent = r.id
 where stop_at(t.id, 101) is null
)
search breadth first by id set ord
--search depth first by id set ord
select *
from rec;

       LVL          ID         ORD
---------- ---------- ----------
         1           0           1
         1         100           2
         2           1           3

exec dbms_application_info.set_client_info('');

PL/SQL procedure successfully completed.

with rec(lvl, id) as
(
select 1, id
  from t_two_branches where id_parent is null
```

```
union all
select r.lvl + 1, t.id
  from t_two_branches t
  join rec r on t.id_parent = r.id
 where stop_at(t.id, 101) is null
)
--search breadth first by id set ord
search depth first by id set ord
select *
from rec;
```

LVL	ID	ORD
1	0	1
2	1	2
1	100	3

Oracle 11.2 and 12.1 return only 3 rows in both cases; however it was expected that a query will return all nodes for the first branch for depth-first search because none of them equals 101. So it looks like irrespective of whatever approach we specify in the search clause, Oracle always does a breadth-first search and after that orders a result accordingly. On the other hand, Oracle 12.2 returns the following results.

LVL	ID	ORD
1	0	1
1	100	2
2	1	3
3	2	4
4	3	5
5	4	6
6	5	7

7	6	8
8	7	9
9	8	10
10	9	11
11	10	12

12 rows selected.

LVL	ID	ORD
1	0	1
2	1	2
3	2	3
4	3	4
5	4	5
6	5	6
7	6	7
8	7	8
9	8	9
10	9	10
11	10	11
1	100	12

12 rows selected.

This means that it does a depth-first search regardless of whatever is specified in the search_clause – in both cases all the nodes for the first branch are returned.

Let's now check the result for connect by.

```
select rownum rn, level lvl, id, id_parent
  from t_two_branches
 start with id_parent is null
connect by prior id = id_parent
       and stop_at(id, 101) is null;
```

RN	LVL	ID	ID_PARENT
1	1	0	
2	2	1	0
3	3	2	1
4	4	3	2
5	5	4	3
6	6	5	4
7	7	6	5
8	8	7	6
9	9	8	7
10	10	9	8
11	11	10	9
12	1	100	

```
12 rows selected.
```

It's the same as for the recursive subquery factoring on 12.2 and depth-first search.

To summarize, connect by always traverses a hierarchy using a depth-first search while the behavior for he recursive subquery factoring has changed from for breadth-first to depth-first search in version 12.2. The search_clause has an impact only on the final order, not on the algorithm Oracle uses to traverse the hierarchy. For connect by it's easy to mimic a breath-first search by ordering a result by level.

Once Again About Cycles

Let's investigate how to handle a cycle using recursive subquery factoring and a graph table from the previous chapter (Figure 5-1).

Listing 6-7. Detecting cycle by ID

```
with t(id, id_parent) as
(
select * from graph where id_parent = 1
union all
select g.id, g.id_parent
  from t
  join graph g on t.id = g.id_parent
)
search depth first by id set ord
cycle id set cycle to 1 default 0
select * from t;
```

ID	ID_PARENT	ORD	CYCLE
2	1	1	0
3	1	2	0
4	3	3	0
5	4	4	0
3	5	5	1

"**cycle id set cycle to 1 default 0**" instructs Oracle to set the "cycle" column to 1 if cycle by id is detected. Oracle will not look for child rows for the offending row, but it will continue to look for other noncyclic rows. <u>A row is considered to form a cycle if one of its ancestor rows has the same values for the cycle columns.</u> In other words, if row is marked as a cycle,

151

then one of the existing rows in the result set has the same value in the specified column.

In the above example, the row with ID = 3 was marked as a cycle because ID = 3 already existed in a result. In the case of a "connect by" clause the row with ID = 5 was marked as a cycle because its child (row with ID = 3) is also its ancestor – see Figure 5-1 in the previous chapter.

Unlike connect by, we can specify which column to use to detect a cycle. So if we specify id_parent in a cycle_clause, then the result will be a bit different – the execution stops when we face a node with ID_PARENT = 3 for a second time.

Listing 6-8. Detecting cycle by ID_PARENT

```
with t(id, id_parent) as
(
select * from graph where id_parent = 1
union all
select g.id, g.id_parent
  from t
  join graph g on t.id = g.id_parent
)
search depth first by id set ord
cycle id_parent set cycle to 1 default 0
select * from t;
```

ID	ID_PARENT	ORD	C
2	1	1	0
3	1	2	0
4	3	3	0
5	4	4	0
3	5	5	0
4	3	6	1

We may notice that cycle by ID was identified in the same row as it was for the connect by query and condition "nocycle prior id = id_parent **and prior id_parent is not null**" (see Listing 5-8). However, it's not always the case. If the root node is part of the cycle, then results may differ. Let's have a look at the result when we start from the node with ID = 3.

Listing 6-9. Building hierarchy from the node which is part of the cycle

```
select level lvl, graph.*, connect_by_iscycle cycle
  from graph
 start with id = 3
connect by nocycle prior id = id_parent;
```

LVL	ID	ID_PARENT	CYCLE
1	3	1	0
2	4	3	0
3	5	4	1
1	3	5	0
2	4	3	0
3	5	4	1

```
select level lvl, graph.*, connect_by_iscycle cycle
  from graph
 start with id = 3
connect by nocycle prior id = id_parent
       and prior id_parent is not null;
```

```
       LVL          ID  ID_PARENT       CYCLE
---------- ---------- ---------- ----------
         1          3           1           0
         2          4           3           0
         3          5           4           0
         4          3           5           1
         1          3           5           0
         2          4           3           0
         3          5           4           1
```

```
with t(id, id_parent) as
(
select * from graph where id = 3
union all
select g.id, g.id_parent
  from t
  join graph g on t.id = g.id_parent
)
search depth first by id set ord
cycle id set cycle to 1 default 0
select * from t;
```

```
        ID  ID_PARENT          ORD C
---------- ---------- ---------- -
         3          1          1 0
         4          3          2 0
         5          4          3 0
         3          5          4 1
         3          5          5 0
         4          3          6 0
         5          4          7 0
         3          5          8 1
```

The node with ID = 3 has two parents so we traverse the cycle two times.

In the last query in the second cycle, edge (5, 3) appears twice because ID with the same value must appear twice to detect a cycle. On the other hand, the result of the second query from Listing 6-9 looks the most natural because for both cycles it <u>contains all the edges forming the cycle without any recurrences</u>.

In addition to built-in capabilities to detect cycles we can implement our own logic as shown in Listing 6-10. cnt1 is the number of occurrences of ID in the concatenation of ancestor IDs, similarly cnt2 is the number of occurrences of ID in the concatenation of ancestor PARENT_IDs. If you uncomment filters by cnt1/cnt2, then the result will be the same as for recursive subquery factoring/connect by queries from Listing 6-9. There is no need to specify cycle_clause when such filters are used.

Listing 6-10. Manual implementation of the logic to detect cycles

```
with t(id, id_parent, path_id, path_id_parent, cnt1, cnt2) as
(
select g.*,
       cast('->' || g.id as varchar2(4000)),
       cast('->' || g.id_parent as varchar2(4000)),
       0,
       0
  from graph g
 where id = 3
union all
select g.id,
       g.id_parent,
       t.path_id || '->' || g.id,
       t.path_id_parent || '->' || g.id_parent,
       regexp_count(t.path_id || '->', '->' || g.id || '->'),
```

```
        regexp_count(t.path_id_parent || '->', '->' || g.id
        || '->')
   from t
   join graph g
     on t.id = g.id_parent
-- and t.cnt1 = 0
-- and t.cnt2 = 0
)
search depth first by id set ord
cycle id set cycle to 1 default 0
select * from t;
```

ID	ID_PARENT	PATH_ID	PATH_ID_PARENT	CNT1	CNT2	ORD	C
3	1	->3	->1	0	0	1	0
4	3	->3->4	->1->3	0	0	2	0
5	4	->3->4->5	->1->3->4	0	0	3	0
3	5	->3->4->5->3	->1->3->4->5	1	1	4	1
3	5	->3	->5	0	0	5	0
4	3	->3->4	->5->3	0	0	6	0
5	4	->3->4->5	->5->3->4	0	1	7	0
3	5	->3->4->5->3	->5->3->4->5	1	1	8	1

Limitations of the Current Implementation

The query in a recursive member has a number of limitations; in
particular, you cannot use distinct, group by, having, connect by, aggregate
functions, model, etc., in it. One may ask whether this is a limitation of
the current implementation or the recursive execution does not make
sense when such a complex logic is used. My inclination is that some of
these limitations will be removed in the future. On the other hand, we can

use workarounds for some limitations even in the current version, but that may look a bit awkward. In particular, we can use analytic functions and additional filters to get an aggregated result – although this is not something to be used in real-life tasks.

The following will be demonstrated mainly for academic purposes. So, let's assume we need to build a parent–child hierarchy where the parent is the sum of all IDs on the current level.

```
with t0(id, id_parent, letter) as
(select 1, 0, 'B' from dual
union all select 2, 1, 'D' from dual
union all select 3, 1, 'A' from dual
union all select 10, 5, 'C' from dual
union all select 66, 6, 'X' from dual),
t(id, id_parent, sum_id, lvl, str, rn) as
(select id, id_parent, id, 1, letter, 1 from t0 where
id_parent = 0
 union all
 select
   t0.id,
   t0.id_parent,
   sum(t0.id) over (),
   t.lvl + 1,
   listagg(letter, ', ') within group (order by letter) over
(),
   rownum
 from t
 join t0 on t.sum_id = t0.id_parent and t.rn = 1)
select * from t;
```

ID	ID_PARENT	SUM_ID	LVL	STR	RN
1	0	1	1	B	1
3	1	5	2	A, D	2
2	1	5	2	A, D	1
10	5	10	3	C	1

Analytic functions were used instead of aggregate ones and "t.rn = 1" was added to the join condition to avoid duplicates, because the value of the analytic function is the same for all rows and they are not grouped into one row per group.

If we are interested only in an aggregated result for each level, then it can be achieved using a query like this:

```
select sum_id, lvl, str from t where rn = 1;
```

Analytic functions in a recursive member would cause «ORA-32486: unsupported operation in recursive branch of recursive WITH clause» in Oracle 11.2.0.1; however it was fixed in 11.2.0.3.

Summary

"Recursive with" is defined in standard SQL:1999 while the "connect by" clause is an Oracle-specific feature. Nevertheless, it makes sense to use connect by instead of recursive subquery factoring in all cases where it's possible, because it's better optimized and works faster. As it was mentioned previously, it's not possible to reference calculated expressions in "connect by" queries while recursive with provides this facility. So if any cumulative-like calculations are required while traversing a hierarchy, then recursive subquery factoring may be the best option.

Traversing hierarchies is not the only application of recursive subquery factoring. It can be used for various tasks when the same logic has to be applied to a recordset multiple times. It's important to highlight that the final result contains recordsets from all the iterations while on current iteration it's possible to access rows only from the previous one. The necessity to return recordsets from all the iterations may cause intensive work area usage and other overhead costs. So if you do not need recordsets from all iterations but only from the last one, then it's reasonable to use PL/SQL loops and collections or temporary tables.

Even though recursive subquery factoring and connect by have built-in capabilities to handle cycles, it makes sense to use them only in trivial cases. For more complex cases, procedural approaches are better. Anyway, connect by and recursive subquery factoring handle cycle a bit differently so it may be important to know the details.

CHAPTER 7

Model

One may say that the model clause is the most powerful SQL feature, meaning that it can be used to solve numerous tasks that otherwise would not be resolvable using SQL. This can be accomplished not only because the model clause considerably extends possibilities of declarative SQL, but in addition to that it introduces ability of iterative computations in SQL on top of a recordset. On the other hand, the model clause has some issues with scalability and, in general, a class of problems where the model shines is quite limited. In many cases PL/SQL is preferable even though a result can be achieved using a model clause, but first things first.

A model clause allows you to treat a recordset as a multidimensional cube by mapping columns into three groups: partitions, dimensions, and measures.

- Partitions specify logical groups and rules of the model are applied to partitions independently. Specifying partitions may help to dramatically leverage power of parallel execution.

- Dimension columns are used to define a multidimensional cube and, by default, a combination of all the dimensions uniquely identifies cells in the cube. From another perspective we may say – to uniquely identify a row in a spreadsheet or a value in a multidimensional array.

© Alex Reprintsev 2018
A. Reprintsev, *Oracle SQL Revealed*, https://doi.org/10.1007/978-1-4842-3372-6_7

- Measures are values of multidimensional cubes
  that can be calculated using model rules. As a rule,
  measures are numeric values but, unlike many others
  tools for multidimensional analysis, Oracle supports
  dates and strings or even RAW values as measures.

Partitions, dimensions, and measures can be specified not only as
mappings to columns of the query but also as expressions.

Let's see how it works using an example from Listing 7-1.

Listing 7-1. Basic example of the model clause

```
with t(id, value) as
(
select 1, 3 from dual
union all select 2, 9 from dual
union all select 3, 8 from dual
union all select 5, 5 from dual
union all select 10, 4 from dual
)
select * from t
model
-- return updated rows
dimension by (id)
measures (value, 0 result)
-- rules
(
  result[id >= 5] = sum(value)[id <= cv(id)],
  result[0] = value[10] + value[value[1]]
);
```

ID	VALUE	RESULT
1	3	0
2	9	0
3	8	0
5	5	25
10	4	29
0		12

We defined a single dimension by ID column and two measures: one as mapped to a value column and another one as a zero.

Rule `result[id >= 5] = sum(value)[id <= cv(id)]` is applied only to rows with dimension values greater or equal to 5, which means two rows in our example – with ID = 5 and ID = 10. The value of the expression is a summarized measure for all the rows with dimension value equal or less than the current dimension value. The function `cv` is used on the right side of the rule to access current dimension value when multiple rows are referenced on the left side of the rule.

Note   You may also see function `currentv` in documentation for Oracle 10g Release 1, but it does not appear in documentation for later versions although it looks like it still works. Similarly `model` keyword is interchangeable with `spreadsheet` keyword but the latter is no longer documented.

Rule `result[0] = value[10] + value[value[1]]` means that the measure value for a cell with dimension value 0 is a sum of measure value for ID = 10 and ID = value[1], which is 3. Please note that the cell with dimension value 0 did not exist in original recordset and was added during the model clause evaluation. As will be shown later, this behavior may be adjusted. `value[value[1]]` is an example of nested cell reference.

So we can consider measures as values of multidimensional arrays and dimensions as indices to address the values; however, measure values also can be used to access the cells.

If we uncomment the `return updated rows` in Listing 7-1, then the result will contain only rows with applied rules – that is, with IDs 5, 10, and 0. The default value is `return for all rows`. The `rules` keyword is optional unless you want to specify iterations.

There are two notations to address cells – *symbolic dimension reference* and *positional dimension reference*. In case of a symbolic dimension reference, there must be a predicate containing the name of the dimension; otherwise the dimension reference is positional – for example, constant value, expression, or even a for loop. Differences between the notations are important for the left side of the rule which identifies the cells that are updated with the values from the right side of the rule.

The way how Oracle treats missing cells can be specified using keywords `update/upsert all/upsert`. `Update` only updates existing cells, `upsert` (default value) updates existing cells and creates missing cells in case of a positional reference while `upsert all` also creates missing cells for mixed references if the dimension values used in the symbolic reference existed in the original recordset. Let's see how it works for specific example as shown in Listing 7-2.

Listing 7-2. Upsert all in action

```
with t(dim1, dim2, value) as
(
select 0, 0, 1 from dual
union all select 0, 1, 2 from dual
union all select 1, 0, 3 from dual
)
select * from t
model
```

```
dimension by (dim1, dim2)
measures (value, cast(null as number) result)
rules upsert all
(
  result[0, 0] = -1,
  result[dim1=1, dim2=0] = -3,
  result[-1, for dim2 in (select count(*) from dual)] = -4,
  result[-2, dim2=1] = -10,
  result[-3, dim2=-1] = -100,
  result[-4, -1] = -1000
)
order by dim1, dim2;
```

DIM1	DIM2	VALUE	RESULT
-4	-1		-1000
-2	1		-10
-1	1		-4
0	0	1	-1
0	1	2	
1	0	3	-3

There are 3 original rows and 3 created ones in the query output from Listing 7-2. Cells with values -4 and -1000 have been added because the positional notation was used for both dimensions. The cell with value -10 was added because the value for symbolic notation dim2=1 existed in the original recordset even though the positional value for dim1 did not exist. The measure with value -100 was not added because the value -1 used in symbolic notation for dim2 did not exist. The measure value for cell [0, 1] is unknown because no rule was specified for it. And finally, the result for cells [0, 0] and [dim1=1, dim2=0] was calculated because they existed in the original recordset.

If we specify `upsert` then measure -10 will be excluded from the result set, and if we specify `update` then cells with the result values -4 and -1000 will also disappear.

Simply speaking, symbolic references are used when we aim to work with existing data only while positional references can be used if there may be a necessity to add new cells – for example, in case of forecasting or interpolation. Mixed reference makes sense when some dimensions are supposed to be fixed while another can be extended with new members.

If we want to reference all the members of the dimension then we can use the keyword `any` for positional reference or the `is  any` predicate for symbolic reference. The behavior is the same in both cases – the rule is applied to all the members of the dimension and new ones cannot be created.

When the left side of the rule references multiple rows, the order may be very important as demonstrated in Listing 7-3.

Listing 7-3. Specifying order on the left side of the rule

```
with t(id, value) as
(select rownum, rownum from dual connect by level <= 3)
select *
from t
model
dimension by (id)
measures (value, 100 r1, 100 r2)
(
  r1[any] order by id asc  = nvl(r1[cv(id)-1], 0) + value[cv(id)],
  r2[id is any] order by id desc = nvl(r2[cv(id)-1], 0) +
  value[cv(id)]
)
```

```
order by id;
```

ID	VALUE	R1	R2
1	1	1	1
2	2	3	102
3	3	6	103

When we specify ascending order the result is a cumulative sum while for descending order, the result is completely different. We got 102 and 103, which are the sum of the measure value for current row and measure r2 for the previous row, which was initialized as 100. There is no previous row for the first row so the result is simply a measure value for that row.

It always makes sense to specify the order on the left side of the rule if it's applied for multiple rows because

- It improves performance;

- It adds clarity to the solution;

- It helps to avoid ORA-32637: Self cyclic rule in sequential order MODEL.

Listing 7-4 shows an example of recursive measure. Oracle cannot resolve this dependency but if we uncomment "order by id," then the result will be calculated successfully. Try to guess what the result is without running the query.

Listing 7-4. Recursive measure

```
with t as
(select rownum id from dual connect by level <= 3)
select *
from t
model
dimension by (id)
```

```
measures (id result)
rules
(
  result[any] /*order by id*/ = sum(result)[any]
);
(select rownum id from dual connect by level <= 3)
                              *
ERROR at line 2:
ORA-32637: Self cyclic rule in sequential order MODEL
```

By default, all the rules are evaluated in the order they are specified in a query. This also can be explicitly specified using an optional keyword sequential order. This behavior may be changed if we specify automatic order so that dependencies among the cells are taken into account.

Listing 7-5. Model with automatic rule ordering

```
with t as
(select rownum id from dual connect by level <= 3)
select *
from t
model
dimension by (id)
measures (0 t1, 0 x, 0 t2)
rules automatic order
(
  t1[id] = x[cv(id)-1],
  x[id] = cv(id),
  t2[id] = x[cv(id)-1]
)
```

```
order by id;
```

ID	T1	X	T2
1		1	
2	1	2	1
3	2	3	2

If you omit automatic order in Listing 7-5, then values for t1 would be NULL, 0, 0.

As it was already shown, you can specify multiple rules for the same measure; moreover Oracle will not complain even if you specify multiple rules for the same measure and the same cells; however this should be avoided. For example, we can add fourth rule t1[id] = x[cv(id)] + t2[cv(id)] into the query from Listing 7-5, but after that, rule t1[id] = x[cv(id)-1] is completely overridden and should be removed.

Whatever order is specified, rules are calculated one by one. This means the first rule is evaluated for all cells referenced on the left side and then the second rule is evaluated for all cells referenced on its left side and so on. In other words, *rules are applied by columns and not by rows*.

The keywords automatic/sequential order define a query plan. For sequential order you'll see SQL MODEL ORDERED in the plan, and in the case of automatic order it can be SQL MODEL CYCLIC/SQL MODEL ACYCLIC depending on whether cyclic dependencies exist or not.

In a simple case cyclic dependency may be in the scope of the same measure (when one cell references another in the first rule and the other way round in the second rule) or for different measures and the same cell. Frankly speaking, I did not come across useful examples of models with cyclic dependencies so I'd suggest that you always specify rules in correct order and use default value sequential order; and in addition to that, specify the order on the left-hand side of each rule that references multiple cells.

In case of ORDERED/ACYCLIC models you also may see FAST in the plan if all the rules use a single cell reference.

For example, for this rule

```
rules automatic order (x[1] = cv(id), x[-1] = cv(id))
```

there will be SQL MODEL ACYCLIC **FAST** in the plan while for this one

```
rules automatic order (x[for id in (1, -1)] = cv(id))
```

or this one

```
rules automatic order (x[id in (1, -1)] = cv(id))
```

it will be SQL MODEL ACYCLIC.

The logical difference between the second and third examples is that the second one uses positional reference while the third one uses symbolic reference, so if some cells are missing in the source recordset, then the result will differ.

If we specify automatic order for the query from Listing 7-4, then Oracle will throw an exception that the model does not converge.

Listing 7-6. Model with cyclic rule and automatic order

```
with t as
(select rownum id from dual connect by level <= 3)
select *
from t
model
dimension by (id)
measures (id result)
rules automatic order
(
  result[any] /*order by id*/ = sum(result)[any]
);
```

```
from t
    *
ERROR at line 4:
ORA-32634: automatic order MODEL evaluation does not converge
```

According to documentation, «*Convergence is defined as the state in which further executions of the model will not change values of any of the cell in the model*». Empirically we can figure out that, and at most three (four) steps are used to check convergence.

Listing 7-7. Checking convergence

```
select * from (select 1 x from dual)
model dimension by (x) measures (0 as result, 64 tmp)
rules automatic order
(result[1]=ceil(tmp[1]/4), tmp[1]=result[1]);
```

```
         X      RESULT        TMP
---------- ---------- ----------
         1          1          1
```

```
select * from (select 1 x from dual)
model dimension by (x) measures (0 as result, 65 tmp)
rules automatic order
(result[1]=ceil(tmp[1]/4), tmp[1]=result[1]);
select * from (select 1 x from dual)
                           *
ERROR at line 1:
ORA-32634: automatic order MODEL evaluation does not converge
```

In the first case values for (result, tmp) were 16, 4, 1, and 1 again – model converged; in the second case values on the third and fourth steps did not match, which led to an exception.

automatic order may change the plan operation from MODEL ORDERED to MODEL ACYCLIC when there are no cyclic dependencies (refer, for example, to Listing 7-5 to check that), but the desired result can be achieved by just specifying rules in a proper order.

In all the examples so far (strictly speaking excluding acyclic model example), model rules have been evaluated only once; however it's possible to evaluate rules iteratively until the termination condition is satisfied. To demonstrate iterative computations let's implement a bisection method using the same interval and function as in Listing 6-5.

Listing 7-8. Implementation of bisection method using iterative model

```
with t as (select 0 id from dual)
select *
from t
model
dimension by (id)
measures ((1+2)/2 x, 1 x0, 2 x1)
rules iterate (1e2) until abs(x[0]-previous(x[0])) < 1e-2
 (
   x[iteration_number+1] = x[0],
   x0[iteration_number+1] = case when sign(y(x[0])) =
                                      sign(y(x0[iteration_number]))
                                 then x[0]
                                 else x0[iteration_number]
                            end,
   x1[iteration_number+1] = case when sign(y(x[0])) =
                                      sign(y(x1[iteration_number]))
                                 then x[0]
                                 else x1[iteration_number]
                            end,
   x[0] = (x0[iteration_number+1] + x1[iteration_number+1])/2
 )
```

order by id;

ID	X	X0	X1
0	1.4140625	1	2
1	1.5	1	1.5
2	1.25	1.25	1.5
3	1.375	1.375	1.5
4	1.4375	1.375	1.4375
5	1.40625	1.40625	1.4375
6	1.421875	1.40625	1.421875

7 rows selected.

Iteration_number is a function that returns an integer representing the completed iteration through the model rules starting with 0. The maximum possible iteration number in the above example is limited with 100 (this can be specified only using a constant, not an expression); however, there is termination condition abs(x[0]-previous(x[0])) < 1e-2 that means the absolute difference between root on current iteration and on the previous iteration should be less than 0.01. So computation stopped on the 6th step and the result is the same as the one calculated using the subquery factoring clause - 1.4140625. The previous function is used to refer the value on the previous iteration.

There is no way to figure out whether a model is iterative or not based on a query plan. Query plan operations are the same as for non-iterative models. Moreover, a stats column in the plan does not reflect the number of iterations with enabled runtime execution statistics. A query plan for Listing 7-8 will be the following.

```
select * from dbms_xplan.display_cursor(format => 'IOSTATS LAST');
```

```
-------------------------------------------------------------------
| Id | Operation               | Name | Starts | E-Rows | A-Rows |   A-Time    |
-------------------------------------------------------------------
|  0 | SELECT STATEMENT        |      |      1 |        |      7 | 00:00:00.01 |
|  1 |  SORT ORDER BY          |      |      1 |      1 |      7 | 00:00:00.01 |
|  2 |   SQL MODEL ORDERED FAST |      |      1 |      1 |      7 | 00:00:00.01 |
|  3 |    FAST DUAL            |      |      1 |      1 |      1 | 00:00:00.01 |
-------------------------------------------------------------------
```

In the model clause we can define reference model(s) that can be used as "lookup arrays."

Listing 7-9. Using reference models

```
with sales(year, currency, value) as
(select '2015', 'GBP', 100 from dual
union all select '2015', 'USD', 200 from dual
union all select '2015', 'EUR', 300 from dual
union all select '2016', 'GBP', 400 from dual
union all select '2016', 'EUR', 500 from dual)
, usd_rates(currency, rate) as
(select 'GBP', 1.45 from dual
union all select 'USD', 1 from dual
union all select 'EUR', 1.12 from dual)
select *
from sales
model
  reference usd_rates_model on (select * from usd_rates)
  dimension by (currency)
  measures (rate)
```

```
main sales_model
dimension by (year, currency)
measures (value, 0 usd_value)
(
  usd_value[any, any] order by year, currency =
    value[cv(year), cv(currency)] * usd_rates_model.
    rate[cv(currency)]
)
order by 1, 2;

YEAR CUR     VALUE  USD_VALUE
---- ---  ---------- ----------
2015 EUR        300        336
2015 GBP        100        145
2015 USD        200        200
2016 EUR        500        560
2016 GBP        400        580
```

As was stated at the beginning of this chapter, a combination of all the dimensions uniquely identifies the cell in the cube, but this rule can be relaxed if you specify unique single reference keyword. Query from Listing 7-10 would throw an exception ORA-32638: Non unique addressing in MODEL dimensions with the default value for addressing which is unique dimension.

Listing 7-10. Model with unique single reference

```
with t(id, value) as
(select trunc(rownum/2), rownum from dual connect by level <= 3)
select *
from t
model
unique single reference
```

```
dimension by (id)
measures (value, 0 result)
(result[0] = 111)
order by id;
```

ID	VALUE	RESULT
0	1	111
1	2	0
1	3	0

The last thing to mention regarding basic functionality is the treatment of null values. There are two special functions for model clause presentv/presentnnv that work similarly to nvl2. Presentv checks if the value existed in the recordset prior to execution of the model clause while presentnnv in addition to that also checks if the value was not null. Listing 7-11 shows differences between presentv, presentnnv, and nvl2.

Listing 7-11. Comparing results for presentv, presentnnv, and nvl2

```
with t(id) as
(select cast('base' as varchar2(10)) from dual)
select *
from t
model
ignore nav
dimension by (id)
measures (cast(null as varchar2(10)) msr_base,
          cast(null as varchar2(10)) msr_calc,
          to_number(null) num)
(
  msr_base['calc'] = '1',
  msr_base['presentv'] = presentv(msr_base['base'], '+', '-'),
  msr_base['presentnnv'] = presentnnv(msr_base['base'], '+', '-'),
```

```
  msr_base['nvl2'] = nvl2(msr_base['base'], '+', '-'),
  msr_calc['presentv'] = presentv(msr_base['calc'], '+', '-'),
  msr_calc['presentnnv'] = presentnnv(msr_base['calc'], '+', '-'),
  msr_calc['nvl2'] = nvl2(msr_base['calc'], '+', '-'),
  num[any] = num[-1]
)
order by id;
```

ID	MSR_BASE	MSR_CALC	NUM
base			0
calc	1		0
nvl2	-	+	0
presentnnv	-	-	0
presentv	+	-	0

Missing numeric measures are treated as zeros instead of nulls when you specify ignore nav. All values for the num column would be nulls with the default behavior - keep nav.

Analytic functions can be used in a model clause to implement advanced logic. Listing 7-12 demonstrates a usage example.

Listing 7-12. Analytic functions in model clause

```
with t(value) as
(select column_value from table(sys.odcivarchar2list('A','B',
'C','D','E')))
select *
from t
model
ignore nav
dimension by (row_number() over (order by value) id)
measures (value, cast(null as varchar2(4000)) result, count(*)
over () num)
```

```
(
  result[mod(id, 2) = 1] = listagg(value, ', ') within group
(order by id) over (),
  num[mod(id, 2) = 1] = count(*) over (order by id desc)
)
order by id;
```

	ID VALUE	RESULT	NUM
1	A	A, C, E	3
2	B		5
3	C	A, C, E	2
4	D		5
5	E	A, C, E	1

The same logic can be implemented using aggregate functions in the following way:

```
result[mod(id, 2) = 1] = listagg(value, ', ') within group
(order by null)[mod(id, 2) = 1],
num[mod(id, 2) = 1] = count(*)[mod(id, 2) = 1 and id >= cv(id)]
```

The crucial difference between aggregate functions in a model clause and an regular aggregate functions is that aggregate functions in model clauses do not require grouping. Instead you need to specify the range of cells for the aggregate function.

Aggregate functions allow flexible addressing of cells' ranges unlike analytic functions. But analytic functions accept both measures and dimensions as arguments while an aggregate function can be applied only to measures. Also it's not possible to specify ordering on the left side of the rule when an analytic function is used. Rule 1 and rule 3 from Listing 7-13 demonstrate limitations of analytic and aggregate functions correspondingly.

Listing 7-13. Limitation of analytic and aggregate functions in model clause

```
select *
from (select rownum id from dual connect by rownum <= 3) t
model
dimension by (id)
measures (id value, 0 r1, 0 r2)
(
  -- 1)
  -- ORA-30483: window  functions are not allowed here
  -- r1[any] order by id = sum(id) over (order by id desc)
  -- 2)
  r1[any] /*order by id*/ = sum(id) over (order by id desc),
  -- 3) ORA-00904: : invalid identifier
  -- r2[any] order by id desc = sum(id)[id >= cv(id)]
  -- 4)
  r2[any] = sum(value)[id >= cv(id)]
)
```

To explore flexibility of addressing for aggregate functions, let's get back to the example regarding limitations of analytic functions shown in Listing 3-6. The first limitation is not an issue at all. Listing 7-14 shows how to calculate the number of points within the distance of 5 by two coordinates.

Listing 7-14. Aggregate functions in model clause with conditional addressing by multiple dimensions

```
with points as
 (select rownum id, rownum * rownum x, mod(rownum, 3) y
    from dual
  connect by rownum <= 6)
, t as
```

```
(select p.*,
        -- the number of points within the distance of 5 by x
           coordinate
        -- cannot be solved with analytic functions for more
           than one coordinate
        count(*) over(order by x range between 5 preceding and 5
        following) cnt,
        -- sum of the distances to the point (3, 3) for all rows
        -- between unbounded preceding and current row ordered
           by id
        -- cannot be solved using analytic function if required
           to calculate
        -- distance between other rows and current row rather
           than a constant point
        round(sum(sqrt((x - 3) * (x - 3) + (y - 3) * (y - 3)))
              over(order by id),
              2) dist
   from points p)
select *
from t
model
dimension by (x, y)
measures (id, cnt, dist, 0 cnt2)
rules
(
   cnt2[any, any] = count(*)[x between cv(x) - 5 and cv(x) + 5,
                             y between cv(y) - 1 and cv(y) + 1]
)
order by id;
```

However, there is no straightforward solution for the second limitation because it's not possible to refer a measure for the current row in the expression for an aggregate function. As a workaround we can use an iterative model and do as many iterations as the number of rows to maintain two auxiliary measures with coordinates for the current row. The idea is shown in Listing 7-15, but this approach looks a bit awkward and performance is inefficient.

Listing 7-15. Using iterative model as a workaround for limitation of aggregate functions

```
with points as
  (select rownum id, rownum * rownum x, mod(rownum, 3) y
     from dual
   connect by rownum <= 6)
select *
from points
model
dimension by (id)
measures (id i, x, y, 0 x_cur, 0 y_cur, 0 dist2)
rules iterate (1e6) until i[iteration_number+2] is null
(
  x_cur[any] = x[iteration_number + 1],
  y_cur[any] = y[iteration_number + 1],
  dist2[iteration_number + 1] =
  round(sum(sqrt((x - x_cur) * (x - x_cur) +
                (y - y_cur) * (y - y_cur)))[id <= cv(id)], 2)
)
order by id;
```

As you see, auxiliary measures x_cur and y_cur have to be initialized for all the rows on all the iterations. To populate (x_cur, y_cur) with values (x, y) for the current row, we use [iteration_number + 1] because row numbering starts with 1 while interation_number starts with 0. Measure dist2 is calculated only for a single row on each iteration.

Given that sometimes aggregate and analytic functions are
interchangeable in a model clause, we will discuss this question a bit
further during performance analysis.

Let's proceed to specific tasks. Listing 7-16 shows how to use the model
to generate recursive sequences discussed in previous chapters.

Listing 7-16. Generation of recursive sequences using model clause

```
select *
from dual
model
dimension by (0 id)
measures (1 result)
rules
(
  result[for id from 1 to 20 increment 1] =
  round(100 * sin(result[cv(id)-1] + cv(id) - 1))
);

select *
  from (select rownum lvl, rownum - 1 result
          from dual connect by level <= 2)
model
ignore nav
dimension by (lvl)
measures (result)
rules
(
  result[for lvl from 3 to 15 increment 1] =
  result[cv(lvl)-1] + result[cv(lvl)-2]
);
```

The model allows us to use values calculated on previous stages likewise recursive subquery factoring. The crucial difference from a logical perspective between the two is that a model applies rules and calculates values (measures) by columns and not by rows, while recursive subquery factoring evaluates all the expressions for a current row before processing the next row. You can find additional details in the quiz "Baskets" in Chapter 12.

Also, unlike recursive subquery factoring, a model provides an easy way to reference measures from any other row; thus there is no need to use an auxiliary column to generate Fibonacci, for example. Visibility for recursive subquery factoring is limited to the recordset on the previous iteration.

Even though recursive subquery factoring and a model can be used to solve the same tasks, these capabilities are completely different and designed for different purposes so using the same terminology is not quite appropriate. Speaking about recursive subquery factoring, we can say "referring value calculated on a previous level" or "referring calculated value for parent record" while for the model clause, a more correct statement would be "referring measure value for a previous dimension member."

Recursive subquery factoring was designed to be able to apply the same logic multiple times and to work with hierarchical data in particular, while the model clause was designed for spreadsheet-like computations and to work with multidimensional data.

Summarizing use cases, it makes sense to use the model in the following situations:

1.   Spreadsheet-like calculations.

Simply speaking, this means calculating cells based on values for other cells or their ranges.

Trivial expressions can often be rewritten to use other SQL capabilities: analytic functions and/or additional joins.

For example, if we have information about monthly sales and want to calculate a ratio to the first month, we can use the model

```
with t as
(select rownum id, 100 + rownum - 1 value from dual connect by
level <= 12)
select *
from t
model
dimension by (id)
measures (value, 0 ratio)
rules
(ratio[any] order by id = value[cv(id)]/value[1])
```

At the same time, it can be easily calculated using analytic functions

```
select id, value, value / first_value(value) over(order by id)
ratio from t
```

Here is a more synthetic example: calculate the ratio between the current row value and the value from the row referenced by ref_id.

```
exec dbms_random.seed(100);
create table t as
select rownum id,
       100 + rownum - 1 value,
       trunc(dbms_random.value(1, 10 + 1)) ref_id
  from dual
connect by level <= 10;
```

Model solution is below:

```
select *
from t
model
```

```
dimension by (id)
measures (value, ref_id, 0 ratio)
rules
(
 ratio[any] order by id =
 round(value[cv(id)] / value[ref_id[cv(id)]], 3)
);
```

```
        ID       VALUE      REF_ID        RATIO
---------- ---------- ---------- ----------
         1       100          6         .952
         2       101          7         .953
         3       102          7         .962
         4       103          8         .963
         5       104          3        1.02
         6       105          5        1.01
         7       106         10         .972
         8       107          4        1.039
         9       108          2        1.069
        10       109          7        1.028
```

The same can be achieved with self join (or analytic function using approach from Listing 3-3):

```
select t1.*, round(t1.value / t2.value, 3) ratio
  from t t1
  join t t2
    on t1.ref_id = t2.id
order by t1.id
```

However, sometimes more complex expressions might require multiple joins and extensive usage of analytic and aggregate functions as well as other SQL capabilities, while the same can be done using a model clause and compact rules.

It's worth mentioning that the model has some scalability issues so, even if the solution is concise and simple, it always makes sense to test it on real-data volumes and switch to alternative approaches including PL/SQL if the model does not scale enough.

On the other hand, client applications for spreadsheet-like calculations, like Excel, are not designed to work with large data volumes. For example, the max number of rows for Excel 2016 is 1 million, which a model can easily handle without notable performance degradation, not to mention that the result can be calculated on the server side without fetching data to the client.

2. Calculating a complicated result that otherwise cannot be achieved using pure SQL.

Sometimes Oracle accounts for reporting systems have only select privileges so that you cannot create a table function and type for its result. Of course, that can be created in another schema and granted to a reporting system user, but the model reduces the number of cases when it's really necessary. Also the model may be a good solution to implement complex logic for materialized views – even though model calculations can be expensive this may be unnoticeable for end users.

Quite often people use a model clause when it's not the best option:

- Generation of sequences where the current value may be derived based on an initial value – for example, date ranges. In this case generation would be faster with `connect by`.

- Various char data treatment from splitting string into tokens to calculating expression in a string. To split strings you can use `connect by`; for more complex manipulations it's better to encapsulate logic in PL/SQL or even C function.

- Finding specific sequences in a data – for example, subsequences of integers without gaps. The better instrument for this is pattern matching or analytic functions.

- Calculation of totals and subtotals. Group by rollup/ grouping sets/cube designed for this purpose.

- Transposing. This is the job for pivot/unpivot operators.

- All other cases when you can avoid using it. ☺

Brief Analysis of the Performance

The specific of the model clause is that a full recordset used for modeling is getting loaded into memory. The number of result columns is fixed and predefined (equals to partitions + dimensions + measures), but he number of rows varies and may be more than or less than the number of rows in the initial recordset as well as equal to it.

To analyze scalability, let's measure performance of the different approaches to generate a recursive sequence with `sin` function initially introduced in the chapter about `connect by` (Chapter 5). The approaches are PL/SQL function, recursive subquery factoring, and model. You can find all the code in the corresponding chapters.

For a PL/SQL function, we will calculate the sum of all elements for an increasing number of rows: 1e5, 2e5, 3e5, 4e5, 5e5, 1e6. The performance of recursive and non-recursive implementation of function `f` is approximately the same so you can use any of them for reproducing.

```
select sum(value(t)) result from table(f(1e5)) t;
```

Similarly, we will measure timings for recursive subquery factoring and model approaches instead of the PL/SQL function.

Aggregate function was used to get a single row result and avoid fetching; our primary goal is to generate a sequence though. To complete the picture, let's also consider an iterative model that does not generate a sequence but calculates the sum of the elements.

```
select cumul
from dual
model
dimension by (0 id)
measures (1 result, 1 cumul)
rules iterate (1e5)
(
  result[0] = round(100 * sin(result[0] + iteration_number)),
  cumul[0] = cumul[0] + result[0]
);
```

For all the approaches, most of the time is spent on CPU and execution statistics are shown in Table 7-1.

Table 7-1. *Execution statistics for sequence generation*

Number of rows	PL/SQL	Recursive with	Model	Iterative model
1e5	01.18	02.29	03.22	01.86
2e5	02.43	04.52	12.68	03.35
3e5	03.47	07.58	27.93	05.00
4e5	04.70	10.31	53.45	06.90
5e5	05.82	12.85	01:18.57	08.58
1e6	11.80	27.32	05:01.87	17.00

Also a lot of PGA memory is consumed during generation; on the other hand, temporary tablespace was involved only for recursive with (this can be avoided using manual memory management as will be shown later in this section – so performance from recursive with may be a bit better).

Memory category (v$process_memory.category) for the model and recursive subquery factoring is SQL and for PL/SQL function it's PL/SQL, which is quite expected. You can drill down and check v$sql_workarea. operation_type, it will be SPREADSHEET for model clause and CONNECT-BY (SORT) for recursive with.

v$active_session_history.pga_allocated and v$active_session_history. temp_space_allocated are good sources to track memory usage growth in dynamics. If more detailed analysis is required, then you may want to use v$process_memory_detail performance view.

So as you see, the model demonstrated worse performance and moreover nonlinear growth of elapsed time depending on the number of rows. The iterative model looks much better, but strictly speaking it does not solve the original task – to generate the sequence; it only calculates the sum of elements. On the other hand, as a rule, the model is used on top of existing data instead of generating new data, but anyway large data volumes remain an issue.

Performance and scalability of recursive with for this task was much better than for the model clause, but the model may be a better approach for many other tasks. As it was mentioned earlier, recursive with adds a new recordset on each iteration, but this is not necessary for a model so if you need to iteratively apply a set of transformations to some recordset then model may be a much better approach.

Query plans for a model clause to generate a recursive sequence were trivial - SQL MODEL ORDERED FAST and SQL MODEL ORDERED for iterative and non-iterative model respectively.

Listing 7-17 shows a query with a model clause that requires some additional operations because of the analytic/aggregate function in it. Let's execute the query with an analytic function for 1e6 and 1.2e6 (20% more) number of rows and do the same for the aggregate function. There is no need for the model in this query at all, and it's used purely for performance analysis.

Listing 7-17. Analytic/aggregate functions in model clause

```
select *
from
(select *
from (select rownum id from dual connect by rownum <= 1e6) t
model
dimension by (id)
measures (id value, 0 result)
(
  -- analytic version
  result[any] = sum(value) over (order by id desc)
  -- aggregate version
  -- result[any] = sum(value)[id >= cv(id)]
)
order by id
)
where rownum <= 3;
```

ID	VALUE	RESULT
1	1	500000500000
2	2	500000499999
3	3	500000499997

Execution time for 1e6 rows was 4 seconds in both cases – this is not surprising because plans for aggregate and analytic functions are the same. But elapsed time jumped to 8 seconds when we increased the number of rows by 20%.

Listing 7-18. Execution time for model with analytic/aggregate function

```
---------------------------------------------------------
| Id  | Operation                            | Name |
---------------------------------------------------------
|   0 | SELECT STATEMENT                     |      |
|   1 |  COUNT STOPKEY                       |      |
|   2 |   VIEW                               |      |
|   3 |    SORT ORDER BY STOPKEY             |      |
|   4 |     SQL MODEL ORDERED                |      |
|   5 |      VIEW                            |      |
|   6 |       COUNT                          |      |
|   7 |        CONNECT BY WITHOUT FILTERING| |
|   8 |         FAST DUAL                    |      |
|   9 |      WINDOW (IN SQL MODEL) SORT      |      |
---------------------------------------------------------
```

There was not enough memory for the query execution when we increased the number of rows so Oracle started using temporary tablespace – this is the reason for nonlinear elapsed time growth. You can check that by running the query below for the corresponding SQL_ID.

```
select pga_allocated / (1024 * 1024) pga_mb,
       temp_space_allocated / (1024 * 1024) temp_mb,
       ash.*
  from v$active_session_history ash
 where sql_id = '<sql_id>'
 order by sample_time desc
```

Let's switch to manual memory management and increase memory for sorting to the max possible value – 2GB.

```
alter session set workarea_size_policy = manual;
alter session set sort_area_size = 2147483647;
```

Elapsed time after this change is 5 second, which means linear dependency on the record count. It's better to let Oracle manage memory though and use manual memory management only for specific queries and when there is a strong reason for it.

The last thing to mention is that execution time for 1.2e6 rows without a model and with default memory settings is just 2 seconds. Let me reiterate that you should avoid using a model clause when the required result can be achieved without it.

```
select *
  from (select t.*, sum(id) over(order by id desc) result
          from (select rownum id from dual
                  connect by rownum <= 1.2e6) t
         order by id)
 where rownum <= 3;
```

Summarizing observations regarding performance:

- Model clause causes intensive memory usage. There is always "SPREADSHEET" work area operation, but for core complex logic there may be "WINDOW (SORT)" and others.

- Rule evaluation and operating on huge work areas may require a lot of CPU resources.

- Of course, a query plan with runtime execution statistics is an invaluable source of information – it shows which operation was the most resource consumptive as well as memory usage per operation.

- In some cases, the partitioned model and parallel execution may dramatically improve the performance – this will be investigated further in the next section.

Model Parallel Execution

To analyze model parallel execution, let's consider the following task: for each partition we need to calculate a running sum that drops to zero when reaches some predefined limit.

Listing 7-19 shows the model query to calculate running for limit 3e3 (3000).

Listing 7-19. Model clause for conditional running sum calculation

```
create table t (part int, id int, value int);
begin
  for i in 1 .. 80 loop
    dbms_random.seed(i);
    insert into t
      select i, rownum id, trunc(dbms_random.value(1, 1000 + 1))
      value
        from dual
      connect by rownum <= 1e5;
  end loop;
  commit;
end;
/

select --+ parallel(2)
*
from t
model
partition by (part)
```

```
dimension by (id)
measures (value, 0 x, 0 sid)
rules
(
  x[any] order by id = case when cv(id)=1 then value[cv(id)]
                            when x[cv(id)-1] > 3e3 then
                            value[cv(id)]
                            else x[cv(id)-1] + value[cv(id)]
                       end,
  sid[any] order by id = userenv('sid')
)
```

The same logic can be implemented using a parallel pipelined function. A weak REF CURSOR parameter allows only partitioning by ANY so we created a strong REF CURSOR to partition by the hash(part). The column part also specified in order by clause because there is no guarantee that there will be one partition per slave. Also the table function requires an SQL collection type for result.

Listing 7-20. Pipelined function for parallel processing

```
create or replace type to_3int as object (part int, x int, sid int)
/
create or replace type tt_3int as table of to_3int
/
create or replace package pkg as
type refcur_t is ref cursor return t%rowtype;
end;
/
create or replace function f_running(p in pkg.refcur_t) return
tt_3int
  pipelined
  parallel_enable(partition p by hash(part)) order p by(part, id) is
```

```
rec  p%rowtype;
prev p%rowtype;
x    int := 0;
begin
  loop
    fetch p
      into rec;
    exit when p%notfound;
    if rec.id = 1 then
      x := rec.value;
    elsif x > 3e3 then
      x := rec.value;
    else
      x := x + rec.value;
    end if;
    pipe row(to_3int(rec.part, x, userenv('sid')));
    prev := rec;
  end loop;
  return;
end;
/
```

Performance testing was done on a server with **80 CPU cores** for granular analysis of parallel execution impact on the performance. The following query was executed with a different DOP (degree of parallelism) to measure elapsed time for a PL/SQL approach.

```
select count(distinct sid) c, sum(x*part) s
  from table(f_running(cursor(select /*+ parallel(2) */ * from t)));
```

Similarly, an inline view with a model clause was used instead of a table operator to test the model approach.

Table 7-2 represents execution statics for two approaches and a ratio between elapsed times. As you see, the model clause is faster than a PL/SQL approach even for serial execution; moreover it leverages parallel execution more efficiently. For a DOP 20 model runs more than 3 times faster than a PL/SQL function. Increasing DOP to 40 negatively impacts performance of a PL/SQL because overhead costs to manage parallel execution stifle the benefit.

Table 7-2. *Parallel execution statistics*

DOP	Actual DOP	PL/SQL	Model	Ratio
Serial	1	01:47.37	53.34	2.01
4	4	36.59	15.83	2.31
10	10	19.78	08.72	2.27
20	19	16.22	05.24	3.1
40	34	18.72	04.35	4.3

It's important to note that a PL/SQL approach for sequence generation was better, while for this task the model is faster. This is because we used a collection of numbers in the first case but a collection of objects in the second case. Oracle requires additional CPU resources to construct the object for every single row. Also sequence generation required sin and round functions, while only primitive operations were used in the logic for the conditional running sum. The more complex the logic is, the less the impact of constructing an object for each row.

Another key detail for parallel processing is partitioning. When we specify partitioning for a model clause, then data for them becomes completely isolated and rules are evaluated independently for each partition; but in case of a pipelined function there is no guarantee that there will be a single partition per slave so we need to keep that in mind when implementing the logic.

The is one last detail to mention – actual DOP was the same for both approaches, which is not surprising because DOP was specified in SQL queries and eventually the SQL engine is responsible for splitting data across slave sessions.

Summary

Model clause is the most powerful Oracle SQL feature. Theoretically iterative models allow us to implement an algorithm of any complexity (see Chapter 10, "Turing Completeness"). On the other hand, the model clause may cause excessive CPU and memory consumption, and it it's not linearly scalable for tasks where some other approaches, including PL/SQL, demonstrate linear scalability depending on data volumes. However, it's possible to leverage parallel execution for partitioned models, which makes SQL modeling a perfect instrument for some tasks.

It makes sense to use a model for spreadsheet-like computations, allowing implementation of complicated rules while avoiding multiple joins. Also a model may be the right tool for implementing complex logic when it's preferable to avoid using a procedural approach, especially if a model is used in materialized views so the response time is not critical.

CHAPTER 8

Row Pattern Matching: match_recognize

The ability to find and analyze the patterns in the data was widely desired but not possible with SQL until Oracle 12c.

This is required in many business areas, for example, security applications and fraud detection or financial applications and pricing analysis. Native pattern-matching capabilities in SQL help to avoid complex bespoke solutions on the client side or within the middle-tier application server and use easy-to-share SQL queries instead.

This is the last one of Oracle's specific SQL features, but before diving into it, let's briefly recall the evolution of SQL.

Basic SQL – the one that implements five main operations of relational algebra – allows only row-level visibility.

Aggregate functions introduce group-level visibility, but a group is defined by a specific expression that must be the same for all rows in the group and each row belongs to exactly one group.

Analytic functions allow window-level visibility. The window definition is the same for all rows; however the windowing_clause adds some flexibility so that attributes of the current row may be specified as shift values by range/rows.

© Alex Reprintsev 2018
A. Reprintsev, *Oracle SQL Revealed*, https://doi.org/10.1007/978-1-4842-3372-6_8

Pattern matching is the next level of flexibility; to match a pattern across a recordset it's treated as a sequence of rows – the idea is similar to regular expressions when an input string is considered as a sequence of chars. Each row may belong to zero, one, or more matches.

Let's reuse the table atm from Listing 3-4. We can get all the rows where the amount equals to 5 using the query below.

```
select * from atm where amount = 5
```

The same can be achieved using match_recognize.

```
select *
from atm
match_recognize
( all rows per match
  pattern (five)
  define
    five as five.amount = 5
) mr
order by ts;

TS              AMOUNT
--------- ----------
03-JUL-16            5
03-JUL-16            5
```

Obviously, pattern matching was not designed not for such kind of tasks and, for example, if there was an index for the amount column, Oracle would not use it (although the index can be used if you specify the pattern matching and where clauses together). The query plan looks as follows (FINITE AUTOMATON was trimmed in the output of dbms_xplan).

```
-------------------------------------------------------------------
| Id  | Operation                                          | Name |
-------------------------------------------------------------------
|   0 | SELECT STATEMENT                                   |      |
|   1 |   SORT ORDER BY                                    |      |
|   2 |    VIEW                                            |      |
|   3 |     MATCH RECOGNIZE BUFFER DETERMINISTIC FINITE AU|      |
|   4 |      TABLE ACCESS FULL                             | ATM  |
-------------------------------------------------------------------
```

Let's proceed to an example that is a bit more complex.

```
alter session set NLS_DATE_FORMAT = 'mi';

Session altered.

select *
from atm
match_recognize
( order by ts
  measures
    strt.amount start_amount,
    final last(up.amount) end_amount,
    running count(*) as cnt,
    match_number() as match,
    classifier() as cls
  all rows per match
  after match skip past last row
  pattern (strt down* up*)
  define
    down as down.amount < prev(down.amount),
    up as up.amount > prev(up.amount)
) mr
order by ts;
```

TS	START_AMOUNT	END_AMOUNT	CNT	MATCH	CLS	AMOUNT
01	85	100	1	1	STRT	85
03	85	100	2	1	DOWN	15
05	85	100	3	1	UP	100
07	40	85	1	2	STRT	40
09	40	85	2	2	DOWN	30
11	40	85	3	2	UP	50
13	40	85	4	2	UP	85
15	60	100	1	3	STRT	60
17	60	100	2	3	DOWN	5
19	60	100	3	3	UP	100
21	25	80	1	4	STRT	25
23	25	80	2	4	UP	30
25	25	80	3	4	UP	80
27	5	35	1	5	STRT	5
29	5	35	2	5	UP	35

Here a pattern is defined as one row with label strt, zero, or more rows with label down and zero or more rows with label up. Actually strt, down, and up are called pattern variables. A row is marked as down when an amount is less than in the previous row and correspondingly marked as up when an amount is greater than in the previous row. If we visualize the relation between an amount and ts, then each match will be V-shape or just an ascending or descending part of it if the other one is missing.

all rows per match means every row that is matched is included in the pattern-match output. If you specify one row per match instead, then for every pattern match found, there will be one row in the resultset. In the first case, the way output is generated is similar to analytic functions while in the second case – it's similar to the aggregate ones.

There are two specific built-in measures for pattern matching. match_number numbers matches starting with one and assigns the same number for all rows in a specific match. classifier shows which row mapped to which pattern variable. All the measures except match_number function are evaluated within the scope of a given match.

Note   You can define a union of pattern variables using the subset keyword to reference them in measures together. For example, SUBSET STDN = (STRT, DOWN). These groupings also can be referenced in the define clause to specify definitions of other pattern variables. See Listing 8-3 for usage example.

Expression running count(*) was used for row numbering within the matches. final count(*) can be used to show the total row count in the match. Similarly, the expression final last(up.amount) means that for all rows in the match we display the last (maximal) value mapped to the up pattern variable.

after match skip past last row means that whenever a match is completed, a new search is restarted from the row right after the last row in the match. This behavior may be changed so that a new search starts from some row at a completed match; thus rows may belong to more than one match. New search cannot start from the same row as the previous one; otherwise Oracle would throw an exception ORA-62517: Next match starts at the same point the last match started. In the edge case, a new search can start from the second row of the current match.

The same matched groups and classifiers can be easily calculated using analytic functions as shown in Listing 8-1.

Listing 8-1. Implementing pattern matching logic using analytic functions

```
select ts,
       amount,
       count(decode(cls, 'STRT', 1)) over(order by ts) match,
       cls
  from (select ts,
               amount,
               case
                 when lag(cls) over(order by ts) = 'UP' and cls
                 <> 'UP' then
                  'STRT'
                 else
                  cls
               end cls
          from (select atm.*,
                       nvl(case
                             when amount < lag(amount)
                             over(order by ts) then
                              'DOWN'
                             when amount > lag(amount)
                             over(order by ts) then
                              'UP'
                           end,
                           'STRT') cls
                  from atm))
 order by ts;
```

If we change a pattern so only complete V-shapes (with ascending and descending branches) are matched - strt down+ up+, then some rows will not be part of any matched pattern. If want to see them as part of the

result, then we can specify either alternative in the pattern: strt down+
up+|dummy+? or use an option with unmatched rows, that is, all rows
per match with unmatched rows.

```
select *
from atm
match_recognize
( order by ts
  measures
    strt.amount start_amount,
    final last(up.amount) end_amount,
    running count(*) as cnt,
    match_number() as match,
    classifier() as cls
  all rows per match
  after match skip past last row
  pattern (strt down+ up+|dummy+?)
  define
    down as down.amount < prev(down.amount),
    up as up.amount > prev(up.amount)
) mr
order by ts;
```

TS	START_AMOUNT	END_AMOUNT	CNT	MATCH	CLS	AMOUNT
01	85	100	1	1	STRT	85
03	85	100	2	1	DOWN	15
05	85	100	3	1	UP	100
07	40	85	1	2	STRT	40
09	40	85	2	2	DOWN	30
11	40	85	3	2	UP	50
13	40	85	4	2	UP	85
15	60	100	1	3	STRT	60

17	60	100	2	3 DOWN	5
19	60	100	3	3 UP	100
21			1	4 DUMMY	25
23			1	5 DUMMY	30
25	80	35	1	6 STRT	80
27	80	35	2	6 DOWN	5
29	80	35	3	6 UP	35

I believe there is no need to say that this query can also be rewritten to use analytic functions instead.

Listing 8-2 shows the query that marks Fibonacci numbers in a sequence.

Listing 8-2. Marking Fibonacci numbers using pattern matching

```
with t as (select rownum id from dual connect by rownum <= 55)
select * from t
match_recognize
( order by id
  all rows per match
  pattern ((fib|{-dummy-})+)
  define fib as (id = 1 or id = 2 or id = last(fib.id, 1) +
  last(fib.id, 2)));
```

```
        ID
----------
         1
         2
         3
         5
         8
        13
        21
        34
```

This query cannot be rewritten with an analytic function because when we mark a row, we need to consider rows marked so far.

There are a few more interesting details to mention here. Functions like last in the define clause work in the scope of a matched group. This means that if we want to access two previous values for a matched variable, then the whole sequence must be one match. To avoid interrupting the match, we used an alternative in the pattern. Syntax {--} means that rows marked with this label will not be part of the result even though they are part of the match. Finally, a crucial point is that rows were pre-generated and pattern matching just helped to mark the required rows. So pattern matching cannot be used to generate data based on some rules unlike model or recursive subquery factoring; however it can be used to fill data gaps, for example.

Let's say we have a table with intervals and the goal is to add missing ones. For the data below, the missing intervals are (5, 6), (15, 19), and (26, 29).

```
with t(s, e) as (
select 1, 4 from dual
union all select 7, 8 from dual
union all select 9, 10 from dual
union all select 11, 14 from dual
union all select 20, 25 from dual
union all select 30, 40 from dual)
```

Listing 8-3 shows how missing intervals can be added using pattern matching. The X pattern variable is used to mark consecutive intervals in the match and Y marks the interval if there is a gap between it and the previous one. We start searching for the next match from Y so intervals with the preceding gaps appear in the result twice – marked as Y and as STRT. For those marked as Y, we use them to calculate the start and end for missing intervals, and the number of rows marked as Y equals to the number of missing intervals. To correctly handle the last row we added a fake interval (1e10, 1e10).

Listing 8-3. Filling data gaps using pattern matching

```
select mr.*
from (select * from t union all
      select 1e10, 1e10 from dual)
match_recognize
( order by s
  measures
    classifier() cls,
    decode(classifier(), 'Y', last(cont.e) + 1, s) strt,
    decode(classifier(), 'Y', s - 1, e) end
  all rows per match with unmatched rows
  after match skip to last y
  pattern (strt x* y)
  subset cont = (strt, x)
  define x as x.s = prev(x.e) + 1
) mr
where s <> 1e10
order by strt, end;

        S CLS          STRT        END           E
---------- ----- ---------- ---------- ----------
         1 STRT           1          4          4
         7 Y              5          6          8
         7 STRT           7          8          8
         9 X              9         10         10
        11 X             11         14         14
        20 Y             15         19         25
        20 STRT          20         25         25
        30 Y             26         29         40
        30 STRT          30         40         40

9 rows selected.
```

It was already mentioned that in some cases the logic for pattern matching can be re-implemented using analytic functions. Let's now compare the performance between two approaches based on a specific task: find all consecutive combinations of 1, 2, and 3 for table that contains digits from 0 to 9.

```
exec dbms_random.seed(1);
create table digit as
select rownum id, trunc(dbms_random.value(0, 9 + 1)) value
  from dual
connect by rownum <= 2e6;
```

Listing 8-4 shows a solution using pattern matching. Unlike all previous examples, we specified one row per match to group three matched rows for each match into one.

Listing 8-4. Finding combinations of elements (1, 2, 3) using pattern matching

```
select decode(v_id, v1_id, 1, v2_id, 2, v3_id, 3) v1,
       decode(v_id + 1, v1_id, 1, v2_id, 2, v3_id, 3) v2,
       decode(v_id + 2, v1_id, 1, v2_id, 2, v3_id, 3) v3,
       count(*) cnt
  from digit
match_recognize
( order by id
  measures
    least(v1.id, v2.id, v3.id) v_id,
    (v1.id) v1_id,
    (v2.id) v2_id,
    (v3.id) v3_id
  one row per match
  after match skip to next row
```

```
pattern (permute (v1, v2, v3))
define
  v1 as v1.value = 1,
  v2 as v2.value = 2,
  v3 as v3.value = 3)
group by decode(v_id, v1_id, 1, v2_id, 2, v3_id, 3),
        decode(v_id + 1, v1_id, 1, v2_id, 2, v3_id, 3),
        decode(v_id + 2, v1_id, 1, v2_id, 2, v3_id, 3)
order by 1, 2, 3;
```

V1	V2	V3	CNT
1	2	3	2066
1	3	2	1945
2	1	3	2027
2	3	1	1971
3	1	2	1962
3	2	1	2015

Keywords after match skip to next row were specified in order to catch all the combinations. For example, there are two overlapping sequences 1, 3, 2 and 3, 2, 1 on the ID interval (709, 719) and the rows with ID 715 and 716 are part of two different matches.

```
select * from digit where id between 709 and 719;
```

ID	VALUE
709	9
710	3
711	2
712	4
713	6
714	1

715	3
716	2
717	1
718	5
719	0

Keyword permute means that we consider all possible combinations of v1, v2, v3. To define which permutation was matched we derive matching IDs and use logic with decode. The number of rows after pattern matching equals to the number of matched groups and the number of rows after group by is not more than 6 – the number of permutations of 1, 2, and 3.

Listing 8-5 shows an approach using analytic functions. For each row we derive two previous rows and check that all of them are unique and members of the set (1, 2, 3).

Listing 8-5. Finding combinations of elements (1, 2, 3) using analytic functions

```
select v1, v2, v3, count(*) cnt
  from (select row_number() over(order by id) rn,
               value v3,
               lag(value, 1) over(order by id) v2,
               lag(value, 2) over(order by id) v1
          from digit)
 where rn > 2
   and v1 in (1, 2, 3)
   and v2 in (1, 2, 3)
   and v3 in (1, 2, 3)
   and v1 <> v2
   and v1 <> v3
   and v2 <> v3
 group by v1, v2, v3
 order by 1, 2, 3;
```

By the way, similar logic can be used for pattern matching as well; in such case we can avoid decode, permute, and grouping.

```
pattern (v1 v2 v3)
define
  v1 as v1.value = any (1, 2, 3),
  v2 as v2.value = any (1, 2, 3)
        and v2.value <> v1.value,
  v3 as v3.value = any (1, 2, 3)
        and v3.value <> v2.value
        and v3.value <> v1.value)
```

Listing 8-6 shows query plans with runtime execution statistics (starts column always equals to 1 and is manually removed for formatting purposes)

Listing 8-6. Query plans for finding combinations of elements (1, 2, 3)

```
select * from table(dbms_xplan.display_cursor(format =>
'IOSTATS LAST'));
```

Id	Operation	Name	E-Rows	A-Rows	A-Time	Buffers
0	SELECT STATEMENT			6	00:00:04.85	3712
1	SORT GROUP BY		10	6	00:00:04.85	3712
* 2	VIEW		2000K	11986	00:00:04.85	3712
3	WINDOW SORT		2000K	2000K	00:00:03.91	3712
4	TABLE ACCESS FULL	DIGIT	2000K	2000K	00:00:00.16	3712

Id	Operation	Name	E-Rows	A-Rows	A-Time	Buffers
0	SELECT STATEMENT			6	00:00:02.74	3712
1	SORT GROUP BY		2000K	6	00:00:02.74	3712
2	VIEW		2000K	11986	00:00:02.73	3712
3	MATCH RECOGNIZE SORT		2000K	11986	00:00:02.72	3712
4	TABLE ACCESS FULL	DIGIT	2000K	2000K	00:00:00.16	3712

As you see, time spent on pattern matching and aggregation in the first query is less than elapsed time only for analytics in the second query. Please also note that the Reads column is absent, which means that all table blocks were in the buffer cache.

Speaking about performance, it's worth it to mention that, similar to a model clause, you can leverage the power parallel execution – especially if data can be partitioned. In the section "Model Parallel Execution," I compared model vs. PL/SQL. Let's complete the picture by adding a pattern-matching solution.

```
select --+ parallel(10)
  *
from t
model
match_recognize
(
  partition by part
  order by id
  measures
    sum(value) x,
    userenv('sid') sid
```

```
all rows per match
pattern(x+)
define
  x as sum(value) - value <= 3e3
) mr;
```

It runs about 3 times faster than the model approach with the same degree of parallelism.

Pattern matching is based on state machines and the pattern itself defines whether the state machine is

- Deterministic Finite Auto (DFA) - each of the transitions is uniquely determined by its source state and event;

- Nondeterministic Finite Auto (NFA) - next state depends not only on the current event, but also possibly on an arbitrary number of subsequent events.

In the first case, an efficient algorithm is used and you will see MATCH RECOGNIZE SORT DETERMINISTIC FINITE AUTOMATON in the plan while in the second case, backtracking is required and the plan will contain an operation MATCH RECOGNIZE SORT. There may be the keyword BUFFER instead of SORT if a recordset is ordered as required before applying pattern matching.

Listing 8-7 contains a query that generates NFA, because of the quantifier for pattern variable y. If y was matched 3 times but the test for z fails, then the state machine walks back and tries to match z again – this is exactly what is happening during recognition of the second group. If we specify pattern (x y{3} z) instead, then DFA will be used but there will be only one match.

Listing 8-7. Pattern matching with backtracking

```
with t as (select rownum id from dual connect by rownum <= 10)
select * from t
match_recognize
( order by id
  measures
    match_number() match,
    classifier() cls
  all rows per match with unmatched rows
  pattern (x y{2, 3} z)
  define
    z as x.id + z.id <= 15
) mr;
```

```
       ID      MATCH CLS
---------- ---------- -----
        1          1 X
        2          1 Y
        3          1 Y
        4          1 Y
        5          1 Z
        6          2 X
        7          2 Y
        8          2 Y
        9          2 Z
       10
```

10 rows selected.

Nevertheless, even with all the power, pattern matching currently has some limitations. In particular

- It's possible to use only a limited subset of aggregate functions in the define clause and measures clause. For example, you cannot use listagg or UDAG. It causes `ORA-62512: This aggregate is not yet supported in MATCH_RECOGNIZE clause`. Additional details regarding aggregate function in pattern matching can be found in Chapter 12 in the quiz "Resemblance Group."

- You can use subqueries in a define clause but they cannot be correlated. Otherwise the query fails with `ORA-62510: Correlated subqueries are not allowed in MATCH_RECOGNIZE clause`. I believe the reason is to not mix up execution of finite automata and the SQL engine.

Summary

Row pattern matching significantly extends capabilities of SQL for data analysis. This feature allows us to perform complex analysis that otherwise would require analytic and aggregate functions, joins, and subqueries. In some cases match_recognize is the only way to get a result using SQL in an efficient and scalable way. Even for cases when pattern matching can be rewritten using analytic functions, it shows better performance. An analogy could be drawn with pivot/unpivot operators that can be replaced with cross join/group by, but new capability performs a bit better than old-school methods.

Regular expression-like syntax allows defining patterns in a concise way, which simplifies maintainability and improves readability. Eventually, pattern matching is a considerable breakthrough in SQL capabilities and definitely a useful feature.

CHAPTER 9

Logical Execution Order of Query Clauses

Oracle allows the combining of various query clauses on the same layer of a single query, from basic features like joins, filtering, and grouping to advanced constructions like model clause or pattern matching. Sometimes it's not possible to achieve the result using single select ... from query block so you may have to create additional inline views in the query – for example, when you want to filter by the value of an analytic function. However, even if you can implement the entire logic using a single query block – it's not always necessary, because Oracle can eliminate inline views during the query transformations. Moreover, in some cases additional inline views may help to improve the performance as it will be shown in the end of the chapter.

This chapter covers the execution order of query clauses in a query block from a logical point of view, which helps to implement complex logic in a concise way.

Let's assume we have one single select statement containing only one select keyword – thus there are no subqueries or inline views. Basically the execution order is following:

1. from, join, where

2. connect by

3. group by

© Alex Reprintsev 2018
A. Reprintsev, *Oracle SQL Revealed*, https://doi.org/10.1007/978-1-4842-3372-6_9

4. having

5. analytic functions

6. select-list (distinct, scalar subqueries etc)

7. order by

However this requires a number of clarifications.

1. Specifics of the combination of join, where, and
    connect by was covered in Chapter 5, "Hierarchical
    queries: Connect by.". In addition, as it was
    demonstrated in the section "Pseudocolumn
    Generation in Detail," strictly speaking, it's not
    correct to say that predicates in the where clause
    are executed either before or after connect by.

2. Even though, logically post-join predicates are
    supposed to be evaluated after pre-join predicates,
    in fact they may be applied before if that leads to the
    plan with a lower cost.

3. Query transformations may affect the actual
    execution order even for a single query block. For
    example, distinct may be applied before join if
    Distinct Placement transformation takes place –
    technically Oracle creates additional inline view.

4. An invaluable source of information about the
    execution order for a specific query is, of course,
    a query plan. It will show when predicates are
    applied, when aggregate and analytic functions are
    executed, and when various sorts are performed, if
    any, and much more.

All the transformations and optimizations can take place only if this does not change the result, but what is more important, the actual execution order may change after CBO transformations – a simple case is Distinct Placement transformation.

Sometimes developers write a code, making wrong assumptions about execution order, which may be dangerous. Below are some caveats.

1. You should not build the logic with an assumption that some filters will be applied before others in the same query block or rely on a specific plan. The example below demonstrates how a query may fail if the query plan changes.

```
create table t01(id, value, constraint pk_t01 primary
key(id)) as
select 1, '1' from dual union all
select 2, '2' from dual union all
select 0, 'X' from dual;

create table t02(id, value) as
select 1, 1 from dual union all
select 2, 2 from dual;

select
* from t01 join t02 using (id, value);
select *
  from table(dbms_xplan.display_cursor(format =>
  'basic predicate'));
select --+ no_index(t01)
* from t01 join t02 using (id, value);
select *
  from table(dbms_xplan.display_cursor(format =>
  'basic predicate'));
```

In the first case, Oracle does nested loops with an
access by ID and applies a filter by value on top of
a joined recordset, while in the second case there
is a hash join and the query fails with ORA-01722:
invalid number because of an implicit conversion
when it tries to convert X into a number.

```
select
* from t01 join t02 using (id, value);
        ID      VALUE
---------- ----------
         1          1
         2          2


-----------------------------------------------------
| Id  | Operation                    | Name   |
-----------------------------------------------------
|   0 | SELECT STATEMENT             |        |
|   1 |  NESTED LOOPS                |        |
|   2 |   NESTED LOOPS               |        |
|   3 |    TABLE ACCESS FULL         | T02    |
|*  4 |     INDEX UNIQUE SCAN        | PK_T01 |
|*  5 |    TABLE ACCESS BY INDEX ROWID| T01   |
-----------------------------------------------------

Predicate Information (identified by operation id):
-----------------------------------------------------

   4 - access("T01"."ID"="T02"."ID")
   5 - filter("T02"."VALUE"=TO_NUMBER("T01"."VALUE"))

select --+ no_index(t01)
* from t01 join t02 using (id, value);
ERROR:
```

ORA-01722: invalid number

```
------------------------------------
| Id  | Operation          | Name |
------------------------------------
|   0 | SELECT STATEMENT   |      |
|*  1 |  HASH JOIN         |      |
|   2 |   TABLE ACCESS FULL| TO2  |
|   3 |   TABLE ACCESS FULL| TO1  |
------------------------------------

Predicate Information (identified by operation id):
---------------------------------------------------

   1 - access("TO2"."VALUE"=TO_NUMBER("TO1"."VALUE") AND
             "TO1"."ID"="TO2"."ID")
```

2. You should not rely on the order of evaluation of
    predicates in compound conditions. For example,
    in both queries below, predicates were applied in
    the same order as they were specified so that the
    first query failed and the second one is executed
    successfully. Given that id < 3 is false for the third
    row, Oracle did not evaluate the second condition.

```
select id, case when 1 / (id - 3) < 0 and id < 3 then 1 end x
  from (select rownum id from dual connect by level <= 3);
ERROR:
ORA-01476: divisor is equal to zero
```

```
select id, case when id < 3 and 1 / (id - 3) < 0 then 1 end x
  from (select rownum id from dual connect by level <= 3);
```

```
          ID            X
---------- ----------
           1            1
           2            1
           3
```

The key point is that there is no guarantee for such
evaluation. For example, both queries below fail,
irrespective of how the predicates are specified.

```
create table t03 as
select 'A' id from dual union all select '123' from dual;

Table created.

select * from t03
 where id >= 100 and regexp_like(id, '\d+');
 where id >= 100 and regexp_like(id, '\d+')
       *
ERROR at line 2:
ORA-01722: invalid number

select * from t03
 where regexp_like(id, '\d+') and id >= 100;
 where regexp_like(id, '\d+') and id >= 100
                                   *
ERROR at line 2:
ORA-01722: invalid number
```

To make sure that some predicates are evaluated
before others, we can use case expressions.

```
select * from t03
 where case when regexp_like(id, '\d+') then id end >= 100;

ID
---
123
```

3. There is no guarantee how many times a scalar
   subquery or deterministic function will be executed.
   Of course, you may want to use various optimization
   techniques like scalar subquery caching or reduce
   the number of executions for a specific function by
   making it deterministic, but you should not ever rely
   that there will be a specific number of executions, in
   particular a single execution.

Let's get back to the execution order of query clauses and have a look
at mix of connect by with analytic and aggregate functions.

```
select
 id,
 count(*) cnt,
 max(level) max_lvl,
 max(rownum) max_rn,
 sum(id + count(*)) over(order by id) summ
  from (select column_value id from table(numbers(0, 0, 1)))
 group by id
 start with id = 0
connect by prior id + 1 = id;
```

ID	CNT	MAX_LVL	MAX_RN	SUMM
0	2	1	3	2
1	2	2	4	5

Initially Oracle built a tree 0, 1, 0, 1 (four rows, two levels) and generated values for rownum and level pseudocolumns. After that, the recordset has been grouped, and finally the analytic function was calculated.

As stated in the list regarding execution order, analytic functions are executed after group by but before distinct. So using an analytic function with distinct in a select list is one of the examples when distinct cannot be replaced with group by without additional inline views.

Let's create a table and demonstrate a few more examples when group by cannot be used instead of distinct.

```
create table tt as
select rownum id, mod(rownum, 2) value
  from dual connect by level <= 3;
```

These two queries are logically identical and produce the same output:

```
select distinct value from tt
select value from tt group by value
```

However, in the following cases, group by cannot be used without an additional inline view, because expressions in the select list are evaluated after group by.

```
select distinct row_number() over(partition by id order by
null) rn, value
  from tt;
```

```
        RN        VALUE
---------- ----------
         1          0
         1          1
```

```
select distinct (select count(*) from tt) cnt, value from tt;
```

```
    CNT        VALUE
---------- ----------
         3          1
         3          0
```

```
select distinct sys_connect_by_path(value, '->') path, value
   from tt
connect by 1 = 0;
```

```
PATH                VALUE
---------- ----------
->1                    1
->0                    0
```

To check the behavior of distinct and filter by rownum, let's create another table:

```
create table tt1 as
(select trunc(rownum / 2) id from dual connect by level <= 5);
select * from tt1;
```

```
        ID
----------
         0
         1
         1
         2
         2
```

Even though the filtering condition was specified to return three rows, the following query returns only two rows because three rows returned after a filter is applied and only two of them are unique. Inline view was used in the from clause to guarantee an order.

```
select distinct id
  from (select * from tt1 order by id)
 where rownum <= 3;
```

```
        ID
----------
         0
         1
```

The same can be done using group by without additional inline views because all expressions for grouping as well as filter conditions can be evaluated before group by.

```
select id
  from (select * from tt1 order by id)
 where rownum <= 3
 group by id;
```

Let's analyze in more detail a situation when aggregate and analytic functions are mixed together in the same query block. First query from Listing 9-1 returns two rows as in the original table, but the second one returns only a single row because the entire recordset was aggregated before analytics.

Listing 9-1. Mixing aggregate and analytic functions

```
select count(*) over() cnt1
  from (select column_value id from table(numbers(1, 1)));
```

```
      CNT1
----------
         2
         2
```

```
select count(*) over() cnt1, count(*) cnt2
  from (select column_value id from table(numbers(1, 1)));

    CNT1        CNT2
---------- ----------
        1           2
```

Aggregate and analytic functions can be nested. To understand the result of Listing 9-2, keep in mind that aggregate functions are evaluated first and analytics are applied after that.

Listing 9-2. Nesting aggregate and analytic functions

```
select value,
       count(*) agg,
       count(*) over() an,
       sum(count(*)) over(order by value) agg_an
  from tt
 group by value;

    VALUE         AGG          AN       AGG_AN
---------- ----------- ----------- ----------
        0           1           2           1
        1           2           2           3
```

Some developers try to avoid inline views with no particular reason; however in other cases it makes a difference from a performance point of view. Listing 9-3 shows a query from Listing 9-2 rewritten with an inline view and a bit simplified query (without analytic count) along with their versions after transformations and plans.

Listing 9-3. Inline view instead of nested aggregate and analytic functions

```
select t.*, sum(agg) over(order by value) agg_an
  from (select value, count(*) agg, count(*) over() an
          from tt
          group by value) t;

select "T"."VALUE" "VALUE",
       "T"."AGG" "AGG",
       "T"."AN" "AN",
       sum("T"."AGG") over(order by "T"."VALUE"
       range between unbounded preceding and current row) "AGG_AN"
  from (select "TT"."VALUE" "VALUE",
               count(*) "AGG",
               count(*) over() "AN"
          from "TT" "TT"
          group by "TT"."VALUE") "T";
```

```
-------------------------------------
| Id  | Operation            | Name |
-------------------------------------
|   0 | SELECT STATEMENT     |      |
|   1 |  WINDOW SORT         |      |
|   2 |   VIEW               |      |
|   3 |    WINDOW BUFFER     |      |
|   4 |     HASH GROUP BY    |      |
|   5 |      TABLE ACCESS FULL| TT  |
-------------------------------------
```

```
select t.*, sum(agg) over(order by value) agg_an
  from (select value, count(*) agg
          from tt
          group by value) t;
```

```
select "TT"."VALUE" "VALUE",
       count(*) "AGG",
       sum(count(*)) over(order by "TT"."VALUE"
       range between unbounded preceding and current row) "AGG_AN"
  from "TT" "TT"
 group by "TT"."VALUE";


-------------------------------------
| Id | Operation            | Name |
-------------------------------------
|  0 | SELECT STATEMENT     |      |
|  1 |  WINDOW BUFFER       |      |
|  2 |   SORT GROUP BY      |      |
|  3 |    TABLE ACCESS FULL | TT   |
-------------------------------------
```

As you see, Oracle did not manage to eliminate an inline view for the first query, but what is more important – plans differ. The plan for the second query is the same as the plan for the original query with nested functions; however column "an" is not calculated. On the other hand, the first query returns the identical result as the original one, but as we see from the plan there are two WINDOW operations and a top-level function requires its own sort. This means that in this case you may want to use nested functions for performance reasons. Technically, a complex view merging transformation was applied for the second query but could not be applied for the first one.

Aggregate functions also can be nested. As you may remember it's not possible to use a distinct keyword in listagg function, but if result is supposed to be a single row, then nested aggregates can help to remove duplicates from concatenation as shown in Listing 9-4.

Listing 9-4. Nested aggregate functions

```
select listagg(id, ',') within group(order by id) list
  from (select column_value id, rownum rn
         from table(numbers(1, 2, 3, 5, 2)));

LIST
----------

1,2,2,3,5

select listagg(max(id), ',') within group(order by max(id)) list
  from (select column_value id, rownum rn
         from table(numbers (1, 2, 3, 5, 2)))
group by id;

LIST
----------

1,2,3,5
```

To perform aggregation by id before concatenation it's enough to specify aggregate function max just in one place.

```
listagg(id, ',') within group(order by max(id)) list
listagg(max(id), ',') within group(order by id) list
```

When aggregate functions are nested, then the result is always a single row and only one level deep nesting makes sense and is allowed.

This capability may be quite useful if we want to concatenate unique values in a correlated scalar subquery. Listing 9-5 demonstrates a couple of approaches but the second one works only in 12c while on 11g it fails with ORA-00904: "T1"."ID": invalid identifier because correlation names scoped only to one level deep.

Listing 9-5. Concatenating unique values in correlated scalar subquery

```
select t1.*,
       (select listagg(max(t2.name), ', ') within group(order
       by t2.name)
          from t2
        where t1.id = t2.id
          group by t2.name) x1,
       (select listagg(t2.name, ', ') within group(order by t2.name)
          from (select distinct name from t2 where t1.id =
          t2.id) t2) x2
  from t1;
```

As was mentioned in the beginning of the chapter, sometimes an inline view may be mandatory, for example, if you want to use the result of the analytic function in a where clause. In other cases it may be optional as was shown in a query with mixed analytic and aggregate functions. In such situations it's up to you to decide whether to use an inline view and make a query easier to read or get rid of it to make it more concise and avoid unnecessary layers.

It's not possible to figure out in a general case whether a query contains (mergeable) inline views or not based on the plan. As was demonstrated, getting rid of an inline view can change the plan and have a positive impact on the performance; however additional inline views also may lead to improved performance.

Let's create a function with an execution time close to one second to demonstrate such a case.

```
create or replace function f return number is
begin
  dbms_lock.sleep(1);
  return 1;
end f;
/
```

The first query from Listing 9-6 takes 6 seconds because functions are evaluated twice for each row. The second query takes 2 seconds because of scalar subquery caching – the function is evaluated twice for the first row and the result is cached. Finally, the third query takes only a second because we can reuse the cached scalar from the inline view in both expressions.

Listing 9-6. Improving performance with inline views and scalar subquery caching

```
select id, value, f + 1 f1, f - 1 f2 from tt t;
```

ID	VALUE	F1	F2
1	1	2	0
2	0	2	0
3	1	2	0

```
Elapsed: 00:00:06.04
select id, value, (select f from dual) + 1 f1, (select f from
dual) - 1 f2
  from tt t;
```

ID	VALUE	F1	F2
1	1	2	0
2	0	2	0
3	1	2	0

```
Elapsed: 00:00:02.02
select id, value, ff + 1 f1, ff - 1 f2
  from (select tt.*, (select f from dual) ff from tt) t;
```

ID	VALUE	F1	F2
1	1	2	0
2	0	2	0
3	1	2	0

Elapsed: 00:00:01.02

Even specific Oracle clauses like pattern matching or model may be combined in the same query block.

```
select * from dual
match_recognize (all rows per match pattern (x) define x as 1 = 1)
model dimension by (1 id) measures (0 result) rules ();
```

In this case match_recognize will be applied first and the model will be executed on top of it; furthermore each clause is isolated to another so if you want to treat a recordset in a specific way before applying the logic, you may have to specify partitioning and ordering for each clause.

Summary

Some details regarding logical execution of query clauses, along with the examples, have been examined. When logic is quite complicated it makes sense to use multiple query blocks even if that is not necessary - for maintainability purposes. However you have to make sure that inline views are merged as expected so there is no negative impact on the performance. It's not always possible to avoid inline views – for example, when filtering by result of an analytic function is required. Moreover, in some cases inline views may improve the performance as was demonstrated in the end of the chapter. Also inline views may be useful as workarounds for bugs (for example, there were a lot of bugs on old versions when connect by and analytic functions have been mixed in the same query block) and to control transformations – you can disable view merging and control transformations in each subqeury separately.

CHAPTER 10

Turing Completeness

Turing completeness is a very important notion in computer science because being Turing complete means that your model of computations can execute any algorithm no matter how complex it's, what data structures are used, and how much storage or time would be needed to evaluate it. SQL can be considered as yet another example of a model of computations and even though it's not supposed to be used to implement any algorithm or business logic, it's interesting to analyze whether it's Turing complete or not for the sake of completeness. Moreover, as will be shown in the next chapter "When PL/SQL Is Better Than Vanilla SQL," sometimes pure SQL is not the best way to get the result even if an algorithm can be easily implemented using it.

In computation theory, a system of data-manipulation rules (or model of computations) is said to be Turing complete if it can be used to simulate any Turing machine. The examples of such systems are the following: processor's instruction set, a programming language, a cellular automaton, or even an ultimate reduced instruction set computer (URISC). On the other hand, some widely known models of computations are not Turing complete – for instance, deterministic finite automaton (DFA).

According to the Church–Turing thesis, "All physically computable functions are Turing-computable," or in other words, if some model of computations can simulate a Turing machine then it can implement any computable function.

© Alex Reprintsev 2018
A. Reprintsev, *Oracle SQL Revealed*, https://doi.org/10.1007/978-1-4842-3372-6_10

One of the easiest ways to prove whether language is Turing complete is to implement an elementary cellular automaton called Rule 110, which is Turing complete – proof can be found in note [7] in the Appendix.

In an elementary cellular automaton, a one-dimensional pattern of 0s and 1s evolves according to a simple set of rules. Whether a point in the pattern will be 0 or 1 in the new generation depends on its current value, as well as on those of its two neighbors as described in Table 10-1. The left neighbor for the first symbol is the last symbol in the tape and the right neighbor for the last symbol is the first symbol.

Table 10-1. *The set of rules for Rule 110 automaton*

Current pattern	111	110	101	100	011	010	001	000
New start for the center cell	0	1	1	0	1	1	1	0

Rule 110 is called like that because if a binary sequence for new states 01101110 interpreted as a binary number corresponds to the decimal value 110.

Listing 10-1 shows the example of an evaluation for the first 19 steps of Rule 110 for the initial tape 00000000001000000000000010000.

Listing 10-1. Example of evaluation for Rule 110

```
  PART STR
--------- ---------------------------------------
        1 00000000001000000000000010000
        2 00000000011000000000000110000
        3 00000000111000000000001110000
        4 00000001101000000000011010000
        5 00000011111000000000111110000
        6 00000110001000000001100010000
```

```
 7 000011100110000000011100110000
 8 000110101110000000110101110000
 9 001111111010000001111111010000
10 011000001110000011000001110000
11 111000011010000111000011010000
12 101000111110001101000111110001
13 111001100010011111001100010011
14 001011100110110001011100110110
15 011110101111110011110101111110
16 110011111000010110011111000010
17 110110001000111110110001000111
18 011110011001100011110011001100
19 110010111011100110010111011100
20 110111101110101110111101110101
```

Listing 10-2 shows how Rule 110 can be implemented using recursive subquery factoring and analytic functions. In a nutshell, the tape is transformed into a recordset where one row is one symbol and analytic functions are used to derive neighbors for each value, after symbols for the required steps are generated, they getting concatenated into strings.

Listing 10-2. Implementation of Rule 110 using recursive subquery factoring

```
with t0 as
 (select '00000000001000000000000010000' str from dual),
t1 as
 (select 1 part, rownum rn, substr(str, rownum, 1) x
    from t0
  connect by substr(str, rownum, 1) is not null),
t2(part, rn, x) as
 (select part, rn, cast(x as char(1))
    from t1
```

```
union all
select part + 1,
        rn,
        case nvl(lag(x) over(order by rn),
             last_value(x) over(order by rn rows
             between current row and unbounded following))
             || x ||
             nvl(lead(x) over(order by rn),
             first_value(x) over(order by rn rows
             between unbounded preceding and current row))
          when '111' then '0'
          when '110' then '1'
          when '101' then '1'
          when '100' then '0'
          when '011' then '1'
          when '010' then '1'
          when '001' then '1'
          else '0'
        end
    from t2
  where part < 20)
select part, listagg(x) within group(order by rn) str
  from t2
 group by part
 order by 1;
```

Without analytic functions it's not possible to derive values for neighbors because a recursive query name must be referenced only once in a recursive branch, so self joins of subqueries with a recursive query name are not allowed. Therefore I do not think that SQL is Turing complete without support of analytic functions in a recursive branch; however this has to be proven.

After it's proven that cellular automaton can be used to implement any algorithm, one may ask "how to actually use it for that? For example, to implement a very simple routine that sums up two numbers." In order to do that, pattern of 0s and 1s must be treated as data and code so the tape has to be constructed in a specific manner. In other words, the algorithm has to be coded in input tape – not in SQL.

The last thing to mention about Rule 110 is that it can be implemented relatively simply for a tape of arbitrary length using a model clause even without iterations. Such imitations using SQL are quite slow and can be used only for academic purposes though.

A model clause has yet another interesting feature from an academic point of view – it can be used to implement any algorithm if you get rid of nested loops, which is theoretically always possible. To demonstrate this let's have a look at a bubble sort algorithm shown in Listing 10-3.

Listing 10-3. Bubble sort for string of symbols

```
declare
  s varchar2(4000) := 'abcd c*de 01';
  n number := length(s);
  j number := 1;
  k number := 1;
  x number := 1;
  i number := 1;
begin
  while x > 0 loop
    x := 0;
    for j in 1 .. n - k loop
      i := i + 1;
      if substr(s, j + 1, 1) < substr(s, j, 1) then
        s := substr(s, 1, j - 1) || substr(s, j + 1, 1) ||
              substr(s, j, 1) || substr(s, j + 2);
```

```
       x := 1;
     end if;
   end loop;
   k := k + 1;
  end loop;
  dbms_output.put_line(i || s);
end;
```

We repeat nested loops until there is at least one swap on the current iteration of the while loop, which is flagged in an x variable.

After conversion to a single while loop in Listing 10-4, we introduced an additional flag – c. This flag is an analogue to x from Listing 10-3 while x itself always equals to 1 and may reset to zero only when an "inner loop" is completed so algorithms can terminate only if we processed all the symbols on the current step and there were no swaps (i.e., c = 0).

Listing 10-4. Bubble sort using single while loop

```
declare
  s varchar2(4000) := 'abcd c*de 01';
  n number := length(s);
  j number := 1;
  k number := 1;
  x number := 1;
  i number := 1;
  c number := 0;
begin
  while x > 0 loop
    i := i + 1;
    c := case when substr(s, j + 1, 1) < substr(s, j, 1)
              then 1
              else case when j = 1 then 0 else c end
         end;
```

```
    s := case when substr(s, j + 1, 1) < substr(s, j, 1)
            then substr(s, 1, j - 1) || substr(s, j + 1, 1) ||
                substr(s, j, 1) || substr(s, j + 2)
            else s
        end;
    x := case when j = n - k and c = 0 then 0 else 1 end;
    k := case when j = n - k then k + 1 else k end;
    j := case when j - 1 = n - k then 1 else j + 1 end;
  end loop;
  dbms_output.put_line(i || s);
end;
```

To implement this logic using a model clause we have to

- Declare necessary variables (columns);

- Replace assignment operators ":=" with equality signs "=";

- Replace semicolon, which separates statements with a comma, to separate rules in the model;

- Add [0] for addressing – logic is applied to a single string that is identified with rn = 0.

Listing 10-5 shows an SQL approach. In all three cases the result is the same and 64 iterations have been performed to get it.

Listing 10-5. Bubble sort using model clause

```
with t as (select 'abcd c*de 01' s from dual)
select i, s
from t
model
dimension by (0 rn)
measures (length(s) n, 1 j, 1 k, 1 x, 1 i, 0 c, s)
rules iterate(60) until x[0]=0
```

```
(
  i[0] = i[0] + 1,
  c[0] = case when substr(s[0], j[0] + 1, 1) < substr(s[0], j[0], 1)
            then 1
            else case when j[0] = 1 then 0 else c[0] end
        end,
  s[0] = case when substr(s[0], j[0] + 1, 1) < substr(s[0], j[0], 1)
            then substr(s[0], 1, j[0] - 1) || substr(s[0],
            j[0] + 1, 1) ||
                substr(s[0], j[0], 1) || substr(s[0], j[0] + 2)
            else s[0]
        end,
  x[0] = case when j[0] = n[0] - k[0] and c[0] = 0 then 0 else 1 end,
  k[0] = case when j[0] = n[0] - k[0] then k[0] + 1 else k[0] end,
  j[0] = case when j[0] - 1 = n[0] - k[0] then 1 else j[0] + 1 end
);

        I S
---------- ------------
        64   *01abccdde
```

Summary

It has been shown that recursive subquery factoring makes SQL Turing complete. Moreover it was demonstrated how an iterative model can be used to implement an arbitrary algorithm. Nevertheless with all the power, SQL is not a language for iterative computations. Also as was shown in the subsection "Brief Analysis of the Performance" in Chapter 7 about the model clause, even for trivial algorithms PL/SQL may be faster than recursive subquery factoring or model clauses. Additional details when PL/SQL is a more preferable approach than SQL can be found in the next chapter – "When PL/SQL Is Better Than Vanilla SQL."

PART II

PL/SQL and SQL solutions

The list of tasks and demonstrated solutions in Chapter 12 correspond to the following Oracle features:

#	Quiz	CB	AF	RW	M	PM	PL
1	Converting into decimal	+					+
2	Connected components	+					+
3	Ordering dependencies	+					+
4	Percentile with shift		+				
5	N consequent 1s		+		+	+	
6	Next value		+		+	+	
7	Next branch		+		+	+	
8	Random subset			+	+		+
9	Covering ranges	+	+			+	
10	Zeckendorf representation	+		+	+	+	
11	Top paths		+			+	
12	Resemblance group				+	+	
13	Baskets			+	+		
14	Longest increasing subsequence				+		+
15	Quine						

Legend

AF: analytic functions

CB: connect by

RW: recursive with

M: model

PM: pattern matching

PL: PL/SQL

CHAPTER 11

When PL/SQL Is Better Than Vanilla SQL

It was already mentioned a few times that for many tasks, instead of using advanced Oracle features like a model clause or recursive subquery factoring, you can implement the logic in PL/SQL with better performance and scalability. However PL/SQL may be a better choice to get a recordset even if the challenge can be addressed with basic SQL features only. As a rule, the reason is because of limitations or current implementation of SQL or specifics of SQL queries. SQL is declarative language and its implementation in Oracle RDBMS is not open source; thus what is happening under the hood can be controlled only to some extent. Below is an attempt to categorize cases when PL/SQL solution is better than vanilla SQL; please keep in mind that this categorization is quite relative and some cases may fall into multiple categories.

© Alex Reprintsev 2018
A. Reprintsev, *Oracle SQL Revealed*, https://doi.org/10.1007/978-1-4842-3372-6_11

Specifics of Analytic Functions

Analytic functions are extremely powerful features and they significantly extend a set of tasks that can be efficiently solved using pure SQL. On the other hand, analytic functions have some functional limitations as was shown in the corresponding chapter (Chapter 3) as well as some specifics in implementation that may be a reason for not achieving the optimal performance.

Fetch Termination

The core of the first problem in this subsection is the inability to efficiently specify in a query that rows should be fetched until some condition is false. Analytic functions are just a feature that helps to achieve this with pure SQL, but not always in an efficient way.

Let's consider a case when it's required to terminate fetching or stop returning the rows based on some condition. Listing 11-1 shows a table with information about transactions, and the goal is to return all the latest transactions unless the total reaches limit X (or unless N *specific* rows are returned).

At least three different approaches may be proposed right off the bat:

- Using analytic functions;

- Implementing logic in table (pipelined) function;

- Fetch data and validate termination condition on client side.

Listing 11-1. Transaction table

```
exec dbms_random.seed(1);
create table transaction(id int not null, value number not null);
insert --+ append
into transaction
select rownum, trunc(1000 * dbms_random.value + 1) value
  from dual
connect by rownum <= 3e6;
create index idx_tran_id on transaction(id);
exec dbms_stats.gather_table_stats(user, 'transaction');
```

Tests are performed on Oracle 12.1.0.2 with

1) Enabled runtime execution statistics.

```
alter session set statistics_level = all;
```

2) Disabled adaptive plans.

```
alter session set "_optimizer_adaptive_
plans" = false;
```

Plans were displayed using command

```
select *
  from table(dbms_xplan.display_cursor(format => 'IOSTATS LAST'));
```

IOSTATS was used instead of ALLSTATS mainly due to formatting purposes – so that plans can fit the page width. Statistics about memory usage can be displayed by using MEMSTATS or ALLSTATS.

First of all let's consider a bit simplified task when we need to return just 10 of the latest transactions. The first approach is an inline view with order by and filter by rownum. See Listing 11-2.

Listing 11-2. Limiting rows with rownum

```
select *
  from (select * from transaction order by id desc)
 where rownum <= 10;
```

ID	VALUE
3000000	875
2999999	890
2999998	266
2999997	337
2999996	570
2999995	889
2999994	425
2999993	64
2999992	140
2999991	638

```
10 rows selected.
```

Query returns the result almost immediately – less than in a centisecond.

Id	Operation	Name	Starts	E-Rows	A-Rows	A-Time	Buffers
0	SELECT STATEMENT		1		10	00:00:00.01	7
* 1	COUNT STOPKEY		1		10	00:00:00.01	7
2	VIEW		1	10	10	00:00:00.01	7
3	TABLE ACCESS BY INDEX ROWID	TRANSACTION	1	3000K	10	00:00:00.01	7
4	INDEX FULL SCAN DESCENDING	IDX_TRAN_ID	1	10	10	00:00:00.01	4

This is achieved by reading the index in descending order and accessing the table by rowid to get the value, but the crucial point is that reading stops after getting 10 rows.

Let's now implement the logic using analytic functions. See Listing 11-3.

Listing 11-3. Limiting rows with row_number

```
select t1.id, t1.value
  from (select row_number() over(order by id desc) rn, t0.*
          from transaction t0) t1
 where rn <= 10;
```

Even though the Reads column is missing in the plan, which means that all data was read from memory and not from disk - Buffers, it took more than 2 seconds to execute (which is multiple times longer than the first approach).

Id	Operation	Name	Starts	E-Rows	A-Rows	A-Time	Buffers
0	SELECT STATEMENT		1		10	00:00:02.05	6047
* 1	VIEW		1	10	10	00:00:02.05	6047
* 2	WINDOW SORT PUSHED RANK		1	3000K	10	00:00:02.05	6047
3	TABLE ACCESS FULL	TRANSACTION	1	3000K	3000K	00:00:00.46	6047

WINDOW SORT **PUSHED RANK** operation means that ordering is performed until a specified number of rows is returned, but input data for this operation is all the rows from the table. In other words, this means that the full table is scanned but order is guaranteed only for a specified number of rows.

When using analytic functions we also can take advantage of the fact that data in an index is ordered, but in this case we have to use an additional join as shown in Listing 11-4.

Listing 11-4. Limiting rows with row_number - optimized version

```
select t2.*
  from (select --+ cardinality(10) index_desc(t0 idx_tran_id)
          row_number() over(order by id desc) rn, rowid row_id
            from transaction t0) t1
  join transaction t2
    on t1.row_id = t2.rowid
 where t1.rn <= 10;
```

We explicitly specified an access method in the inline view to avoid a full scan and hinted at low cardinality so that Oracle does nested loops. Execution time is less than a centisecond – similar to the approach with filter by rownum. An additional join acts as TABLE ACCESS BY USER ROWID instead of TABLE ACCESS BY INDEX ROWID as in the first approach.

Id	Operation	Name	Starts	E-Rows	A-Rows	A-Time	Buffers
0	SELECT STATEMENT		1		10	00:00:00.01	6
1	NESTED LOOPS		1	10	10	00:00:00.01	6
* 2	VIEW		1	10	10	00:00:00.01	4
* 3	WINDOW NOSORT STOPKEY		1	10	10	00:00:00.01	4
4	INDEX FULL SCAN DESCENDING	IDX_TRAN_ID	1	3000K	11	00:00:00.01	4
5	TABLE ACCESS BY USER ROWID	TRANSACTION	10	1	10	00:00:00.01	2

The last thing to mention about a simplified task is that an optimal plan can be achieved if a limit is specified using a constant or bind variable. If we use a scalar subquery (`select 10 from dual`), then the plan will look like the one below.

Id	Operation	Name	Starts	E-Rows	A-Rows	A-Time	Buffers
0	SELECT STATEMENT		1		10	00:00:03.37	6971
1	NESTED LOOPS		1	10	10	00:00:03.37	6971
* 2	VIEW		1	10	10	00:00:03.37	6969
3	WINDOW NOSORT		1	10	3000K	00:00:02.91	6969
4	INDEX FULL SCAN DESCENDING	IDX_TRAN_ID	1	3000K	3000K	00:00:01.11	6969
5	FAST DUAL		1	1	1	00:00:00.01	0
6	TABLE ACCESS BY USER ROWID	TRANSACTION	10	1	10	00:00:00.01	2

You may note that operation WINDOW NOSORT **STOPKEY** became WINDOW NOSORT, which means that the index was fully scanned. So if a limit is calculated using a subquery, then you may want to split the query into two and use a bind variable for the limit.

Let's proceed to the original task: we need to fetch the latest rows until the total amount reaches the limit; let it be 5000.

Obviously, filter by rownum cannot be used in this case. Listing 11-5 shows an analytic approach to limit rows by a cumulative sum.

Listing 11-5. Limiting rows with sum

```
select t1.id, t1.value
  from (select sum(value) over(order by id desc) s, t0.*
          from transaction t0) t1
 where s <= 5000;
```

ID	VALUE
3000000	875
2999999	890
2999998	266
2999997	337
2999996	570
2999995	889
2999994	425
2999993	64
2999992	140

```
9 rows selected.
```

You can see in the execution plan that elapsed time is much longer than for the original query with row_number from Listing 11-3. This is because all rows have been ordered even though we need only 9 rows in the result.

Id	Operation	Name	Starts	E-Rows	A-Rows	A-Time	Buffers	Reads	Writes
0	SELECT STATEMENT		1		9	00:00:13.59	6055	12746	11861
* 1	VIEW		1	3000K	9	00:00:13.59	6055	12746	11861
2	WINDOW SORT		1	3000K	3000K	00:00:13.07	6055	12746	11861
3	TABLE ACCESS FULL	TRANSACTION	1	3000K	3000K	00:00:00.47	6047	0	0

Columns Reads/Writes signify that temporary tablespace was used for sort. Let's re-run the test after increasing the sort area size to its maximum possible value.

```
alter session set workarea_size_policy = manual;
alter session set sort_area_size = 2147483647;
```

Id	Operation	Name	Starts	E-Rows	A-Rows	A-Time	Buffers
0	SELECT STATEMENT		1		9	00:00:04.95	6047
* 1	VIEW		1	3000K	9	00:00:04.95	6047
2	WINDOW SORT		1	3000K	3000K	00:00:04.48	6047
3	TABLE ACCESS FULL	TRANSACTION	1	3000K	3000K	00:00:00.44	6047

After this change there is enough memory to perform a sort, and the execution time significantly dropped, but there is no need to order all the rows from the table anyway.

With an assumption that there is continuous numbering for ID (which happens extremely rarely for real data), we can use the next approach with recursive subquery factoring.

Listing 11-6. Limiting rows with recursive subquery factoring – for continuous numbering

```
with rec(id, value, s) as
(
  select id, value, value
    from transaction
   where id = (select max(id) from transaction)
  union all
  select t.id, t.value, rec.s + t.value
    from transaction t
    join rec on rec.id - 1 = t.id
   where rec.s + t.value <= 5000
)
select * from rec;
```

Execution time again dropped to 1 centisecond.

Id	Operation	Name	Starts	E-Rows	A-Rows	A-Time	Buffers
0	SELECT STATEMENT		1		9	00:00:00.01	35
1	VIEW		1	2	9	00:00:00.01	35
2	UNION ALL (RECURSIVE WITH) BREADTH FIRST		1		9	00:00:00.01	35
3	TABLE ACCESS BY INDEX ROWID BATCHED	TRANSACTION	1	1	1	00:00:00.01	7
* 4	INDEX RANGE SCAN	IDX_TRAN_ID	1	1	1	00:00:00.01	6
5	SORT AGGREGATE		1	1	1	00:00:00.01	3
6	INDEX FULL SCAN (MIN/MAX)	IDX_TRAN_ID	1	1	1	00:00:00.01	3
7	NESTED LOOPS		9	1	8	00:00:00.01	28
8	NESTED LOOPS		9	1	9	00:00:00.01	19
9	RECURSIVE WITH PUMP		9		9	00:00:00.01	0
* 10	INDEX RANGE SCAN	IDX_TRAN_ID	9	1	9	00:00:00.01	19
* 11	TABLE ACCESS BY INDEX ROWID	TRANSACTION	9	1	8	00:00:00.01	9

For Oracle 12c it's easy to handle gaps in ID numbering (for older versions, you can use methods described in the subsection "Correlated Inline Views and Subqueries" in the first chapter) as shown in Listing 11-7.

Listing 11-7. Limiting rows with recursive subquery factoring – generic case

```
with rec(id, value, s) as
(
  select id, value, value
    from transaction
   where id = (select max(id) from transaction)
  union all
  select t.id, t.value, rec.s + t.value
    from rec
   cross apply (select max(id) id from transaction where id <
   rec.id) t0
    join transaction t on t0.id = t.id
   where rec.s + t.value <= 5000
)
cycle id set c to 1 default 0
select * from rec;
```

Id	Operation	Name	Starts	E-Rows	A-Rows	A-Time	Buffers
0	SELECT STATEMENT		1		9	00:00:00.01	54
1	VIEW		1	2	9	00:00:00.01	54
2	UNION ALL (RECURSIVE WITH) BREADTH FIRST		1		9	00:00:00.01	54
3	TABLE ACCESS BY INDEX ROWID BATCHED	TRANSACTION	1	1	1	00:00:00.01	7
* 4	INDEX RANGE SCAN	IDX_TRAN_ID	1	1	1	00:00:00.01	6
5	SORT AGGREGATE		1	1	1	00:00:00.01	3
6	INDEX FULL SCAN (MIN/MAX)	IDX_TRAN_ID	1	1	1	00:00:00.01	3
7	NESTED LOOPS		9	1	8	00:00:00.01	47
8	NESTED LOOPS		9	1	9	00:00:00.01	38
9	NESTED LOOPS		9	1	9	00:00:00.01	19
10	RECURSIVE WITH PUMP		9		9	00:00:00.01	0
11	VIEW	VW_LAT_EC725798	9	1	9	00:00:00.01	19
12	SORT AGGREGATE		9	1	9	00:00:00.01	19
13	FIRST ROW		9	1	9	00:00:00.01	19
* 14	INDEX RANGE SCAN (MIN/MAX)	IDX_TRAN_ID	9	1	9	00:00:00.01	19
* 15	INDEX RANGE SCAN	IDX_TRAN_ID	9	1	9	00:00:00.01	19
* 16	TABLE ACCESS BY INDEX ROWID	TRANSACTION	9	1	9	00:00:00.01	9

You may note the cycle clause in the query. Even though cycle mark is zero for all the rows, without a cycle clause, the query fails with «ORA-32044: cycle detected while executing recursive WITH query». This is not quite correct behavior and it will be discussed later on in the current chapter.

Well, recursive subquery factoring helps to get a result in quite an efficient way on the last versions, but what if we need to implement more complex logic than the limit for the cumulative sum or we use the old version that does not support recursive subquery factoring. Listing 11-8 shows how logic can be encapsulated in a PL/SQL function as well as create statements for required types.

Listing 11-8. Types and function for limiting rows

```
create or replace type to_id_value as object(id int, value
number)
/
create or replace type tt_id_value as table of to_id_value
/

create or replace function f_transaction(p_limit in number)
  return tt_id_value
  pipelined is
  l_limit number := 0;
begin
  for i in (select --+ index_desc(transaction idx_tran_id)
              *
            from transaction
            order by id desc) loop
    l_limit := l_limit + i.value;
    if l_limit <= 5000 then
      pipe row(to_id_value(i.id, i.value));
```

```
    else
      exit;
    end if;
  end loop;
end f_transaction;
/
```

The average execution time is a two hundredth of a second.

Listing 11-9. Limiting rows with PL/SQL function

```
select * from table(f_transaction(p_limit => 5000));
        ID      VALUE
---------- ----------
   3000000        875
   2999999        890
   2999998        266
   2999997        337
   2999996        570
   2999995        889
   2999994        425
   2999993         64
   2999992        140
```

```
9 rows selected.
```

```
Elapsed: 00:00:00.02
```

Let's add a unique combination of symbols into hint «--+ *index_desc(transaction idx_tran_id) zzz*» and recompile the function so that we can easily find details for the required statement in v$sql. After a couple of executions, the stats are the following.

```
column sql_text format a50
select executions, rows_processed, sql_text
  from v$sql v
 where sql_text like '%index_desc(transaction idx_tran_id) zzz%'
   and sql_text not like '%v$sql%';

EXECUTIONS ROWS_PROCESSED SQL_TEXT
---------- -------------- -----------------------------------
         2             20 SELECT --+ index_desc(transaction
                                    idx_tran_id) zzz
                           * FROM TRANSACTION ORDER BY ID DESC
```

Even though there is no filter in a query, only 20 rows have been processed (fetched), which means 10 rows per execution as expected.

A similar approach can be implemented in a client application, but the ability to encapsulate the logic into a PL/SQL function is quite important.

The last thing to note regarding queries with limits is that the so-called Top-N Queries have been introduced in Oracle 12c. No fundamental changes have been made in the SQL engine for this functionality, and if you have a look at the final query after transformation for Ton-N syntax, you will see analytic functions. So in a nutshell Top-N is just syntactic sugar and avoiding it makes it possible to write more efficient queries in many cases – in particular, you can apply an optimization technique as shown in Listing 11-4. I suppose this functionality was introduced due to following reasons:

- Marketing reasons. Other RDBMSs have this feature and now it's in Oracle as well;

- Simplifying migration from other RDBMSs;

- Simplicity to write ad hoc queries for non-expert database developers;

  Using this feature for complex performance-critical queries is not reasonable.

Avoiding Multiple Sorts

The second use case regarding analytic functions will be about ordering that is caused by analytics. Listing 11-10 shows a fact table with low cardinality dimensions.

Listing 11-10. Fact table with low cardinality dimensions

```
exec dbms_random.seed(1);
create table fact_a as
select date '2010-01-01' + level / (60 * 24) dt,
       trunc(3 * dbms_random.value()) dim_1_id,
       trunc(3 * dbms_random.value()) dim_2_id,
       trunc(1000 * dbms_random.value()) value
  from dual
connect by level <= 3e6;
exec dbms_stats.gather_table_stats(user, 'fact_a');
```

The goal is to calculate a cumulative sum by each dimension and their combination - dim_1_id, dim_2_id with ordering by date.

```
select dt,
       dim_1_id,
       dim_2_id,
       value,
       sum(val) over(partition by dim_1_id order by dt) dim1_sum,
       sum(val) over(partition by dim_2_id order by dt) dim2_sum,
       sum(val) over(partition by dim_1_id, dim_2_id order by dt)
       dim1_dim2_sum
  from fact_a
 order by dt
```

To minimize fetch let's use the following query, which returns only a single row.

```
select to_char(sum(dim1_sum), lpad('9', 20, '9')) d1,
       to_char(sum(dim2_sum), lpad('9', 20, '9')) d2,
       to_char(sum(dim1_dim2_sum), lpad('9', 20, '9')) d12
  from (select dt,
               dim_1_id,
               dim_2_id,
               value,
               sum(value) over(partition by dim_1_id order by
               dt) dim1_sum,
               sum(value) over(partition by dim_2_id order by
               dt) dim2_sum,
               sum(value) over(partition by dim_1_id, dim_2_id
               order by dt)
               dim1_dim2_sum
          from fact_a
         order by dt);
```

D1	D2	D12
749461709848354	749461230723892	249821726573778

There are three sorts in the query plan even though ordering always by dt. This is because the expression for partitioning differs.

Id	Operation	Name	Starts	E-Rows	A-Rows	A-Time	Buffers	Reads	Writes
0	SELECT STATEMENT		1		1	00:01:21.85	9272	96051	90717
1	SORT AGGREGATE		1	1	1	00:01:21.85	9272	96051	90717
2	VIEW		1	3000K	3000K	00:01:21.06	9272	96051	90717
3	SORT ORDER BY		1	3000K	3000K	00:01:20.05	9272	96051	90717
4	WINDOW SORT		1	3000K	3000K	00:01:11.46	9267	82098	76764
5	WINDOW SORT		1	3000K	3000K	00:00:42.91	9257	48721	45685
6	WINDOW SORT		1	3000K	3000K	00:00:20.28	9249	21504	20284
7	TABLE ACCESS FULL	FACT_A	1	3000K	3000K	00:00:00.49	9240	0	0

Total execution time is approximately 1 minute and 20 seconds and as we see in columns Reads/Writes, all three sorts cause reads/writes from temporary tablespace. Let's set the maximum possible memory for sort and re-run the query.

```
alter session set workarea_size_policy = manual;
alter session set sort_area_size = 2147483647;
```

The elapsed time dropped four times and all the sorts have been performed in memory.

Id	Operation	Name	Starts	E-Rows	A-Rows	A-Time	Buffers
0	SELECT STATEMENT		1		1	00:00:21.08	9240
1	SORT AGGREGATE		1	1	1	00:00:21.08	9240
2	VIEW		1	3000K	3000K	00:00:20.41	9240
3	SORT ORDER BY		1	3000K	3000K	00:00:19.59	9240
4	WINDOW SORT		1	3000K	3000K	00:00:17.50	9240
5	WINDOW SORT		1	3000K	3000K	00:00:11.83	9240
6	WINDOW SORT		1	3000K	3000K	00:00:06.58	9240
7	TABLE ACCESS FULL	FACT_A	1	3000K	3000K	00:00:00.47	9240

Taking into account the specifics of analytic widows in this query, we can implement the required logic using PL/SQL associative arrays and a cursor with a single order by. Listing 11-11 shows this approach and the required types.

Listing 11-11. Avoiding multiple sort operations

```
create or replace function f_fact_a return tt_fact_a
  pipelined is
  type tt1 is table of number index by pls_integer;
  type tt2 is table of tt1 index by pls_integer;
  l_dim1  tt1;
  l_dim2  tt1;
  l_dim12 tt2;
begin
  for r in (select /*+ lvl 0 */
              dt, dim_1_id, dim_2_id, value
               from fact_a
              order by dt) loop
    -- NoFormat Start
    l_dim1(r.dim_1_id) := case
                           when l_dim1.exists(r.dim_1_id)
                           then l_dim1(r.dim_1_id)
                           else 0
                         end + r.value;
    l_dim2(r.dim_2_id) := case
                           when l_dim2.exists(r.dim_2_id)
                           then l_dim2(r.dim_2_id)
                           else 0
                         end + r.value;
```

```
    l_dim12(r.dim_1_id)(r.dim_2_id) :=
    case
      when l_dim12.exists(r.dim_1_id)
       and l_dim12(r.dim_1_id).exists(r.dim_2_id)
      then l_dim12(r.dim_1_id)(r.dim_2_id)
      else 0
    end + r.value;
    -- NoFormat End
    pipe row(to_fact_a(r.dt,
                       r.dim_1_id,
                       r.dim_2_id,
                       r.value,
                       l_dim1(r.dim_1_id),
                       l_dim2(r.dim_2_id),
                       l_dim12(r.dim_1_id) (r.dim_2_id)));
  end loop;
end;
/

create or replace type to_fact_a as object
(
  dt             date,
  dim_1_id       number,
  dim_2_id       number,
  value          number,
  dim1_sum       number,
  dim2_sum       number,
  dim1_dim2_sum number
)
/
create or replace type tt_fact_a as table of to_fact_a
/
```

Let's compile a function with disabled PL/SQL optimization.

```
alter session set plsql_optimize_level = 0;
alter function f_fact_a compile;
set timing on
select to_char(sum(dim1_sum), lpad('9', 20, '9')) d1,
       to_char(sum(dim2_sum), lpad('9', 20, '9')) d2,
       to_char(sum(dim1_dim2_sum), lpad('9', 20, '9')) d12
  from table(f_fact_a)
 order by dt;
```

The average execution time is around 45 seconds, which is worse than an SQL approach.

Let's now change the parameter value «plsql_optimize_level» to 2 (this is default value) and compile the function after replacing «/*+ lvl 0 */» with «/*+ lvl 2 */» in the code.

The average execution time became 12-14 seconds, which is better than the SQL approach.

The reason for such a significant improvement is that the fetch size for the default optimization level is 100 rows. You can easily check that in v$sql view.

```
select regexp_substr(sql_text, '/.*/') hint,
       executions,
       fetches,
       rows_processed
  from v$sql s
 where sql_text like '%FROM FACT_A%'
   and sql_text not like '%v$sql%';
```

HINT	EXECUTIONS	FETCHES	ROWS_PROCESSED
/*+ lvl 0 */	2	6000002	6000000
/*+ lvl 2 */	2	60002	6000000

So the PL/SQL approach is approximately 35% faster for this task, but for a larger number of cumulative sums the difference would be more substantial, and more importantly, it's possible to increase the fetch size, which would make the PL/SQL approach several times faster. Additional information about that can be found in "Doing SQL from PL/SQL: Best and Worst Practices" [9].

Iterative-Like Computations

Oracle provides at least two ways to perform iterative-like computations in SQL on top of recordset: iterative model and recursive subquery factoring. The source data for an iterative model is a single recordset and you cannot use any additional data structures like list or stack; and, secondly, there may be only one loop counter (for academic interest implementation of bubble sort using iterative model was shown in Chapter 10, "Turing Completeness"). The specifics of recursive subquery factoring are that on each iteration you can use data only from the previous iteration even though the result set contains data from all the iterations. Briefly speaking, the field of application for these features is quite limited, not to mention issues with scalability and intensive memory and CPU usage.

You can find in the next chapter some solutions with iterative models or recursive subquery factoring and their comparison with PL/SQL approaches. In this chapter, however, we will consider a couple of tasks that can be solved in pure SQL without those advanced features and their alternatives in PL/SQL.

When There Is No Effective Built-In Access Method

Let's assume the goal is to return distinct values for a not nullable column with low cardinality.

```
create table t_str(str varchar2(30) not null, padding
varchar2(240));
insert into t_str
select 'AAA', lpad('x', 240, 'x') from dual
union all
select 'BBB', lpad('x', 240, 'x') from dual
union all
select lpad('C', 30, 'C'), lpad('x', 240, 'x') from dual
connect by rownum <= 3e6
union all
select 'DDD', lpad('x', 240, 'x') from dual;
create index t_str_idx on t_str(str);
exec dbms_stats.gather_table_stats(user,'t_str');
```

Of course, a trivial solution is using a distinct keyword.

```
select distinct str from t_str;

STR
------------------------------
BBB
AAA
CCCCCCCCCCCCCCCCCCCCCCCCCCCCCC
DDD
```

Id	Operation	Name	Starts	E-Rows	A-Rows	A-Time	Buffers
0	SELECT STATEMENT		1		4	00:00:01.04	17662
1	HASH UNIQUE		1	4	4	00:00:01.04	17662
2	INDEX FAST FULL SCAN	T_STR_IDX	1	3000K	3000K	00:00:00.53	17662

Execution time is more than 1 second and it required almost 18k logical reads.

Listing 11-12 shows how recursive subquery factoring can be used for getting a list of distinct values for a column.

Listing 11-12. Using recursive subquery factoring to get distinct values for a column

```
with rec(lvl, str) as
(
  select 1, min(str) from t_str
  union all
  select lvl + 1, (select min(str) from t_str where str > rec.str)
    from rec
   where str is not null
)
select * from rec where str is not null;
```

Id	Operation	Name	Starts	E-Rows	A-Rows	A-Time	Buffers
0	SELECT STATEMENT		1		4	00:00:00.01	13
* 1	VIEW		1	2	4	00:00:00.01	13
2	UNION ALL (RECURSIVE WITH) BREADTH FIRST		1		5	00:00:00.01	13
3	SORT AGGREGATE		1	1	1	00:00:00.01	3
4	INDEX FULL SCAN (MIN/MAX)	T_STR_IDX	1	1	1	00:00:00.01	3
5	SORT AGGREGATE		4	1	4	00:00:00.01	10
6	FIRST ROW		4	1	3	00:00:00.01	10
* 7	INDEX RANGE SCAN (MIN/MAX)	T_STR_IDX	4	1	3	00:00:00.01	10
8	RECURSIVE WITH PUMP		5		4	00:00:00.01	0

The execution time dropped more than 100 times and the number for logical reads reduced more than 1000 times. This was achieved by performing a few "INDEX RANGE SCAN (MIN/MAX)" operations instead of "INDEX FAST FULL SCAN".

Listing 11-13 shows how similar logic can be implemented using PL/SQL function for old Oracle versions.

Listing 11-13. PL/SQL function to get distinct values for a column

```
create or replace function f_str return strings
  pipelined is
  l_min t_str.str%type;
begin
  select min(str) into l_min from t_str;
  pipe row(l_min);
  while true loop
    select min(str) into l_min from t_str where str > l_min;
    if l_min is not null then
      pipe row(l_min);
    else
      return;
    end if;
  end loop;
end f_str;
/
```

Let's analyze performance using a dbms_hprof package:

```
exec dbms_hprof.start_profiling('UDUMP', '1.trc');

PL/SQL procedure successfully completed.
```

```
select column_value str from table(f_str);
STR
--------------------------------
AAA
BBB
CCCCCCCCCCCCCCCCCCCCCCCCCCCCCCC
DDD
exec dbms_hprof.stop_profiling;

PL/SQL procedure successfully completed.

select dbms_hprof.analyze('UDUMP', '1.trc') runid from dual;

     RUNID
----------
         4
```

Listing 11-13 shows profiling results. As you see, the query on the 5th line was executed once and the query from the 8th line was executed 4 times, and the total elapsed time is 931 microseconds or approximately 0.01 second, which is very close to the approach with recursive subquery factoring.

Listing 11-14. Execution statistics using dbms_hprof

```
select pci.runid,
       level depth,
       rpad(' ', (level - 1) * 3, ' ') || fi.function as name,
       fi.subtree_elapsed_time,
       fi.function_elapsed_time,
       fi.calls
  from (select runid, parentsymid, childsymid
          from dbmshp_parent_child_info
         union all
        select runid, null, 2 from dbmshp_runs) pci
```

```
 join dbmshp_function_info fi
   on pci.runid = fi.runid
  and pci.childsymid = fi.symbolid
  and fi.function <> 'STOP_PROFILING'
connect by prior childsymid = parentsymid
        and prior pci.runid = pci.runid
 start with pci.parentsymid is null
        and pci.runid in (4);
```

RUNID	DEPTH	NAME	SUBTREE_ELAPSED_TIME	FUNCTION_ELAPSED_TIME	CALLS
4	1	__plsql_vm	931	16	3
4	2	__anonymous_block	77	77	1
4	2	F_STR	838	110	2
4	3	__static_sql_exec_**line5**	198	198	1
4	3	__static_sql_exec_**line8**	530	530	4

Additional statistics for SQL statements can be found in v$sql as was shown in a previous example.

Problems of a Combinatorial Nature

Combinatorial problems related to data may require generating permutations to analyze combinations of elements. SQL provides various ways to generate recordsets – connect by, recursive subquery factoring, and a model clause; but if you want to refer or reuse during the generation process the data generated so far, then this may be either tricky or inefficient.

Let's consider a specific example: for a set or rows, generate sums of values for all possible subsets with two or more elements. Listing 11-15 shows the script to generate a recordset of values such as each value is greater than the sum of all values generated so far; thus the sum of values for each subset is unique.

Listing 11-15. Creating input set

```
exec dbms_random.seed(3);

create table t_num as
select id, num
  from dual
model
dimension by (1 id)
measures (1 num)
 (
   num[for id from 2 to 19 increment 1] order by id =
   sum(num)[any] + trunc(dbms_random.value(1, 11))
);
```

All permutations and sums for the first three elements are below:

```
select * from t_num where id <= 3;

        ID         NUM
---------- ----------
         1           1
         2           8
         3          15

1 + 8 = 9
1 + 15 = 16
8 + 15 = 23
1 + 8 + 15 = 24
```

For measuring performance we will calculate the total sum to minimize fetch, but <u>the main goal is to generate all the subsets and calculate sums</u>. The number of all subsets for n elements is 2^n including empty subset, singletons, and original set. The total sum without singletons equals to $\dfrac{2^n}{2}\sum_{i=1}^{n} x_i - \sum_{i=1}^{n} x_i = \left(2^{n-1} - 1\right)\sum_{i=1}^{n} x_i$ or 72 for three rows and 536338548711 for all rows.

```
select sum(num) * (power(2, count(*) - 1) - 1) total from t_num;

     TOTAL
-------------
 536338548711
```

There are at least two straightforward ways to generate all permutations with connect by and calculate their sums as demonstrated in Listing 11-16.

Listing 11-16. Connect by + join to get sums of all subsets

```
with
t1 as
 (select power(2, rownum-1) row_mask, num from t_num),
t2 as
 (select rownum as total_mask
    from (select count(*) as cnt from t1)
  connect by rownum < power(2, cnt)
  -- or the same: from t1 connect by num > prior num
 )
```

```
select count(*) cnt, sum(num) sum_num
  from (select total_mask as id, sum(num) as num
          from t2, t1
          where bitand(row_mask, total_mask) <> 0
          group by total_mask
          having count(*) > 1);
```

```
      CNT        SUM_NUM
---------- --------------
    524268   536338548711
```

With execution time around 25 seconds, most of the time was spent on doing nested loops and re-evaluating subquery t1 524268 times. This can be optimized if we specify the hint materialized in t1; after that the execution time drops to 14 seconds.

Id	Operation	Name	Starts	E-Rows	A-Rows	A-Time	Buffers	Reads	Writes
0	SELECT STATEMENT		1		1	00:00:25.81	1572K	868	868
1	SORT AGGREGATE		1	1	1	00:00:25.81	1572K	868	868
2	VIEW		1	1	524K	00:00:25.70	1572K	868	868
* 3	FILTER		1		524K	00:00:25.54	1572K	868	868
4	HASH GROUP BY		1	1	524K	00:00:25.36	1572K	868	868
5	NESTED LOOPS		1	1	4980K	00:00:22.24	1572K	0	0
6	VIEW		1	1	524K	00:00:01.39	3	0	0
7	COUNT		1		524K	00:00:01.17	3	0	0
8	CONNECT BY WITHOUT FILTERING		1		524K	00:00:00.98	3	0	0
9	VIEW		1	1	1	00:00:00.01	3	0	0
10	SORT AGGREGATE		1	1	1	00:00:00.01	3	0	0
11	VIEW		1	19	19	00:00:00.01	3	0	0
12	COUNT		1		19	00:00:00.01	3	0	0
13	TABLE ACCESS FULL	T_NUM	1	19	19	00:00:00.01	3	0	0
* 14	VIEW		524K	1	4980K	00:00:19.37	1572K	0	0
15	COUNT		524K		9961K	00:00:10.07	1572K	0	0
16	TABLE ACCESS FULL	T_NUM	524K	19	9961K	00:00:07.02	1572K	0	0

We can avoid join if we generate a sum expression with sys_connect_by_path function and implement a function to evaluate it – this approach is shown in Listing 11-17.

Listing 11-17. Connect by + UDF to get sums of all subsets

```
select count(*) cnt, sum(f_calc(path)) sum_num
  from (select sys_connect_by_path(num, '+') || '+' as path
          from t_num
          where level > 1
          connect by num > prior num);
create or replace function f_calc(p_str in varchar2) return
number is
  pragma udf;
  result number := 0;
  i      int := 0;
  n      varchar2(30);
begin
  while true loop
    i := i + 1;
    n := substr(p_str,
                instr(p_str, '+', 1, i) + 1,
                instr(p_str, '+', 1, i + 1) - instr(p_str, '+',
                1, i) - 1);
    if n is not null then
      result := result + n;
    else
      exit;
    end if;
  end loop;
  return result;
end f_calc;
```

Execution takes around 7 seconds if we specify «pragma udf» and 10 seconds otherwise. Most of the resources are used for evaluating an expression for sum, if we comment out «sum(f_calc(path))» then the execution time is less than 1 second.

Let's now use a temporary table to store intermediate results:

```
create global temporary table tmp(lvl int, x int, num number);
```

This makes it possible to generate sums of all the combinations in just half a second!

```
begin
  insert into tmp (lvl, x, num)
    select 1, rownum, num from (select num from t_num order by
    num);
  for c in (select rownum x, num
              from (select num from t_num order by num)) loop
    insert into tmp (lvl, x, num)
      select c.x, 0, tmp.num + c.num from tmp where tmp.x < c.x;
  end loop;
end;
/

PL/SQL procedure successfully completed.

Elapsed: 00:00:00.53
select count(*) cnt, sum(num) sum_num from tmp where lvl > 1;

       CNT        SUM_NUM
---------- --------------
    524268   536338548711

Elapsed: 00:00:00.03
```

Obviously, a PL/SQL approach performs much better that an SQL for this task. PL/SQL code gives an impression that this logic can also be implemented using recursive subquery factoring. But there is one catch – in a PL/SQL loop, we need an entire tmp table that contains data from all the iterations while recursive subquery factoring accesses data only from a previous iteration. We can use a trick with an additional join to add a recordset from a previous iteration to a recordset from the current iteration. This approach is shown in Listing 11-18.

Listing 11-18. Recursive subquery factoring to get sums of all subsets

```
with
r0(x, num) as
 (select rownum, num from (select num from t_num order by num)),
rec(iter, lvl, x, num) as
 (select 1, 1, rownum, num from r0
  union all
  select rec.iter + 1,
         decode(z.id, 1, rec.lvl, rec.lvl + 1),
         decode(z.id, 1, rec.x, 0),
         decode(z.id, 1, rec.num, rec.num + r0.num)
    from rec
    join r0
      on rec.iter + 1 = r0.x
    join (select 1 id from dual union all select 2 id from dual) z
      on (z.id = 1 or rec.x < r0.x))
select count(*) cnt, sum(num) sum_num
  from rec
 where iter = (select count(*) from t_num)
   and lvl > 1;
```

Even though it works and produces a correct result, this approach is quite inefficient because on each iteration, we replicate all the data from previous iterations. If we set sort_area_size to the maximum value, then the elapsed time is around 30 seconds but anyway this was demonstrated mainly for academic purposes to show that even a simple PL/SQL loop may not be efficiently re-implemented using recursive subquery factoring.

If we change join order in the query, then it will fail with «ORA-32044: cycle detected while executing recursive WITH query» and to avoid that cycle clause is required even though this is a logically equivalent query and has the same plan as the query from Listing 11-18 even without a cycle clause.

```
...
    from rec
    cross join (select 1 id from dual union all select 2 id from
    dual) z
    join r0
      on rec.iter + 1 = r0.x
    where (z.id = 1 or rec.x < r0.x))
cycle iter set c to 1 default 0
...
```

Two tasks have been analyzed in this section; in the first case, iterations help to avoid scanning unnecessary data or to "optimize plan," while the second task has an iterative nature itself.

Specifics of Joins and Subqueries

SQL was designed to work with recordsets and, in fact, there are only three join methods – HASH JOIN, NESTED LOOPS, and MERGE JOIN. All of them have pros and cons and various scopes of application; HASH JOIN and MERGE JOIN cannot be used for any arbitrary predicate, unlike NESTED LOOPS.

Speaking about subqueries, there are some limitations, for instance, a nesting limit for correlated subqueries that sometimes makes it impossible to implement complex logic in a subquery. These limitations, along with some other details and examples, will be considered in the following subsections.

Specifics of Joins

In this subsection we will consider a task when PL/SQL helps to implement a look-up in a more efficient way than SQL.

Listing 11-19 shows a script to create a table with information about phone calls containing phone numbers and durations in minutes.

Listing 11-19. Table with information about phone calls

```
create table phone_call (num varchar2(11), duration int);
exec dbms_random.seed(1);
insert --+ append
into phone_call
  select '01' || to_char(trunc(1e9 * dbms_random.value),
'fm099999999'),
         trunc(dbms_random.value(1, 5 + 1))
    from dual
  connect by level <= 1e6;
commit;
exec dbms_stats.gather_table_stats(user, 'phone_call');
```

Listing 11-20 shows a script to create a table with a static list of phone codes for the United Kingdom. You can download this list using http://www.area-codes.org.uk/uk-area-codes.xlsx and import it manually if you do not have permission to get it via httpuritype in Oracle.

Listing 11-20. Table containing a list of phone codes

```
create table phone_code as
with tbl as
 (select regexp_substr(httpuritype('http://www.area-codes.org.
 uk/full-uk-area-code-list.php')
                    .getclob(),
                    '<table class="info">.*?</table>',
                    1,
                    1,
                    'n') c
    from dual)
select *
  from xmltable('/table/tr' passing xmltype((select c from tbl))
             columns
                code varchar2(6) path '/tr/td[1]',
                area varchar2(50) path '/tr/td[2]')
 order by 1;
exec dbms_stats.gather_table_stats(user, 'phone_call');
```

The goal is to calculate the total duration for each code.

There are some specifics in pre-generated data:

1) For simplicity, phone numbers start with 01, but in reality the two first digits can be 01, 02, 03, 05, 07, 08, and 09.

2) Some phone numbers are incorrect, because codes for them do not exist: for example, 0119. This is a side effect of generation and such calls will be excluded from the result.

3) Numbers are not unique, which can be easily checked with the query below.

```
select count(*) cnt_all, count(distinct num)
cnt_dist from phone_call;

 CNT_ALL CNT_DIST

---------- ----------
   1000000   999490
```

Speaking about phone codes, one code may be a prefix for another. In such cases, the longest code that is a prefix for the phone number is the actual code.

```
select *
  from phone_code pc1
  join phone_code pc2
    on pc2.code like pc1.code || '%'
   and pc2.code <> pc1.code
 order by 1, 3;
```

CODE	AREA	CODE	AREA
01387	Dumfries	013873	Langholm
01524	Lancaster	015242	Hornby
01539	Kendal	015394	Hawkshead
01539	Kendal	015395	Grange-Over-Sands
01539	Kendal	015396	Sedbergh
01697	Brampton (6 figure numbers)	016973	Wigton
01697	Brampton (6 figure numbers)	016974	Raughton Head
01697	Brampton (6 figure numbers)	016977	Brampton (4 and 5 figure numbers)
01768	Penrith	017683	Appleby
01768	Penrith	017684	Pooley Bridge
01768	Penrith	017687	Keswick
01946	Whitehaven	019467	Gosforth

```
12 rows selected.
```

The possible length of the prefixes starting with 01 is 4, 5, and 6 digits.

```
select length(code) l, count(*) cnt
  from phone_code
 where code like '01%'
 group by length(code)
 order by 1;
```

```
         L        CNT
---------- ----------
         4         12
         5        582
         6         12
```

For other countries, the range of code lengths may be much wider and the number of cases when one code is a prefix for another may be much greater.

A straightforward solution is below:

```
select code, sum(duration) s
  from (select ca.rowid,
               num,
               duration,
               max(code)
               keep(dense_rank first order by length(code)
               desc) code
          from phone_call ca
          left join phone_code co
            on ca.num like co.code || '%'
         group by ca.rowid, num, duration)
 where code is not null
 group by code
 order by code;
```

To minimize output and fetching, we will be using an aggregate function on top of inline view for performance testing.

```
select sum(code * sum(duration)) s, count(*) cnt
  from (select ca.rowid,
               num,
               duration,
               max(code)
               keep(dense_rank first order by length(code)
               desc) code
          from phone_call ca
          join phone_code co
            on ca.num like co.code || '%'
         group by ca.rowid, num, duration)
 group by code;

         S         CNT
---------- ----------
2884843733         606

select * from table(dbms_xplan.display_cursor(null,null,
'IOSTATS LAST'));
```

Id	Operation	Name	Starts	E-Rows	A-Rows	A-Time	Buffers
0	SELECT STATEMENT		1		1	00:01:08.44	1696K
1	SORT AGGREGATE		1	1	1	00:01:08.44	1696K
2	HASH GROUP BY		1	1	606	00:01:08.44	1696K
3	VIEW		1	2000K	701K	00:01:08.23	1696K
4	SORT GROUP BY		1	2000K	701K	00:01:08.06	1696K
5	NESTED LOOPS		1	2000K	702K	00:01:04.81	1696K
6	TABLE ACCESS FULL	PHONE_CODE	1	611	611	00:00:00.01	4
* 7	TABLE ACCESS FULL	PHONE_CALL	611	3273	702K	00:01:04.57	1696K

As we see from the plan, temporary tablespace was not used during execution (there are no Reads/Writes columns) and all the data was read from memory. The only possible join method is NESTED LOOPS because of a predicate containing the like operator. In fact, most of the time was spent on doing NESTED LOOPS, and further grouping and ordering added just 3 seconds.

To get a table cached in memory you may want to disable direct path reads – "alter session set events '10949 trace name context forever, level 1';".

Given that we know a possible range of code lengths in advance, we can use this fact to achieve a HASH JOIN method with codes if we add an auxiliary join to get all the prefixes for a given range.

```
select sum(code * sum(duration)) s, count(*) cnt
  from (select ca.rowid,
               num,
               duration,
               max(code)
               keep(dense_rank first order by length(code)
               desc) code
          from phone_call ca
        cross join (select rownum + 3 idx
                      from dual connect by rownum <= 3) x
          join phone_code co
            on substr(ca.num, 1, x.idx) = co.code
        group by ca.rowid, num, duration)
  group by code;
```

Id	Operation	Name	Starts	E-Rows	A-Rows	A-Time	Buffers
0	SELECT STATEMENT		1		1	00:00:04.86	2781
1	SORT AGGREGATE		1	1	1	00:00:04.86	2781
2	HASH GROUP BY		1	1	606	00:00:04.86	2781
3	VIEW		1	1000K	701K	00:00:04.65	2781
4	SORT GROUP BY		1	1000K	701K	00:00:04.47	2781
* 5	HASH JOIN		1	1000K	702K	00:00:03.34	2781
6	TABLE ACCESS FULL	PHONE_CODE	1	611	611	00:00:00.01	4
7	MERGE JOIN CARTESIAN		1	1000K	3000K	00:00:01.44	2777
8	VIEW		1	1	3	00:00:00.01	0
9	COUNT		1		3	00:00:00.01	0
10	CONNECT BY WITHOUT FILTERING		1		3	00:00:00.01	0
11	FAST DUAL		1	1	1	00:00:00.01	0
12	BUFFER SORT		3	1000K	3000K	00:00:00.79	2777
13	TABLE ACCESS FULL	PHONE_CALL	1	1000K	1000K	00:00:00.05	2777

The performance considerably improved after this modification and execution time dropped from 68 to 5 seconds – more than 10 times faster!

So cross joins generate three rows for each number to extract the prefix of the corresponding length, and after that we join with phone codes and take the longest prefix for each number. We may note that if join was successful for a code with 6 digits, then there is no reason to join with shorter codes for the current number. Ideally it would be nice to join with an ordered set until the first match but this is not possible in SQL. On the other hand, we can avoid any joins by using the PL/SQL function and associative array for look-up.

```
create or replace package phone_pkg is

  type tp_phone_code is table of int index by varchar2(6);
  g_phone_code tp_phone_code;
  function get_code(p_num in varchar2) return varchar2
  deterministic;

end phone_pkg;
/
create or replace package body phone_pkg is

  function get_code(p_num in varchar2) return varchar2
  deterministic is
    l_num varchar2(6);
  begin
    l_num := substr(p_num, 1, 6);

    while (l_num is not null) and (not g_phone_code.exists(l_
    num)) loop
      l_num := substr(l_num, 1, length(l_num) - 1);
    end loop;

    return l_num;
  end;
```

```
begin
  for cur in (select * from phone_code) loop
    g_phone_code(cur.code) := 1;
  end loop;
end phone_pkg;
/

select sum(code * sum(duration)) s, count(*) cnt
  from (select ca.rowid, num, duration, phone_pkg.get_code(num)
  code
          from phone_call ca
        group by ca.rowid, num, duration)
 group by code;

         S        CNT
---------- ----------
2884843733        607
```

Id	Operation	Name	Starts	E-Rows	A-Rows	A-Time	Buffers
0	SELECT STATEMENT		1		1	00:00:06.34	2777
1	SORT AGGREGATE		1	1	1	00:00:06.34	2777
2	HASH GROUP BY		1	1	607	00:00:06.34	2777
3	VIEW	VM_NWVW_0	1	1000K	1000K	00:00:05.71	2777
4	HASH GROUP BY		1	1000K	1000K	00:00:00.92	2777
5	TABLE ACCESS FULL	PHONE_CALL	1	1000K	1000K	00:00:00.06	2777

As you see, performance is a bit worse than that for an SQL approach with HASH JOIN, but if we add «pragma udf», then the PL/SQL approach will be faster.

Id	Operation	Name	Starts	E-Rows	A-Rows	A-Time	Buffers
0	SELECT STATEMENT		1		1	00:00:03.50	2777
1	SORT AGGREGATE		1	1	1	00:00:03.50	2777
2	HASH GROUP BY		1	1	607	00:00:03.50	2777
3	VIEW	VM_NWVW_0	1	1000K	1000K	00:00:03.03	2777
4	HASH GROUP BY		1	1000K	1000K	00:00:00.85	2777
5	TABLE ACCESS FULL	PHONE_CALL	1	1000K	1000K	00:00:00.05	2777

Further improvement is possible if we make the function deterministic and pass only the first 6 digits of the number as an argument. But with an increasing number and complexity of codes, the PL/SQL approach will be more and more preferable against SQL.

Limitations of the Subqueries

As it was already mentioned in the first chapter, any query that requires joining two and more recordsets may be implemented using explicit joins with a join keyword. However, in some cases subqueries may be preferable – for example, if we need to derive some attribute according to complex logic, we can use scalar subqueries to leverage scalar subquery caching and to avoid aggregate or analytic functions and other complexities in the main query. Subqueries in the where clause also may be more preferable than explicit joins – for instance, when ANTI or SEMI joins are required, please refer to the quiz "Top Paths" in Chapter 12 for a specific example (it does not require multiple nesting levels though).

Sometimes it's not possible to implement complex logic with multiple layers in correlated subquery because of nesting level limitation. These limitations are not well documented but easy to demonstrate.

```
select t1.*,
       (select *
          from (select t2.name
                  from t2 where t2.id = t1.id order by t2.name) t
         where rownum = 1) scalar
  from t1;

        ID N S
---------- - -
         0 X X
         1 A
```

```
select t1.*
  from t1
 where exists
 (select 1
          from t2
        where t2.id = t1.id
          and t2.id =
              (select id
                  from (select id from t3 where t3.id = t1.id
                  order by 1)
                  where rownum = 1));


        ID N
---------- -
         0 X
```

Queries work fine in Oracle 12c but fail on 11g with «ORA-00904: "D1"."DUMMY": invalid identifier»; in Oracle 12c you still may face ORA-00904 for more complex subqueries.

You can implement logic from a subquery in UDF as a workaround when the identifier from the main query is not visible in the subquery. In addition, Oracle 12c provides «pragma udf», which provides additional performance improvement when UDF is called in SQL.

If we have a look at final queries after transformations, we may notice an artificial bind variable introduced instead of a column from the main query.

```
select "T1"."ID" "ID",
       "T1"."NAME" "NAME",
       (select "T"."NAME" "NAME"
          from (select "T2"."NAME" "NAME"
                  from "T2" "T2"
                 where "T2"."ID" = :b1
```

```
                     order by "T2"."NAME") "T"
            where rownum = 1) "SCALAR"
    from "T1" "T1"

select "T1"."ID" "ID", "T1"."NAME" "NAME"
    from "T1" "T1"
 where exists (select 0
            from "T2" "T2"
          where "T2"."ID" = "T1"."ID"
            and "T2"."ID" = (select "from$_subquery$_003"."ID" "ID"
                             from (select "T3"."ID" "ID"
                                   from "T3" "T3"
                                   where "T3"."ID" = :b1
                                   order by "T3"."ID")
                             "from$_subquery$_003"
                             where rownum = 1))
```

The key difference between implementation logic in the UDF and in the subquery is that UDF returns data as of the time of the current call while the subquery returns data as of the time of query start.

To demonstrate the difference, let's create a table and function that takes around 5 seconds to execute.

```
create table t_scn(id, name) as
select 1, 'A' from dual
union all select 2, 'B' from dual
union all select 3, 'C' from dual;

create or replace function f_get_name(p_id in int) return
varchar2 is
begin
  dbms_lock.sleep(5);
  for i in (select * from t_scn where id = p_id) loop
    return(i.name);
```

```
    end loop;
end f_get_name;
/
```

While the query below is running

```
select t_main.*,
        (select name from t_scn where id = t_main.id) name1,
        f_get_name(t_main.id) name2
  from t_scn t_main;
```

Let's update the row in the concurrent session

```
update t_scn set name = 'X' where id = 3;
commit;
```

Result in main session is the following:

```
select t_main.*,
        (select name from t_scn where id = t_main.id) name1,
        f_get_name(t_main.id) name2
  from t_scn t_main;

        ID NAME  NAME1 NAME2
---------- ----- ----- -----
         1 A     A     A
         2 B     B     B
         3 C     C     X
```

This means that changes in a concurrent session during query execution have been picked up by the function. To avoid this we need to create an operator.

```
create operator op_get_name binding (int) return varchar2 using
f_get_name;
```

After repeating the test we see that the operator guarantees the same consistency as the subquery does.

```
select t_main.*,
       (select name from t_scn where id = t_main.id) name1,
       f_get_name(t_main.id) name2,
       op_get_name(t_main.id) name3
  from t_scn t_main;

    ID NAME   NAME1 NAME2 NAME3
---------- ----- ----- ----- -----
     1 A      A     A     A
     2 B      B     B     B
     3 C      C     X     C
```

Summary

If a recordset can be achieved using vanilla SQL, then this is the fastest way to get a result in the absolute majority of cases. However, for some specific tasks, PL/SQL may be more preferable, which was demonstrated based on examples divided into the following categories:

- Specifics of analytic functions;

- Iterative-like computations;

- Specifics of joins and subqueries.

It's important to note that technically one of the below approaches was used in each PL/SQL solution:

- Cursor for loop with processing in PL/SQL;

- Encapsulation in UDF and its usage in a query;

- Iterative execution of SQL statements.

I want to emphasize one more time, then, that the size of the fetch is very important in case of a cursor for loop processing.

In some cases, advanced SQL features like recursive subquery factoring help to efficiently get the result using SQL, which otherwise would require PL/SQL. The next chapter contains a series of tasks and their solutions using advanced SQL features as well as a performance comparison of different approaches.

CHAPTER 12

Solving SQL Quizzes

In this last chapter I'd like to consider specific real-life tasks and their solutions in SQL to demonstrate the power of Oracle SQL. The complexity of the tasks will vary a lot as well as the depth of analysis for different solutions. For a few tasks there will be both SQL and PL/SQL solutions, but the main accent in this chapter is on SQL capabilities.

For the sake of simplicity I tried to eliminate all the unnecessary details and make the problem formulations as simple as possible.

Converting into Decimal Numeral System

We have a string of symbols in some alphabet, and the goal is to convert it into decimal. The first symbol in the alphabet is zero, the value for the second symbol is one, and the value for the third symbol is two, and so on.

Solution

Let's start with the case when the alphabet is hexadecimal. In such a situation we can use the function to_number with the corresponding format model as shown in Listing 12-1.

© Alex Reprintsev 2018
A. Reprintsev, *Oracle SQL Revealed*, https://doi.org/10.1007/978-1-4842-3372-6_12

Listing 12-1. Converting hexadecimal value into decimal

```
var x varchar2(30)
var alphabet varchar2(30)
exec :alphabet := '0123456789ABCDEF';

PL/SQL procedure successfully completed.

exec :x := '1A0A';

PL/SQL procedure successfully completed.

select to_number(:x, 'XXXX') num from dual;

       NUM
----------
      6666
```

Listing 12-2 shows the SQL approach to convert a string from an arbitrary alphabet.

Listing 12-2. Converting string in arbitrary alphabet into decimal in SQL

```
select sum(power(base, level - 1) *
          (instr(:alphabet, substr(:x, -level, 1)) - 1)) num
  from (select length(:alphabet) base from dual)
connect by level <= length(:x);

       NUM
----------
      6666
```

Similar logic can be implemented in PL/SQL as shown in Listing 12-3.

Listing 12-3. Converting from arbitrary alphabet into decimal in PL/SQL

```
create or replace function f_10base(p_x        in varchar,
                                    p_alphabet in varchar
                                    default '0123456789ABCDEF')
   return number is
   result number := 0;
   l_base int := length(p_alphabet);
begin
   for i in 1 .. length(p_x) loop
     result := result + power(l_base, i - 1) *
               (instr(p_alphabet, substr(p_x, -i, 1)) - 1);
   end loop;
   return result;
end f_10base;
```

Let's compare the performance of the two approaches.

```
select sum(f_10base('ABC' || rownum)) f from dual connect by
level <= 1e6;

        F
----------
4.1760E+16

Elapsed: 00:00:16.61

select sum(num) f
  from (select (select sum(power(base, level - 1) *
                    (instr(:alphabet, substr(x,
                        -level, 1)) - 1)) num
          from (select length(:alphabet) base from dual)
        connect by level <= length(x)) num
```

307

```
        from (select 'ABC' || rownum x from dual connect by
        level <= 1e6));
```

```
        F
----------
4.1760E+16
```

```
Elapsed: 00:00:25.53
```

As you see, the PL/SQL solution is faster; nevertheless the context switches. You can use dbms_hprof and dbms_xplan with runtime execution statistics to check in more detail where the time is spent for the PL/SQL and SQL approach correspondingly.

To complete the picture let's measure timing for a built-in function.

```
select sum(to_number('ABC' || rownum, lpad('X', 10, 'X'))) f
  from dual
connect by level <= 1e6;
```

```
         F
----------
4.1760E+16
```

```
Elapsed: 00:00:01.11
```

The performance of an external C function would be approximately the same as for a built-in function. This task demonstrates that in some cases neither SQL nor PL/SQL is the best approach if performance is critical.

Connected Components

Graph theory is a huge subject with a number of terms, list of typical tasks, and various ways of representing the graphs. RDBMSs are not the best tool to work with generic graphs but SQL may be very efficient in working with specific classes of graphs known as hierarchies.

In real life you may face tasks with various types of graphs, and it's quite important to understand how this challenge can be approached, so this and the next quiz are a quick touch on the subject.

In the current task let's consider an undirected graph that is represented as a list of edges and shown on Figure 12-1.

```
create table edge(x1, x2) as
select 10,20 from dual
union all select 50,40 from dual
union all select 20,30 from dual
union all select 20,40 from dual
union all select 60,70 from dual
union all select 80,60 from dual
union all select 20,90 from dual;
```

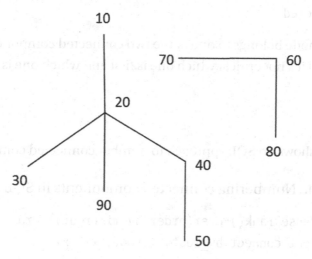

Figure 12-1. *Connected components*

The goal is to number the connected components. The result for the data above is this:

```
        X          GRP
---------- ----------
       10           1
       20           1
       30           1
       40           1
       50           1
       60           2
       70           2
       80           2
       90           1
```

9 rows selected.

So each node belongs to one of the two connected components in this example, and it's not critical which one is first and which one is second.

Solution

Listing 12-4 shows an SQL approach to number connected components.

Listing 12-4. Numbering connected components in SQL

```
select x, dense_rank() over(order by min(root)) grp
  from (select connect_by_root x1 root, x1, x2
          from edge
        connect by nocycle prior x1 in (x1, x2)
                       or prior x2 in (x1, x2))
  unpivot(x for x12 in(x1, x2))
  group by x
  order by 1, 2;
```

Given that the graph is undirected, edge X1 – X2 means that nodes may be traversed from X1 to X2 and the other way around; thus all the combinations of parent–child relations have been specified in the connect by condition to handle this.

Please pay attention that there is no start with clause, so for each edge we are building all connected edges and then use pivot to return all the connected nodes in column X. Finally, for each node we derive a minimal root (which is defined as the starting value for X1 but similarly it may be the starting value for X2) and number the connected components using dense_rank.

The query looks quite concise but in fact it's very inefficient because the same edges are traversed multiple times, but this is the only way to consider all possible connections.

The PL/SQL approach, however, may be very efficient and it's demonstrated in Listing 12-5. The required result can be achieved with a single table scan and fast look-ups in associative arrays.

Listing 12-5. Numbering connected components in PL/SQL

```
create or replace type to_2int as object (x int, grp int)
/
create or replace type tt_2int as table of to_2int
/
create or replace function f_connected_component return tt_2int
  pipelined is
  i_list number := 0;
  i       number;
  n       number;
  k       number;
  type tp1 is table of binary_integer index by binary_integer;
  type tp2 is table of tp1 index by binary_integer;
  t1 tp1;
  t2 tp2;
```

```
begin
  for c in (select x1, x2 from edge) loop
    if not t1.exists(c.x1) and not t1.exists(c.x2) then
      i_list := i_list + 1;
      t1(c.x1) := i_list;
      t1(c.x2) := i_list;
      t2(i_list)(c.x1) := null;
      t2(i_list)(c.x2) := null;
    elsif t1.exists(c.x1) and not t1.exists(c.x2) then
      t1(c.x2) := t1(c.x1);
      t2(t1(c.x1))(c.x2) := null;
    elsif t1.exists(c.x2) and not t1.exists(c.x1) then
      t1(c.x1) := t1(c.x2);
      t2(t1(c.x2))(c.x1) := null;
    elsif t1.exists(c.x1) and t1.exists(c.x2) and t1(c.x1) <>
    t1(c.x2) then
      n := greatest(t1(c.x1), t1(c.x2));
      k := least(t1(c.x1), t1(c.x2));
      i := t2(n).first;
      while (i is not null) loop
        t2(k)(i) := null;
        t1(i) := k;
        i := t2(n).next(i);
      end loop;
      t2.delete(n);
    end if;
  end loop;

  i := t1.first;
  for idx in 1 .. t1.count loop
```

```
    pipe row(to_2int(i, t1(i)));
    i := t1.next(i);
  end loop;
end;
```

The T1 array contains an index of a connected component for each node. The T2 array is the list of components where a component is an array of nodes. In fact, t2 was introduced for performance reasons, because if nodes for some edges belong to different components, then we need to re-renumber nodes for one of the components, and a list of nodes for each component makes this operation very fast.

```
select x, dense_rank() over(order by grp) grp
  from table(f_connected_component)
 order by x;
```

The efficiency of two approaches in non-comparable and, frankly speaking, SQL approach for this task is not reasonable at all. You can use the approach below to generate unique edges:

```
exec dbms_random.seed(11);
create table edge as
select trunc(dbms_random.value(1, 100)) x1,
       trunc(dbms_random.value(1, 100)) x2
  from dual
connect by level <= 61;
select count(distinct least(x1, x2) || ' ' || greatest(x1, x2))
from edge;
```

The PL/SQL approach takes a couple of milliseconds while an SQL query takes more than 3 minutes to execute on my laptop. If you add a few more elements, PL/SQL execution time still will be milliseconds while an SQL approach will take hours.

It's important to note though that if the goal is to return a connected component for a specific node instead of all connected components, then a full table scan may not be the optimal approach if nodes are indexed. In this case a combined SQL and PL/SQL approach to traverse the graph using a breadth-first search may be the best solution. This is not implementable in pure SQL even with recursive subquery factoring because traversing a graph requires maintaining a single list of visited nodes.

Ordering Dependencies

In this task we will implement an algorithm on a directed acyclic graph – DAG. The main difference between DAGs and hierarchies is that each hierarchy node has one parent while there may be multiple parents and children for some nodes in a DAG. This may result in various routes from one node to another in DAG. SQL can be used to traverse directed graphs in much more efficient way than undirected ones and the connect by condition looks the same as for hierarchies, but the issue with multiple possible paths between nodes may cause inefficiency.

A script from Listing 12-6 creates a table where each row represents a dependency between two objects. There are no cycle dependencies but several objects may depend on one specific object, as well as one object may reference a number of other objects. Obviously such data is DAG and not a hierarchy. Graphically it's shown on Figure 12-2, but please note that edges are represented as arrows because the graph is directed.

Listing 12-6. Creating table describing dependencies

```
create table d(name, referenced_name) as
(select null, 'o' from dual
union all select 'o', 'a' from dual
union all select 'o', 'd' from dual
union all select 'a', 'b' from dual
```

```
union all select 'd', 'b' from dual
union all select 'b', 'e' from dual
union all select 'b', 'c' from dual
union all select 'e', 'c' from dual
union all select 'c', 'x' from dual
union all select 'c', 'y' from dual
union all select 'c', 'z' from dual
);
```

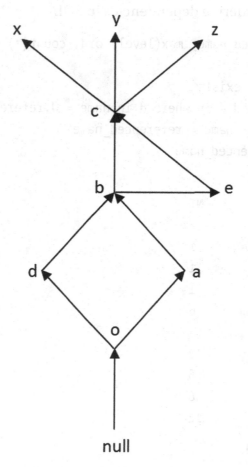

Figure 12-2. *Directed acyclic graph*

The goal is to number dependencies starting with independent objects. So independent objects represent the first level, objects that depend on independent objects and do not have unvisited dependencies represent the second level, and so on.

Solution

Listing 12-7 shows a straightforward approach to order dependencies.

Listing 12-7. Ordering dependencies in SQL

```
select referenced_name, max(level) ord, count(*) cnt
  from d
 start with not exists
 (select 1 from d d_in where d_in.name = d.referenced_name)
connect by prior name = referenced_name
 group by referenced_name
 order by 2, 1;
```

```
R           ORD          CNT
- ---------- ----------
x            1            1
y            1            1
z            1            1
c            2            6
e            3            3
b            4            12
a            5            6
d            5            6
o            6            12

9 rows selected.
```

So x, y, and z represent the first level. The second level contains only node c. Both b and e reference c but b also references e, so e must go before b and this is the only node on the third level. Node b represents the fourth level and so on.

You may notice that there is no «nocycle» keyword because there are no cycles according to requirements. This approach is not quite efficient because it builds all possible routes from independent nodes (we cannot call them leaves because our data is DAG and not a tree) and visits the same nodes multiple times. For example, there are 6 routes to node b: x->c->b, y->c->b, z->c->b, x->c->e->b, y->c-> e->b, z->c-> e->b so it visits two children from b six times each so b appears 12 times in the result set.

On the other hand we can use a breadth-first search algorithm for traversing graphs, but this requires maintaining a list of visited nodes, which is not doable using pure SQL.

Listing 12-8 shows PL/SQL implementation using a pipelined function. We maintain a list of visited nodes in the result collection and use the current collection to refer nodes added on a previous iteration.

Listing 12-8. Ordering dependencies in PL/SQL

```
create or replace type to_node as object (name varchar2(30),
lvl  number)
/
create or replace type tt_node as table of to_node
/
create or replace function f_traverse return tt_node is
  result  tt_node;
  current tt_node;
  tmp     tt_node;
  lvl     int := 1;
begin
```

```
    select to_node(referenced_name, lvl) bulk collect
      into current
      from (select distinct referenced_name
              from d
              where not exists
              (select null from d d_in where d_in.name =
              d.referenced_name));
    result := current;

    while true loop
      lvl := lvl + 1;

      select to_node(name, lvl) bulk collect
        into tmp
        from (select distinct d1.name
                from d d1
                join table(current) cur
                  on d1.referenced_name = cur.name
              -- add only nodes without unvisited children
                where not exists (select null
                        from d d2
                        left join table(result) r
                          on d2.referenced_name = r.name
                      where d1.name = d2.name
                        and r.name is null));

      if tmp.count = 0 then
        return result;
      else
        result  := result multiset union all tmp;
        current := tmp;
      end if;
    end loop;
end f_traverse;
```

This algorithm returns nodes on all levels including the last one, unlike the demonstrated SQL approach.

```
select * from table(f_traverse) order by 2, 1;

NAME           LVL
-----  ----------
x               1
y               1
z               1
c               2
e               3
b               4
a               5
d               5
o               6
                7

10 rows selected.
```

Performance may be further improved by creating indexes on the name and referenced_name and using a temporary table with an index to maintain a list of visited nodes. An SQL approach may be acceptable for relatively simple DAGs, but if there are complex dependencies, then PL/SQL will perform better. For instance, for the data below the PL/SQL approach will be 100 times faster but in fact there is only one DAG with just 65 nodes.

```
create table d as
select decode(type, 'to', 'x' || to_char(x + 1), 'n' || x || y)
name,
       decode(type, 'to', 'n' || x || y, 'x' || x)
       referenced_name
  from (select to_char(trunc((rownum - 1) / 7) + 1) x,
               to_char(mod(rownum, 7) + 1) y
          from dual
```

```
      connect by level <= 8 * 7) n,
   (select 'from' type
      from dual
   union all
   select 'to' from dual);
```

Percentile with Shift

Let's move on to quizzes with analytic functions.

The goal sounds simple: for each row, calculate a percentile for fixed value taking into account rows from the current row to n following.

A detailed explanation on how to calculate percentile can be found in Oracle documentation for percentile_cont function (also you can use Excel function - PERCENTILE).

For x = 0.3 and n = 4 the result is as follows:

Order	Value	Percentile
1	10	64
2	333	95.5
3	100	82
4	55	338.5
5	1000	1000

Solution

It's not possible to specify a windowing clause when using percentile_cont as an analytic function so it's applied to the entire partition. Given that we need to calculate percentile for a specific subset of rows starting with the current row, we can get the required subset using a self join and use an aggregate version of percentile_cont. See Listing 12-9.

Listing 12-9. Calculating percentile with shift using self join and percentile_cont

```
create table flow(ord, value) as
select 1, 10 from dual
union all select 2, 333 from dual
union all select 3, 100 from dual
union all select 4, 55 from dual
union all select 5, 1000 from dual;
select t1.*, percentile_cont(0.3) within group(order by
t2.value) pct
  from flow t1
  join flow t2 on t2.ord between t1.ord and t1.ord + 4
 group by t1.ord, t1.value;
```

```
      ORD      VALUE        PCT
---------- ---------- ----------
        1         10         64
        2        333       95.5
        3        100         82
        4         55      338.5
        5       1000       1000
```

We can get the same without percentile_cont if we implement calculations described in the documentation for that function. See Listing 12-10.

Listing 12-10. Calculating percentile with shift using self join and analytic functions

```
select tt.*,
       decode(frn, crn, frn_value,
              (crn - rn) * frn_value + (rn - frn) * crn_value)
              percentile
```

```
from (select t.ord,
             t.value,
             t.rn,
             t.frn,
             t.crn,
             max(decode(rnum, frn, v)) frn_value,
             max(decode(rnum, crn, v)) crn_value
        from (select t1.*,
                     t2.value v,
                     row_number() over(partition by t1.ord
                     order by t2.value) rnum,
                     1 + 0.3 * (count(*) over(partition by
                     t1.ord) - 1) rn,
                     floor(1 + 0.3 * (count(*) over(partition
                     by t1.ord) - 1)) frn,
                     ceil(1 + 0.3 * (count(*) over(partition
                     by t1.ord) - 1)) crn
                from flow t1
                join flow t2
                  on t2.ord between t1.ord and t1.ord + 4) t
        group by t.ord, t.value, t.rn, t.frn, t.crn) tt
 order by tt.ord;
```

ORD	VALUE	RN	FRN	CRN	FRN_VALUE	CRN_VALUE	PERCENTILE
1	10	2.2	2	3	55	100	64
2	333	1.9	1	2	55	100	95.5
3	100	1.6	1	2	55	100	82
4	55	1.3	1	2	55	1000	338.5
5	1000	1	1	1	1000	1000	1000

So we calculate frn and crn indexes for each subset, derive corresponding values, and perform linear interpolation when necessary. But do we really need self join?

Let's consider the solution when values are ordered in a source table. The result of the Listing 12-11 differs from the two previous queries because values are ordered by ord.

Listing 12-11. Calculating percentile with shift using analytic functions only

```
select ttt.*,
       decode(frn, crn, frn_value, (crn - rn) * frn_value +
       (rn - frn) * crn_value) percentile
  from (select tt.*,
                nth_value(value, ord + frn - 1)
                over(order by ord range between unbounded
                preceding and unbounded following) frn_v,
                nth_value(value, ord + crn - 1)
                over(order by ord range between unbounded
                preceding and unbounded following) crn_v,
                last_value(value)
                over(order by ord range between frn - 1
                following and frn - 1 following) frn_value,
                last_value(value)
                over(order by ord range between crn - 1
                following and crn - 1 following) crn_value
           from (select t.*, floor(rn) frn, ceil(rn) crn
                  from (select t0.*,
                               1 +
                               0.3 * (count(*)
```

```
                            over(order by ord range
                            between current row and 4
                            following) - 1) rn
                      from flow to) t) tt) ttt;
```

ORD	VALUE	RN	FRN	CRN	FRN_V	CRN_V	FRN_VALUE	CRN_VALUE	PERCENTILE
1	10	2,2	2	3	55	100	55	100	64
2	55	1,9	1	2	55	100	55	100	95,5
3	100	1,6	1	2	55	100	100	333	239,8
4	333	1,3	1	2	55	100	333	1000	533,1
5	1000	1	1	1	55	100	1000	1000	1000

Corresponding values for crn and frn indexes for each row have been derived in two completely different ways – nth_value/last_value. Moreover, the function nth_value (crn_v and frn_v columns) returns an incorrect result for Oracle 11g if its second parameter is not a constant (this bug has been fixed in 12c).

We can run a query from Listing 12-9 and get the same result, but, as it was already mentioned, this approach works only if the value ordered by ord. If that is not true, then calculating indexes crn and frn is not a problem at all, but deriving correspondent values is not possible with analytic functions – for each row we need to order its own subset of values (this logic is implemented in Listing 12-10 as «row_number() over(partition by t1.ord order by t2.value) rnum»).

N Consequent 1s

For the table below the goal is to find the number of sequences with 10 consequent 1s ordered by id. If there is, say, 11 consequent 11s, this means two sequences: from the 1st to 10th and from the 2nd to 11th row.

```
exec dbms_random.seed(1);
create table t_sign as
select rownum id,
       case when trunc(dbms_random.value(1, 10 + 1)) > 3
            then 1
            else 0
       end sign
  from dual
connect by rownum <= 1e6;
```

Solution

There are multiple possible approaches to a solution:

- A few layers of analytic functions

- Analytic function with windowing clause

- Model clause

- Pattern matching

Below you can see the code along with the timings. The following statements have been executed to avoid temporary tablespace usage and ensure that there is enough memory for work areas.

```
alter session set workarea_size_policy = manual;
alter session set sort_area_size = 2147483647;
```

Results are the following:

```
select count(*) cnt
  from (select t.*, sum(sign) over(partition by g order by id) s
          from (select id, sign, sum(x) over(order by id) g
                  from (select t0.*,
                               decode(nvl(lag(sign) over(order
                        by id), -1),
                                 sign,
                                 0,
                                 1) x
                    from t_sign t0)
              where sign <> 0) t)
  where s >= 10;

      CNT
----------
    28369

Elapsed: 00:00:03.11

select count(*)
  from (select id,
               sum(sign) over(order by id rows between 9
               preceding and current row) s
          from t_sign)
  where s = 10;

  COUNT(*)
----------
    28369

Elapsed: 00:00:01.45
```

```
select count(*) cnt from
(
  select *
  from t_sign
  model
  ignore nav
  dimension by (id)
  measures (sign, 0 s)
  rules
  (
   s[any] order by id = decode(sign[cv()], 0, 0, s[cv()-1]+
   sign[cv()])
  )
)
where s >= 10;

      CNT
----------
    28369

Elapsed: 00:00:04.64

select count(*)
from t_sign
match_recognize
(
  order by id
  one row per match
  after match skip to first one
  pattern (strt one{9})
  define
     strt as strt.sign = 1,
     one as one.sign = 1
) mr;
```

```
 COUNT(*)
----------
     28369
```

Elapsed: 00:00:01.55

So the fastest approaches are pattern matching and analytics with a windowing clause, next is a solution with several analytic functions that requires two sorts and finally the model cause.

Next Value

For each row from table

```
exec dbms_random.seed(1);
create table t_value as
select trunc(dbms_random.value(1, 1000 + 1)) value
  from dual
connect by level <= 1e5;
```

derive the next largest value.

Sample result:

value	next_value
1	2
2	3
2	3
3	null

Solution

It's not possible to use a lead function given that values may repeat so we cannot use a fixed shift. However, similar to the previous quiz, there are multiple approaches to the solution:

- A few layers of analytic functions

- Analytic function with windowing clause

- Model clause

- Pattern matching

Aggregate function «sum(nvl(next_value, 0) - value)» was used to minimize fetch.

```
select sum(nvl(next_value, 0) - value) s
  from (select value, max(next_value) over(partition by value)
  next_value
        from (select value,
                     decode(lead(value, 1) over(order by
                     value),
                            value,
                            to_number(null),
                            lead(value, 1) over(order by
                            value)) next_value
              from t_value));

         S
----------
     69907

Elapsed: 00:00:02.33
```

```
select sum(nvl(next_value, 0) - value) s
  from (select value,
                min(value) over(order by value range between 1
                following and 1 following) next_value
           from t_value);

        S
----------
    69907

Elapsed: 00:00:01.79

select sum(nvl(next_value, 0) - value) s
from
(
  select value, next_value
  from t_value
  model
  dimension by (row_number () over (order by value desc) rn)
  measures(value, cast(null as number) next_value)
  rules
  (
    next_value[rn > 1] order by rn =
    decode(value[cv()], value[cv()-1], next_value[cv()-1],
    value[cv()-1])
  )
);

        S
----------
    69907

Elapsed: 00:00:05.94
```

```
select sum(nvl(next_value, 0) - value) s
from (select * from t_value union all select null from dual)
match_recognize
(
  order by value nulls last
  measures
    final first (next_val.value) as next_value
  all rows per match
  after match skip to next_val
  pattern (val+ {-next_val-})
  define
    val as val.value = first(val.value)
) mr;
         S
----------
     69907
```

Elapsed: 00:00:01.53

The most efficient solutions for this quiz are also pattern matching and analytics with a windowing clause, then a solution with lead and max functions and finally a model clause. It's quite important to use a minimally required window in a windowing clause. For example, if you specify "range between 1 following and unbounded following," then the result will be correct but the elapsed time will be few orders of magnitude greater than for "range between 1 following and 1 following."

One specific row with null values has been added for a pattern matching solution so that the last row in the original tables has a next row.

Next Branch

Let's define "next branch" as the nearest row after a traversing hierarchy such as its row number greater than for current row while its level is less or equal to the current level. This value may be very useful if we want to apply some logic for all children of a given node.

The goal is to find a solution without joins and subqueries.

This approach with joins is trivial:

```
with t(id, parent_id, description, amount) as
(
  select 1 id, null, 'top', 10  from dual
  union all select 2, 1, 'top-one', 100 from dual
  union all select 3, 2, 'one-one', 2000 from dual
  union all select 4, 2, 'one-two', 3000 from dual
  union all select 5, 1, 'top-two', 1000 from dual
  union all select 6, 2, 'one-three', 300 from dual
  union all select 7, 6, 'three-one', 1 from dual
)
, h as
(
  select id, parent_id, description, amount, level l, rownum rn
    from t
    start with id = 1
  connect by parent_id = prior id
)
select h.*,
       (select min(rn)
          from h h0
         where h0.rn > h.rn
           and h0.l <= h.l) next_branch
  from h;
```

ID	PARENT_ID	DESCRIPTI	AMOUNT	L	RN	NEXT_BRANCH
1		top	10	1	1	
2	1	top-one	100	2	2	7
3	2	one-one	2000	3	3	4
4	2	one-two	3000	3	4	5
6	2	one-three	300	3	5	7
7	6	three-one	1	4	6	7
5	1	top-two	1000	2	7	

7 rows selected.

For rows with ID in (3, 4), the next branch is the next row because it has the same level. For rows with ID in (2, 6, 7), the next branch is row with RN = 7 because it has a lower level.

Solution

It may seem that logic can be easily rewritten with analytic functions, but we face two limitations that have been demonstrated earlier for analytic functions in the corresponding chapter.

1) It's not possible to specify multiple ranges when ordering by multiple columns. In this particular case we cannot specify a range for rn

   rn range between 1 following and unbounded following

   and in the same time range for l

   l range between unbounded preceding and current row

2) If we try to order by only one column whether it's l or rn, we have to limit rows by the second column in a function, but it's not possible to use the current value of that attribute in the expression for a function.

As was already mentioned in the chapter about model clauses, the first case can be easily implemented using a model clause while the second case requires iterations and an auxiliary measure to use it as a value of a given attribute from the current row on each iteration.

Listing 12-12 shows the implementation using the model clause.

Listing 12-12. Finding next branch using model clause

```
select *
from h
model
dimension by (l, rn)
measures (id, parent_id, rn xrn, 0 next_branch)
rules
(
  next_branch[any, any] order by rn, l =
    min(xrn)[l <= cv(l), rn > cv(rn)]
);
```

L	RN	ID	PARENT_ID	XRN	NEXT_BRANCH
1	1	1		1	
2	2	2	1	2	7
3	3	3	2	3	4
3	4	4	2	4	5
3	5	6	2	5	7
4	6	7	6	6	7
2	7	5	1	7	

```
7 rows selected.
```

```
select *
  from h
model
dimension by (rn)
measures (id, parent_id, l, 0 l_cur, rn xrn, 0 next_branch)
rules iterate (1e6) until l[iteration_number+2] is null
(
  l_cur[rn > iteration_number + 1] = l[iteration_number + 1],
  next_branch[iteration_number + 1] =
    min(case when l <= l_cur then xrn end)[rn > cv(rn)]
)
order by rn;
```

RN	ID	PARENT_ID	L	L_CUR	XRN	NEXT_BRANCH
1	1		1	0	1	
2	2	1	2	1	2	7
3	3	2	3	2	3	4
4	4	2	3	3	4	5
5	6	2	3	3	5	7
6	7	6	4	3	6	7
7	5	1	2	4	7	

7 rows selected.

I believe there is no need to say that the first approach is more efficient than the second one with iterations and auxiliary measure, but better solution may be provided with analytic functions as shown in Listing 12-13 if we made some assumptions.

Listing 12-13. Finding next branch using analytic functions

```
select h0.*,
       nullif(max(rn) over(order by s range between current
                 row and x - 1e-38 following),
             count(*) over()) + 1 next_branch
  from (select h.*,
               power(2 * 10, 1 - 1) x,
               sum(power(2 * 10, 1 - 1)) over(order by rn) s
          from h) h0;
```

ID	PARENT_ID	L	RN	X	S	NEXT_BRANCH
1		1	1	1	1	
2	1	2	2	,05	1,05	7
3	2	3	3	,0025	1,0525	4
4	2	3	4	,0025	1,055	5
6	2	3	5	,0025	1,0575	7
7	6	4	6	,000125	1,057625	7
5	1	2	7	,05	1,107625	

```
7 rows selected.
```

If we assume that each node has not more than 10 direct descendants, then the sum of x for all possible descendants for a given node on the nth level can be calculated as the sum of the series below

$$\sum_{i=1}^{\infty} \frac{10^i}{(10*2)^{i+n-1}} = \sum_{i=1}^{\infty} \frac{10^i}{20^{n-1}*10^i*2^i} = \frac{1}{20^{n-1}} \sum_{i=1}^{\infty} \frac{1}{2^i} = \frac{1}{20^{n-1}}$$

In other words, the <u>sum of x for all descendants does not exceed value x for a given node</u>, or more specifically: for the node on the 1st level, the limit of the sum equals to 1; for the node on the 2nd level, the limit of the sum equals to 0.05 and so on.

Practically, depth is limited with number precision and we assume that the difference between x and the sum of x for all descendants is never less than 1e-38, thus the windowing clause is «range between current row and x - 1e-38 following»; so the window spans the current node and all its descendants. If we defined range as «range between 1e-38 following and x - 1e-38 following » then the window covers only all descendants.

Eventually we managed to calculate a columns s that can be used to define a window with a range by x. This technique allows us to solve various tasks that require applying some logic to all descendants for a given node, possible, including the node itself.

For example, if we need to calculate the number of all descendants or their sum, including the value of the current node, then it can be done as shown in Listing 12-14.

Listing 12-14. Applying logic using window by all descendants

```
select h0.*,
       count(*) over(order by s range between 1e-38 following
       and x - 1e-38 following) cnt_children,
       sum(amount) over(order by s range between current row
       and x - 1e-38 following) h_sum
  from (select h.*,
               power(2 * 10, 1 - 1) x,
               sum(power(2 * 10, 1 - 1)) over(order by rn) s
          from h) h0;
```

ID	PARENT_ID	DESCRIPTI	AMOUNT	L	RN	X	S	CNT_CHILDREN	H_SUM
1		top	10	1	1	1	1	6	6411
2	1	top-one	100	2	2	,05	1,05	4	5401
3	2	one-one	2000	3	3	,0025	1,0525	0	2000
4	2	one-two	3000	3	4	,0025	1,055	0	3000
6	2	one-three	300	3	5	,0025	1,0575	1	301
7	6	three-one	1	4	6	,000125	1,057625	0	1
5	1	top-two	1000	2	7	,05	1,107625	0	1000

7 rows selected.

Without an analytic function it would require a join/subquery or model clause. However, Oracle 12c provides one more way of doing that – pattern matching.

```
select *
  from (select h.*, power(2 * 10, 1 - 1) x from h)
match_recognize
(
  order by rn
  measures
    first (id) as id,
    first (parent_id) as parent_id,
    first (l) as l,
    first (rn) as rn,
    final count(*)-1 cnt_children,
    final sum(amount) h_sum
  one row per match
  after match skip to next row
  pattern (y+)
  define
    y as sum(x) < 2 * first(x)
) mr;
```

ID	PARENT_ID	L	RN	CNT_CHILDREN	H_SUM
1		1	1	6	6411
2	1	2	2	4	5401
3	2	3	3	0	2000
4	2	3	4	0	3000
6	2	3	5	1	301
7	6	4	6	0	1
5	1	2	7	0	1000

7 rows selected.

In this solution we used a condition with aggregate function «sum(x) < 2 * first(x)» instead of a cumulative sum. An equivalent condition using both x and s is «last(s) - first(s) < first(x)». If, however, you use «max(s) - min(s) < first(x)», then the query fails with ORA-03113 (versions 12.2.0.1.0, 12.1.0.2.0). Using pattern matching, specific functions first/last is more preferable than aggregate functions min/max because we know that s is monotonically increasing.

It's possible to use a rule with min/max; however if we use all rows instead of one row and apply filtering, this obviously introduces additional costs.

```
select *
  from (select h.*,
               power(2 * 10, 1 - 1) x,
               sum(power(2 * 10, 1 - 1)) over(order by rn) s
          from h) h0
match_recognize
(
  order by rn
  measures
    final count(*)-1 cnt_children,
    final sum(amount) h_sum,
    count(*) cnt
  all rows per match
  after match skip to next row
  pattern (y+)
  define
    y as max(s) - min(s) < first(x)
) mr
where cnt = 1;
```

And finally, the most important detail when using pattern matching is that there is no need to use a trick based on the limit of the sum if we want to find the next branch or apply some logic to all the descendants. We just need to specify a pattern that matches all descendants and start the search from every row -«after match skip to next row».

```
select *
  from h
match_recognize
(
  order by rn
  measures
    classifier() cls,
    first (id) as id,
    first (parent_id) as parent_id,
    first (l) as l,
    first (rn) as rn,
    first (amount) as amount,
    final count(child.*) cnt_children,
    final sum(amount) h_sum
  one row per match
  after match skip to next row
  pattern (strt child+|no_children)
  define
    child as child.l > strt.l
) mr;
```

CLS	ID	PARENT_ID	L	RN	AMOUNT	CNT_CHILDREN	H_SUM
CHILD	1		1	1	10	6	6411
CHILD	2	1	2	2	100	4	5401
NO_CHILDREN	3	2	3	3	2000	0	2000
NO_CHILDREN	4	2	3	4	3000	0	3000
CHILD	6	2	3	5	300	1	301
NO_CHILDREN	7	6	4	6	1	0	1
NO_CHILDREN	5	1	2	7	1000	0	1000

```
7 rows selected.
```

Random Subset

For the table containing n rows with a primary key and values from 1 to n without gaps:

```
create table t_id_value as
select rownum id, 'name' || rownum value from dual connect by
rownum <= 2e6;
alter table t_id_value add constraint pk_t_id_value primary
key (id);
```

The goal is to return k unique random rows such as the probability that a row appears in the result is equal for all rows. For simplicity let's assume k equals 10.

Solution

A trivial solution is below:

```
select *
  from (select * from t_id_value order by dbms_random.value)
 where rownum <= 10;
```

In this case we generate dbms_random.value for all rows and then take the first 10 rows with the lowest value.

If the table is wide – that is, contains many columns or some long strings, then we can optimize sort by ordering only rowids and introducing an additional join.

```
select *
  from t_id_value
 where rowid in
       (select *
          from (select rowid from t_id_value order by
          dbms_random.value)
         where rownum <= 10);
```

For the table introduced in this task, demonstrated optimization does not lead to noticeable improvement though.

Given that all IDs start from 1 and there are no gaps, we can use the approach below with generating 10 random IDs.

```
select *
  from t_id_value
 where id in (select trunc(dbms_random.value(1,
                      (select max(id) from t_id_value) + 1))
                 from dual
              connect by level <= 10);
```

There is some chance though that we generate duplicates. For example, the query below returns 9 rows instead of 10:

```
exec dbms_random.seed(48673);

PL/SQL procedure successfully completed.

select *
  from t_id_value
```

```
where id in (select trunc(dbms_random.value(1,
                  (select max(id) from t_id_value) + 1))
            from dual
            connect by level <= 10);
```

```
        ID VALUE
---------- -------------------------------------------
    564703 name564703
    917426 name917426
   1230672 name1230672
   1837951 name1837951
   1367140 name1367140
    248223 name248223
    873017 name873017
    581109 name581109
   1206874 name1206874
```

9 rows selected.

We can work around it by pre-generating a few reserve rows and by selecting k unique rows. However, to avoid even a theoretical chance of duplicates, we need to validate for the kth row whether all generated rows are unique. If not, then generate a new row and re-validate. This approach with referencing all generated rows can be implemented using a model clause or recursive subquery factoring.

```
select *
  from t_id_value
 where id in
 (
  select distinct x
    from dual
  model return updated rows
```

```
dimension by (0 id)
measures(0 i, 0 x, (select max(id) from t_id_value) max_id)
rules
iterate (1e9) until i[0] = 10
(
 x[iteration_number] = trunc(dbms_random.value(1,
 max_id[0] + 1)),
 i[0] = case when iteration_number < 10 - 1
            then 0 else count(distinct x)[any] end
)
);
```

If we use «exec dbms_random.seed(48673)», then validation will be executed twice: after the 10th generated row and after the 11th, but in mostly all cases their validation will happen only once.

A solution using recursive subquery factoring is below:

```
with rec(lvl, batch)
    as (select 1,
                numbers(trunc(dbms_random.value(1, 2e6 + 1)))
           from dual
        union all
        select lvl + 1,
               batch multiset union all
               numbers(trunc(dbms_random.value(1, 2e6 + 1)))
          from rec
         where case when lvl < 10 then 0
                -- cardinality(set())
                -- does not work in recursive member
                    else (select count(*) from table(set
                    (rec.batch)))
                end < 10)
```

```
select *
  from t_id_value
 where id in (select column_value
                from (select *
                        from (select * from rec t order by lvl
                              desc)
                       where rownum = 1),
                     table(batch));
```

We accumulate generated values in a column batch that has data type numbers and check uniqueness starting from a kth iteration, similarly to a model solution. For simplicity, the maximum value has been hard-coded instead of using a scalar subquery.

The disadvantage of SQL approaches is that we need to scan all generated values to check uniqueness, which may be inefficient for large k. PL/SQL helps to avoid that if we use an associative array (this logic can be encapsulated in a pipelined function and used in SQL).

```
declare
  type tp_arr is table of binary_integer index by binary_integer;
  arr tp_arr;
  i    int := 0;
begin
  while true loop
    arr(trunc(dbms_random.value(1, 2e6 + 1))) := null;
    i := i + 1;
    if i >= 10 and arr.count = 10 then
      exit;
    end if;
  end loop;
```

```
  i := arr.first;
  while (i is not null) loop
    dbms_output.put_line(i);
    i := arr.next(i);
  end loop;
end;
/
```

On the other hand, the more values we need to generate, the more preferable the first approach with ordering by random value. Also I'd like to highlight that all approaches that generate k unique values work only if there are no gaps. So if the primary key is varchar2, then we may need to read all the data and map all the rows to array or integers.

Covering Ranges

For the table containing ranges from a to b such as b > a and a is unique

```
create table t_range(a, b) as
(select 1, 15 from dual
union all select 3, 17 from dual
union all select 6, 19 from dual
union all select 10, 21 from dual
union all select 17, 26 from dual
union all select 18, 29 from dual
union all select 20, 32 from dual
union all select 24, 35 from dual
union all select 28, 45 from dual
union all select 30, 49 from dual);
```

we need to return covering ranges (1:15), (17:26), (28:45), that is, we start from the row with the minimal a and then pick up the row with the minimal a greater than the current b and so on.

Solution

Relatively simple, it can be solved using connect by and analytic functions, but performance is quite inefficient in this case.

```
select a, b
  from (select a,
               b,
               min(a) over(order by a range between b - a
               following
                             and unbounded following) as next_a,
               min(a) over() start_a
          from t_range)
 start with a = start_a
connect by prior next_a = a;
```

```
         A          B
---------- ----------
         1         15
        17         26
        28         45
```

```
select a, b
  from (select a, b, lag(a) over(order by a) as lag_a from
  t_range)
 start with lag_a is null
connect by a >= prior b and lag_a < prior b;
```

```
         A          B
---------- ----------
         1         15
        17         26
        28         45
```

A quite elegant and efficient solution can be demonstrated using pattern matching.

```
select *
 from t_range
match_recognize
(
  order by a
  all rows per match
  pattern((x|{-dummy-})+)
  define
    x as nvl(last(x.b, 1), 0) <= x.a
) mr;
```

```
          A          B
---------- ----------
          1         15
         17         26
         28         45
```

There are some alternative solutions using a model clause but their performance is worse than pattern-matching solutions.

Zeckendorf Representation

Zeckendorf's theorem states that every positive integer can be represented uniquely as the sum of one or more distinct Fibonacci numbers in such a way that the sum does not include any two consecutive Fibonacci numbers.

For any given positive integer, Zeckendorf representation can be found by using a greedy algorithm, choosing the largest possible Fibonacci number at each stage.

Our goal is to find representation that satisfies the conditions of Zeckendorf's theorem for all numbers from table n.

```
create table n(num) as select 222 from dual union all select
3690 from dual;
```

The expected result is

```
    NUM PATH
---------- ------------------------------
    222 144+55+21+2
   3690 2584+987+89+21+8+1
```

For simplicity, let's assume that we have a table fib(lvl, value) with the first 20 Fibonacci numbers. Numbers can be generated using one of many ways described in this book.

Solution

A brute force solution can be implemented using connect by as follows.

- Generate all permutations of Fibonacci numbers that are less than a given number;

- Filter only those with sum value equals to given number;

- Filter permutation with a min number of elements.

Listing 12-15. Zeckendorf representation using connect by

```
with n_fib as
 (select num, value, lvl, max(lvl) over(partition by num)
 max_lvl
    from n
    join fib
      on fib.value <= n.num),
```

```
permutation as
 (select num, sys_connect_by_path(value, '+') path, level p_lvl
    from n_fib
   start with lvl = max_lvl
  connect by prior num = num
         and prior value > value
         and sys_guid() is not null)
select num,
       max(substr(path, 2)) keep(dense_rank first order by
       p_lvl) path
  from (select num, path, p_lvl
          from permutation p
           join fib
             on instr(p.path || '+', '+' || fib.value || '+') > 0
          group by num, path, p_lvl
          having sum(value) = num)
 group by num
 order by num;
```

Obviously this approach is extremely inefficient, and we can instead, for each input number, loop thorough Fibonacci numbers in descending order and on each step mark a current Fibonacci numbers if its sum with the numbers marked so far does not exceed the input number. This iterative logic can be implemented using recursive subquery factoring, for example.

Listing 12-16. Zeckendorf representation using recursive subquery factoring and cross apply

```
with n_fib as
 (select num, value, lvl, max(lvl) over(partition by num) max_lvl
    from n
    join fib
      on fib.value <= n.num),
```

```
rec(lvl, num, f, s) as
 (select 1, n_fib.num, n_fib.value, 0
    from n_fib
   where n_fib.lvl = n_fib.max_lvl
  union all
  select rec.lvl + 1, l.num, l.value, rec.f + rec.s
    from rec
   cross apply (select *
                     from (select *
                             from n_fib
                            where n_fib.num = rec.num
                              and n_fib.value + rec.s + rec.f
                                 <= rec.num
                            order by lvl desc)
                    where rownum = 1) l)
cycle lvl set c to 1 default 0
select num, listagg(f, '+') within group(order by f desc) path
  from rec
 group by num
 order by num;
```

The lateral view has been used in Listing 12-16 in order to get on each step a max Fibonacci number that satisfies a condition. As was mentioned in the previous chapter, "When PL/SQL Is Better Than Vanilla SQL," there may be a false positive cycle detection if there are multiple joins or lateral views in a recursive member; «cycle» clause was used to handle that.

This solution can be simplified and optimized by using a scalar subquery instead of a lateral view – in this case, a query can be executed on Oracle 11g.

Listing 12-17. Zeckendorf representation using recursive subquery factoring. Simplified

```
with rec(lvl, num, f, s) as
  (select 1,
          n.num,
          (select max(fib.value) from fib where fib.value
          <= n.num),
          0
     from n
   union all
   select lvl + 1,
          d.num,
          (select max(fib.value)
              from fib
             where fib.value <= d.num - (d.f + d.s)),
          d.f + d.s
     from rec d
    where d.s + d.f < d.num)
select num, listagg(f, '+') within group(order by f desc) path
  from rec
 group by num
 order by num;
```

As you see, table fib is scanned multiple times for both approaches. To avoid multiple scans we can join tables n and fib and apply a model on top of the joined recordset.

Listing 12-18. Zeckendorf representation using model clause

```
with n_fib as
 (select num, value, lvl
    from n
    join fib
      on fib.value <= n.num)
, m as
(select *
   from n_fib
  model
 ignore nav
 partition by (num part)
 dimension by (lvl)
 measures (num, value, 0 x)
 rules
 (
   x[any] order by lvl desc =
   case when x[cv(lvl)+1] + value[cv(lvl)] <= num[cv(lvl)]
        then x[cv(lvl)+1] + value[cv(lvl)]
        else x[cv(lvl)+1]
   end
 ))
select num, listagg(f, '+') within group(order by f desc) path
  from (select num, max(value) f from m group by num, x)
 group by num
 order by num;
```

And finally the most efficient solution can be implemented using pattern matching.

Listing 12-19. Zeckendorf representation using pattern matching

```
select num,
       (select listagg(value, '+')
               within group(order by value desc) path
          from (select n.num, fib.value from fib) y
        match_recognize
        (
          order by value desc
          all rows per match
          pattern((x|{-dummy-})+)
          define
            x as sum(x.value) <= num
        ) mr
       ) path
  from n;
```

Instead of a scalar subquery we could have used an explicit join with a fib table and «partition by num order by value desc» in a match recognize clause.

Implementation using recursive subquery factoring cannot be done in a correlated scalar subquery because in this case it's not possible to refer columns from the main table.

Let's demonstrate this on a simple example:

```
select t.*,
       (with rec(lvl) as (select /*t.id*/ 5 lvl from dual
                          union all
                          select rec.lvl + 1 from rec where
                          lvl < 10)
        select listagg(lvl, ', ') within group(order by lvl)
          from rec) str
  from (select 5 id from dual) t;
```

If you uncomment t.id the query will fail with «ORA-00904: "T"."ID": invalid identifier».

Top Paths

For the table with the list of paths, return only those that do not have subpaths.

Listing 12-20. The list of paths

```
create table t_path(path) as
select '/tmp/cat/' from dual
union all select '/tmp/cata/' from dual
union all select '/tmp/catb/' from dual
union all select '/tmp/catb/catx/' from dual
union all select '/usr/local/' from dual
union all select '/usr/local/lib/liba/' from dual
union all select '/usr/local/lib/libx/' from dual
union all select '/var/cache/' from dual
union all select '/var/cache/'||'xyz'||rownum||'/' from dual
connect by level <= 1e6;
```

For the data from Listing 12-20, the expected result is the following:

```
PATH
-----------------------------------------------------------
/tmp/cat/
/tmp/cata/
/tmp/catb/
/usr/local/
/var/cache/
```

Solution

A straightforward solution is self join on like and filtering. The main disadvantage of this approach is that the join method can be only NESTED LOOPS because of the join predicate, or technically there will be a full scan of an outer table for each row from the inner table. This can be improved a little bit if we use not exists instead of an outer join – in this case Oracle will scan the outer table until the first match for each record from the inner table is found.

Listing 12-21. Filtering top paths using join/subquery

```
select t_path.path
  from t_path
  left join t_path t_top
    on t_path.path like t_top.path || '%_/'
 where t_top.path is null;

PATH
-----------------------------------------------------------
/tmp/cat/
/tmp/cata/
/tmp/catb/
/usr/local/
/var/cache/

Elapsed: 00:00:34.54
select path
  from t_path
 where not exists (select null
         from t_path t_top
        where t_path.path like t_top.path || '%_/');
```

```
PATH
---------------------------------------------------------
/tmp/cat/
/tmp/cata/
/tmp/catb/
/usr/local/
/var/cache/
```

Elapsed: 00:00:09.63

After rewriting the query with a not exist execution, time dropped more than thrice. If we specify an additional filter «and where rownum = 1» in a subquery, this will have no impact on performance because of the way how filter works.

Apparently most of the time is spent on joining and evaluating the like predicate and it would be good to get rid of it. We can derive all subpaths for each path and if some paths have common subpaths, then return only those with a minimal number of subpaths as shown in Listing 12-22.

Listing 12-22. Filtering top path using lateral and group by

```
with t0 as
 (select path,
         length(path) - length(replace(path, '/')) - 1 depth,
         substr(path, 1, instr(path, '/', 1, l.id + 1)) token
    from t_path,
         lateral (select rownum id
                    from dual
                  connect by level <
                  length(path) - length(replace(path, '/'))) l),
t1 as (select t0.*, min(depth) over(partition by token) m from t0)
select path from t1 group by path, depth having depth = min(m)
 order by path;
```

PATH

```
/tmp/cat/
/tmp/cata/
/tmp/catb/
/usr/local/
/var/cache/
```

Elapsed: 00:00:22.78

In this case the lateral view also causes NESTED LOOPS, which is quite CPU intensive and the final execution time is somewhere between the first and second query from Listing 12-21.

If a maximal possible path depth is known in advance, then we can implement the following approach: for each subpath we check if the current path contains something after subpath (p_i is not null) and there is another path that terminates in this subpath ($m_i = 0$) then the current path is filtered out.

Listing 12-23. Filtering out top path using tricky analytics

```
select path
  from (select t1.*,
              min(nvl2(p2, 1, 0)) over(partition by p1) m2,
              min(nvl2(p3, 1, 0)) over(partition by p1, p2) m3,
              min(nvl2(p4, 1, 0)) over(partition by p1, p2,
              p3) m4,
              min(nvl2(p5, 1, 0)) over(partition by p1, p2,
              p3, p4) m5
```

```
            from (select path,
                       substr(path, i1, i2 - i1) p1,
                       substr(path, i2, i3 - i2) p2,
                       substr(path, i3, i4 - i3) p3,
                       substr(path, i4, i5 - i4) p4,
                       substr(path, i5, i6 - i5) p5
                  from (select path,
                              instr(path, '/', 1, 1) i1,
                              instr(path, '/', 1, 2) i2,
                              instr(path, '/', 1, 3) i3,
                              instr(path, '/', 1, 4) i4,
                              instr(path, '/', 1, 5) i5,
                              instr(path, '/', 1, 6) i6
                         from t_path) t0) t1)
  where not (m2 = 0 and p2 is not null or m3 = 0 and p3 is not
  null or
             m4 = 0 and p4 is not null or m5 = 0 and p5 is not
             null);

PATH
-----------------------------------------------------------
/tmp/cat/
/tmp/cata/
/tmp/catb/
/usr/local/
/var/cache/

Elapsed: 00:00:13.68
```

A solution with not exists is faster than the query from Listing 12-23; nevertheless the latter one is based on some assumptions while the former is a more generic approach. Most of the time for a query with analytics was spent on sorting. Also it's important to note that «sort_area_size» was set to the maximal value and none of the queries required disk IO.

The last solution uses pattern matching.

```
select *
from t_path
match_recognize
(
  order by path
  measures
    first(path) path
  one row per match
  pattern(x+)
  define
    x as path like first(path) || '%'
) mr;

PATH
-----------------------------------------------------------
/tmp/cat/
/tmp/cata/
/tmp/catb/
/usr/local/
/var/cache/

Elapsed: 00:00:00.89
```

Execution time is less than a second! The algorithm is very simple: we check whether he first path from the current group is a subpath of the current path; if not, then a new group starts.

For Oracle versions before 12c, the optimal solution would be a PL/SQL pipelined function with a single table scan and similar logic to pattern matching. In other words, this quiz is yet another great example when the cursor for loop may be a better solution than a vanilla SQL.

Resemblance Group

Combine rows into a resemblance group according to this logic: we move across all rows from min to max and mark the current row if there is a row in the group such as the difference between its value and current value is not more than 1.

For the data below all the rows should be in the group except those with ID = 6 and ID = 8.

```
create table t_resemblance(id, value) as
(select 1, 1 from dual
union all select 2, 2 from dual
union all select 3, 2.5 from dual
union all select 4, 3.4 from dual
union all select 5, 0.4 from dual
union all select 6, 5 from dual
union all select 7, -0.5 from dual
union all select 8, -2 from dual
union all select 9, -1 from dual
union all select 10, 3 from dual
union all select 11, 4 from dual
union all select 12, 5 from dual);
```

The 12th row is part of the group even though its value equals to the 6th row, which has not been marked. That is because the group contained 11th row with a value = 4 when we were checking the 12th row.

Solution

For each element in the group there is another element such as a difference between the two is not more than 1; thus, according to transitivity law we can check a current element only with lower and upper bounds before adding it into the group.

In pure SQL this logic can be implemented using an iterative model.

```
select *
from t_resemblance
model
ignore nav
dimension by (row_number() over (order by id) id)
measures(value, 0 mi, 0 ma, 0 flag)
rules iterate (1e9) until value[iteration_number + 2] = 0
(
  flag[iteration_number + 1] =
  case when value[iteration_number + 1] between
          mi[iteration_number] - 1 and ma[iteration_number] + 1
          or iteration_number = 0
      then 1 end,
  mi[iteration_number + 1] =
  decode(flag[iteration_number + 1], 1, least(mi[iteration_
  number],
        value[iteration_number + 1]), mi[iteration_number]),
  ma[iteration_number + 1] =
  decode(flag[iteration_number + 1], 1, greatest(ma[iteration_
  number],
        value[iteration_number + 1]), ma[iteration_number])
);
```

ID	VALUE	MI	MA	FLAG
1	1	0	1	1
2	2	0	2	1
3	2.5	0	2.5	1
4	3.4	0	3.4	1
5	.4	0	3.4	1
6	5	0	3.4	
7	-.5	-.5	3.4	1
8	-2	-.5	3.4	
9	-1	-1	3.4	1
10	3	-1	3.4	1
11	4	-1	4	1
12	5	-1	5	1

12 rows selected.

An algorithm walks through the recordset and on each iteration changes measures only for one row. It updates the upper and lower bounds for the group and marks the current element.

Iterations are necessary because we have to update multiple measures for each row. If we use rules with ANY instead, then the model would evaluate the first rule for all rows and then the second rule for all rows and so on.

Taking into account the specific of the logic, we can try to approach a solution using a pattern-matching clause but in this case we are facing a couple of limitations.

- If we use an aggregate function in the define clause then it's applied to all rows the <u>including current row.</u> So we cannot compare current value with min/max across <u>values matched so far</u>.

- It's not possible to use measures in the define clause
  and moreover measure values for the previous row. The
  reason is that <u>measures are evaluated after a match is
  found</u>.

We can recall that we can use the next function but in this case we
need to apply it to shifted values by one row. This is demonstrated below
by using a new column vv instead of a value in the define clause.

```
select *
  from (select t.*, lag(value, 1, value) over(order by id) vv
          from (select id, value
                  from t_resemblance t
                  union all select null, null from dual) t)
match_recognize
(
  order by id
  measures
    match_number() match,
    classifier() cls,
    min(x.value) mi,
    max(x.value) ma
  all rows per match
  pattern((x|dummy)+)
  define
    x as (next(x.vv) >= min(x.vv) - 1 and next(x.vv)
    <= max(x.vv) + 1)
    -- x as (next(x.vv) between min(x.vv) - 1 and max(x.vv) + 1)
) mr
where id is not null;
```

ID	MATCH	CLS	MI	MA	VALUE	VV
1	1	X	1	1	1	1
2	1	X	1	2	2	1
3	1	X	1	2.5	2.5	2
4	1	X	1	3.4	3.4	2.5
5	1	X	.4	3.4	.4	3.4
6	1	DUMMY	.4	3.4	5	.4
7	1	X	-.5	3.4	-.5	5
8	1	DUMMY	-.5	3.4	-2	-.5
9	1	X	-1	3.4	-1	-2
10	1	X	-1	3.4	3	-1
11	1	X	-1	4	4	3
12	1	X	-1	5	5	4

12 rows selected.

We also have to add one additional row with a null ID value to properly handle the last row in the original recordset. Functions min/max with x.value as an argument were used to return lower and upper bounds for each step, but this is for information purposes only. All the logic is implemented in one line in the define clause. If we use the next function with the between operator, then the query fails with an exception "ORA-62508: illegal use of aggregates or navigation operators in MATCH_RECOGNIZE clause"; that is why a rule with two conditions was used instead.

The last thing to note about this task is that one more solution can be implemented using a recursive subquery factoring, but a pattern-matching solution is much more efficient.

Baskets

The goal is to allocate items to baskets with defined capacities. We loop through baskets from a min to max identifier and allocate items according to their priority. If some item was allocated to a specific basket, then it cannot be allocated to any other basket. For every basket, the total amount of the items cannot exceed the basket amount.

For the below data

```
with
  baskets(basket_id, basket_amount) as
  ( select 100, 500000 from dual union all
    select 200, 400000 from dual union all
    select 300, 1000000 from dual
  ),
  inventory(item_id, item_amount) as
  ( select 1000001, 50000 from dual union all
    select 1000002, 15000 from dual union all
    select 1000003, 250000 from dual union all
    select 1000004, 350000 from dual union all
    select 1000005, 45000 from dual union all
    select 1000006, 100500 from dual union all
    select 1000007, 200500 from dual union all
    select 1000008, 30050 from dual union all
    select 1000009, 400500 from dual union all
    select 1000010, 750000 from dual
  ),
  eligibility(basket_id, item_id, priority_level) as
  ( select 100, 1000003, 1 from dual union all
    select 100, 1000004, 2 from dual union all
    select 100, 1000002, 3 from dual union all
    select 100, 1000005, 4 from dual union all
```

```
    select 200, 1000004, 1 from dual union all
    select 200, 1000003, 2 from dual union all
    select 200, 1000001, 3 from dual union all
    select 200, 1000005, 4 from dual union all
    select 200, 1000007, 5 from dual union all
    select 200, 1000006, 6 from dual union all
    select 300, 1000002, 1 from dual union all
    select 300, 1000009, 2 from dual union all
    select 300, 1000010, 3 from dual union all
    select 300, 1000006, 4 from dual union all
    select 300, 1000008, 5 from dual
)
```

The expected result is the following

BASKET_ID	PRIORITY_LEVEL	ITEM_ID	BASKET_AMOUNT	ITEM_AMOUNT	RESULT
100	1	1000003	500000	250000	250000
100	2	1000004	500000	350000	0
100	3	1000002	500000	15000	265000
100	4	1000005	500000	45000	310000
200	1	1000004	400000	350000	350000
200	2	1000003	400000	250000	0
200	3	1000001	400000	50000	400000
200	4	1000005	400000	45000	0
200	5	1000007	400000	200500	0
200	6	1000006	400000	100500	0
300	1	1000002	1000000	15000	0
300	2	1000009	1000000	400500	400500
300	3	1000010	1000000	750000	0
300	4	1000006	1000000	100500	501000
300	5	1000008	1000000	30050	531050

```
15 rows selected.
```

Solution

The main complexity of this task is that we need to track allocated times. Otherwise the solution would be quite simple and similar to «Zeckendorf representation». Also this detail makes it impossible to use pattern matching for a solution.

We will use a joined recordset as a source so let's introduce a factored query t.

```
t(basket_id, item_id, basket_amount, item_amount,
priority_level) as
( select e.basket_id,
         e.item_id,
         b.basket_amount,
         i.item_amount,
         e.priority_level
    from eligibility e
    join baskets b
      on b.basket_id = e.basket_id
    join inventory i
      on i.item_id = e.item_id
   order by basket_id, priority_level)
```

Listing 12-24 shows how a task can be solved using a model clause.

Listing 12-24. Allocating items using model clause

```
select *
from t
model
dimension by (basket_id, priority_level, item_id)
measures (basket_amount, item_amount, 0 result)
rules
```

```
(
  result[any, any, any] order by basket_id, priority_level,
  item_id =
  case when max(result)[any, any, cv(item_id)] = 0 and
          nvl(max(result)[cv(basket_id),priority_level
          < cv(priority_level),any],0) +
          item_amount[cv(basket_id),cv(priority_level),
          cv(item_id)]
          <= max(basket_amount)[cv(basket_id),cv(priority_
          level),any]
          then nvl(max(result)[cv(basket_id),priority_level
          < cv(priority_level),any],0) +
          item_amount[cv(basket_id),cv(priority_level),
          cv(item_id)]
       else 0
  end
)
order by 1, 2;
```

The combination of basket_id and priority_level is enough for unique addressing but item_id has been added to the dimensions so that we can figure out whether a specific item has been used or not. The entire logic is implemented in one compact rule but it uses a few aggregates with various addressing, which makes a solution not quite efficient.

We may note that it's possible to use an approach similar to the one for the previous quiz "Resemblance group" when we iterated through recordset in a specific order and calculated several measures for each row. In this case measures are is_used – flag, which identifies whether a specific item has been allocated to a specific basket or not, total – running total for each basket and str – concatenation of allocated items. Implementation may be done using an iterative model (like for previous task) or recursive subquery factoring. The latter is shown in Listing 12-25.

Listing 12-25. Allocating items using recursive subquery factoring

```
with t0 as
(select t.*, row_number() over (order by basket_id,
priority_level) rn
   from t),
rec (basket_id, item_id, basket_amount, item_amount,
priority_level,
     rn, total, is_used, str) as
(select t.basket_id, t.item_id, t.basket_amount,
     t.item_amount, t.priority_level, t.rn,
     case when t.item_amount <= t.basket_amount
          then t.item_amount else 0 end,
     case when t.item_amount <= t.basket_amount then 1 end,
     cast(case when t.item_amount <= t.basket_amount
               then ',' || t.item_id end as varchar2(4000))
from t0 t where rn = 1
union all
select t.basket_id, t.item_id, t.basket_amount,
     t.item_amount, t.priority_level, t.rn,
     case when decode(t.basket_id, r.basket_id, r.total, 0)
               + t.item_amount <= t.basket_amount
          and instr(r.str, t.item_id) = 0
          then decode(t.basket_id, r.basket_id, r.total, 0)
               + t.item_amount
          else decode(t.basket_id, r.basket_id, r.total, 0)
     end,
     case when decode(t.basket_id, r.basket_id, r.total, 0)
               + t.item_amount <= t.basket_amount
          and instr(r.str, t.item_id) = 0
          then 1
     end,
```

```
            case when decode(t.basket_id, r.basket_id, r.total, 0)
                    + t.item_amount <= t.basket_amount
                  and instr(r.str, t.item_id) = 0
                  then r.str || ',' || t.item_id
                  else r.str
            end
    from t0 t
    join rec r on t.rn = r.rn + 1)
select * from rec;
```

Concatenation of allocated items is used to check whether a current item has been allocated or not, but we could have used a collection instead of a string to avoid limitations of varchar2 length. Anyway, we have to populate a list of used items for each row, which has negative impact on memory consumption and overall performance.

Although a solution with a model is quite concise, the performance is reasonable for relatively small data volumes - around thousands of rows. Performance of a recursive subquery factoring may be improved if you insert t0 into a temporary table with index by rn so that Oracle accesses only a single row by index on each iteration.

The most efficient solution would be PL/SQL function that uses a cursor for loop and an associative array of allocated items for the fastest check to determine whether an item was allocated or not.

Longest Increasing Subsequence

The longest increasing subsequence problem is to find a subsequence of a given sequence in which the subsequence's elements are in sorted order, lowest to highest, and in which the subsequence is as long as possible. This subsequence is not necessarily contiguous. With adaptation to a database we will be looking for the longest subsequence in a sequence or rows.

For example, for sequence

```
14, 15, 9, 11, 16, 12, 13
```

The expected result is

```
9, 11, 12, 13
```

For simplicity we will be deriving the length of the longest increasing subsequence without returning the subsequence itself. For the above data the correct answer is 4.

Solution

Unlike all previous tasks let's start with a PL/SQL approach. The problem can be solved in a quite efficient way using dynamic programming.

So, let's assume that we need to calculate length - L of a subsequence for a current element and it's already calculated for elements analyzed so far. In such a case, the L for the current element is max(L) across all previous elements, which are less than current element plus 1. This may sound a bit complicated but implementation is fairly simple. Let's reuse type numbers from the section "Unnesting Collections" and table tmp from the section "Iterative-Like computations," lvl stays for length on current step, x is order, and num is a value.

```
declare
  t numbers := numbers(14, 15, 9, 11, 16, 12, 13);
begin
  delete from tmp;

  for i in 1 .. t.count loop

    insert into tmp
      (lvl, x, num)
```

```
    values
      ((select nvl(max(lvl), 0) + 1 from tmp where num < t(i)),
      i, t(i));

  end loop;

end;
/
```

PL/SQL procedure successfully completed.

select * from tmp;

LVL	X	NUM
1	1	14
2	2	15
1	3	9
2	4	11
3	5	16
3	6	12
4	7	13

7 rows selected.

To get a max(lvl) for all elements we need to scan the tmp table. Another option is using a PL/SQL variable and updating it on each iteration. Given that for each element we scan all previous elements, the computational complexity of the algorithm is $O(n^2)$. Also the necessity to scan all previous elements makes implementation using recursive subquery factoring not reasonable; please check the section "Iterative-Like computations" for additional details.

Back to PL/SQL, an algorithm can be improved if we use an auxiliary array that will contain the longest common subsequence and will be refreshed on each iteration. Refresh is implemented according to the next principle: we look up for the max value that is less than the current value and put the current value after the found value. The binary search runs in logarithmic time $O(\log_2 n)$, thus total computational complexity is $O(n*\log_2 n)$.

```
declare
  x     numbers := numbers(14, 15, 9, 11, 16, 12, 13);
  m     numbers := numbers();
  l     int;
  newl int;
  v     varchar2(4000);
  -- index of the greatest element lower than p in array M
  function f(p in number) return int as
    lo  int;
    hi  int;
    mid int;
  begin
    lo := 1;
    hi := 1;
    while lo <= hi loop
      mid := ceil((lo + hi) / 2);
      if x(m(mid)) < p then lo := mid + 1; else hi := mid - 1;
      end if;
    end loop;
    return lo;
  end;
begin
  m.extend(x.count);
```

```
  l := 0;
  for i in 1 .. x.count loop
    newl := f(x(i));
    m(newl) := i;

    if newl > l then l := newl; end if;

    v := '';
    for j in 1 .. l loop
      v := v || ' ' || x(m(j));
    end loop;
    dbms_output.put_line(i || ' ' || v);
  end loop;
end;
/
1  14
2  14 15
3  9 15
4  9 11
5  9 11 16
6  9 11 12
7  9 11 12 13
```

PL/SQL procedure successfully completed.

The l is the length of the longest increasing subsequence on each iteration.

SQL implementation can be done using the model clause.

```
with t(id, value) as
(select rownum, column_value from table(numbers(14, 15, 9, 11,
16, 12, 13)))
select *
  from t
```

```
model
dimension by (id, value)
measures(0 l)
(l[any, any] order by id = nvl(max(l)[id < cv(id),value
< cv(value)],0) + 1)
order by 1;
```

The approach is similar to the first solution in PL/SQL while there is no way to implement a second solution on pure SQL as efficient as using PL/SQL. When we use the model we work with a flat dataset containing columns and rows (even though we consider it as a multidimensional array), and it's not possible to use any auxiliary data structures to optimize the solution.

Quine

The last quiz is just for fun rather than to demonstrate Oracle SQL features. Quine is a program that takes no input and produces a copy of its own source code as its only output. You can find a lot of solutions on the Internet for various programming languages, and I will not focus on a PL/SQL solution where the approach is quite similar to Pascal language, for example. It's a bit more interesting to demonstrate SQL approaches.

Solution

One of the requirements is that the program (in our case, SQL query) cannot access external sources to read its code. So the query below cannot be treated as a complete solution.

```
set pagesize 0 linesize 90
```

```
select sql_text||';'from v$sqlarea join v$session using(sql_id)
where sid=userenv('sid');
select sql_text||';'from v$sqlarea join v$session using(sql_id)
where sid=userenv('sid');
```

On the other hand, the two following solutions satisfy all requirements.

```
select substr(rpad(1,125,'||chr(39)),26)from
dual;select substr(rpad(1,125,'||chr(39)),26)from
dual;
select substr(rpad(1,125,'||chr(39)),26)from
dual;select substr(rpad(1,125,'||chr(39)),26)from
dual;
```

```
select
replace('@''[@'||chr(93)||''')from dual;','@',q'[select
replace('@''[@'||chr(93)||''')from dual;','@',q]')from dual;
select
replace('@''[@'||chr(93)||''')from dual;','@',q'[select
replace('@''[@'||chr(93)||''')from dual;','@',q]')from dual;
```

Maybe you can write shorter quine in Oracle SQL?

Summary

It was demonstrated using selected tasks that Oracle-specific SQL is much more powerful than standard SQL, and some tasks can be solved in a highly scalable way with very little code. I'd especially like to highlight a new Oracle 12c feature – pattern matching, which makes it possible to solve various tasks in a very efficient manner that otherwise would require a lot of PL/SQL code.

Some complex tasks can be solved using recursive subquery factoring or a model clause with competitive performance in compare to PL/SQL. Both approaches do not require collections of objects unlike the PL/SQL approach with pipelined functions. Advantages of the model are concise code and great scalability when using partitioning and parallel execution. Pros for recursive subquery factoring are execution in the scope of the SQL engine, and there is no need for context switches on each iteration.

If, however, you need to implement a relatively complex algorithm that may require additional data structures and control of execution, then PL/SQL tends to be the preferable approach. But when you switch to procedural language to work with data, you always should have an answer why it's better than SQL for your particular task. The last thing to note: if you have to implement some intensive computations that require a lot of CPU, then external libraries and implementation using C can be the best choice.

Details really matter, so you have to take into account the specifics of a particular task and compare different approaches for your Oracle version before making a decision about the preferable approach.

APPENDIX A

Useful Oracle Links

1. A Look Under The Hood of CBO: THE 10053 Event

    `http://www.centrexcc.com/A%20Look%20under%20`
    `the%20Hood%20of%20CBO%20-%20the%2010053%20`
    `Event.pdf`

2. Closing The Query Processing Loop in Oracle 11g

    `http://www.vldb.org/pvldb/1/1454178.pdf`

3. The Oracle Optimizer Explain the Explain Plan

    `http://www.oracle.com/technetwork/database/`
    `bi-datawarehousing/twp-explain-the-explain-`
    `plan-052011-393674.pdf`

4. Query Optimization in Oracle Database10g Release 2

    `http://www.oracle.com/technetwork/database/`
    `bi-datawarehousing/twp-general-query-`
    `optimization-10gr-130948.pdf`

5. SQL Sucks

    `http://www.nocoug.org/download/2006-08/SQL_`
    `Sucks_NoCOUG_Journal_Article_Part_2.pdf`

6. Explaining the EXPLAIN PLAN

© Alex Reprintsev 2018

A. Reprintsev, *Oracle SQL Revealed*, https://doi.org/10.1007/978-1-4842-3372-6_13

```
https://nocoug.files.wordpress.com/2014/08/
nocoug_journal_201408.pdf
```

7. Universality in Elementary Cellular Automata

```
http://www.complex-systems.com/pdf/15-1-1.pdf
```

8. Absolutely Typical - The Whole Story on Types and How They Power PL/SQL Interoperability

```
https://technology.amis.nl/wp-content/
uploads/images/AbsolutelyTypical_UKOUG2011_
jellema.zip
```

9. Doing SQL from PL/SQL: Best and Worst Practices

```
http://www.oracle.com/technetwork/database/
features/plsql/overview/doing-sql-from-
plsql-129775.pdf
```

Index

A

Adjacency lists model, 119
Aggregate functions
 atomic type result, 104
 Cartesian join, 117
 collect function, 105
 concatenate collection
   elements, 104
 cube, 114
 definition, 103
 EAV model, 107
 grouping and
   grouping_id, 115–117
 parsing pivot XML, 110
 rollup, 114
 UDAG, 106
 unpivot operator, 112
Analytic functions
 aggregate functions, 94
 avoiding joins, 88–89
 definition, 85
 differences and
   interchangeability
  max date, 99–100
  max value
   partition, 98

  unbounded range, 98
 fetch termination
  PL/SQL function, 262–263
  recursive subquery
   factoring, 257, 259, 261
  row_number, 248, 250, 252,
   254–255
  sum, 255–256
  transaction, 247
  types and function, 261–262
 vs. joins
  approaches, 96
  execution plans, 97–98
 last_value and ignore nulls,
   100–101
 limitations, 92
 listagg and stragg, 94–95
 logic implementation, 89–90
 order by, 86
 partition by part, 86
 query rewriting, 87
ANSI joins
 Cloudera Impala, 14
 cross join, 6
 demonstration tables, 6
 full outer join, 10
 inner join

© Alex Reprintsev 2018
A. Reprintsev, *Oracle SQL Revealed*, https://doi.org/10.1007/978-1-4842-3372-6

Get the eBook for only $5!

Why limit yourself?

With most of our titles available in both PDF and ePUB format, you can access your content wherever and however you wish—on your PC, phone, tablet, or reader.

Since you've purchased this print book, we are happy to offer you the eBook for just $5.

To learn more, go to http://www.apress.com/companion or contact support@apress.com.

Apress®

All Apress eBooks are subject to copyright. All rights are reserved by the Publisher, whether the whole or part of the material is concerned, specifically the rights of translation, reprinting, reuse of illustrations, recitation, broadcasting, reproduction on microfilms or in any other physical way, and transmission or information storage and retrieval, electronic adaptation, computer software, or by similar or dissimilar methodology now known or hereafter developed. Exempted from this legal reservation are brief excerpts in connection with reviews or scholarly analysis or material supplied specifically for the purpose of being entered and executed on a computer system, for exclusive use by the purchaser of the work. Duplication of this publication or parts thereof is permitted only under the provisions of the Copyright Law of the Publisher's location, in its current version, and permission for use must always be obtained from Springer. Permissions for use may be obtained through RightsLink at the Copyright Clearance Center. Violations are liable to prosecution under the respective Copyright Law.